READ WRITE TEACH

READ WRITE TEACH

Choice and Challenge in the Reading-Writing Workshop

LINDA RIEF

Foreword by Maja Wilson

HEINEMANN
Portsmouth, NH

Heinemann
145 Maplewood Avenue, Suite 300
Portsmouth, NH 03801
www.heinemann.com

Offices and agents throughout the world

© 2014 by Linda Rief

The author and publisher wish to thank those who have generously given permission to reprint borrowed material:

Maja Wilson's foreword copyright © 2014 by Maja Wilson.

Excerpt from "What's Right with Writing" by Linda Rief. Originally appeared in *Voices from the Middle* (May 2006, Vol. 13, No. 4). Copyright © 2006 by the National Council of Teachers of English. Reprinted with permission.

Credits continue on page vi

Library of Congress Cataloging-in-Publication Data
Rief, Linda.
  Read write teach : choice and challenge in the reading-writing workshop / Linda Rief.
    pages cm
  ISBN 978-0-325-05360-8
  1. English language—Composition and exercises—Study and teaching (Elementary)
2. English language—Composition and exercises—Study and teaching (Middle school)
3. Teachers' workshops.   I. Title.
  LB1576.R5194 2014
  428.0071'2—dc23   2013047428

Editor: Holly Kim Price
Production: Hilary Goff
Art direction: Lisa Fowler
Cover design: Suzanne Heiser
Interior design: Monica Ann Crigler
Photo credits: Dave Ervin, Laura Fant, Linda Rief
Typesetter: Gina Poirier, Gina Poirier Design
Manufacturing: Steve Bernier

Printed in the United States of America on acid-free paper
5 6 7 8 GP 25 24 23 22
PO 33770

I've come to a frightening conclusion that I am the decisive element in the classroom. It's my personal approach that creates the climate. It's my daily mood that makes the weather. As a teacher, I possess a tremendous power to make a child's life miserable or joyous. I can be a tool of torture or an instrument of inspiration. I can humiliate or heal. In all situations, it is my response that decides whether a crisis will be escalated or de-escalated and a child humanized or dehumanized.

—Haim G. Ginott

CONTENTS

CHAPTER 8 *Whole Novels 159*

CHAPTER 9 *Under the Influence of Writers: Author-Genre Studies 186*

CHAPTER 10 *Exhibeo Humanitas (Persuasive Writing) 210*

CHAPTER 11 *A Model of Writing 232*

ONLINE RESOURCES

How to Access the Online Resources

STEP 1: Go to www.heinemann.com.

STEP 2: Click on "Login" to open or create your account. Enter your email address and password or click "Create a New Account" to set up an account.

STEP 3: Enter keycode **RWTEACH** and click "**Register**"

CHAPTER 5 *Resources*

CHAPTER 6 *Resources*

CHAPTER 7 *Resources*

CHAPTER 8 *Resources*

CHAPTER 9 *Resources*

CHAPTER 10 *Resources*

CHAPTER 11 *Resources*

FOREWORD

by Maja Wilson

Giggles and nudges are passing through Linda Rief's eighth-grade language arts classroom faster than a rumor. Linda is reading aloud from Gary Paulsen's *Harris and Me*. In an act of revenge, the narrator is urging Harris to pee on an electric fence. The students are waiting for it—the moment the yellow arc hits the wire and Harris gets what's coming to him, retaliation in the form of an angry stream of electrons going you know where!—but Paulsen and Rief are dragging it out, building a long slow agony of suspense, and these thirteen- and fourteen-year-olds who walked into the room as cool, calm, and collected as high school seniors are now acting their age, sharing their glee with knowing smirks and raised eyebrows and barely contained titters.

There's more going on here than the pleasure of a good yarn about pee and pain. At the beginning of class, Linda told the class about meeting Gary Paulsen in person. He spoke about the difficulties he faced as a child, how a librarian got him off the streets, how it was dark and cold outside when he wandered into a warm, bright library. How the librarian gave him hot chocolate and told him he was welcome anytime—he didn't need to read anything. How, many visits later, he asked if she had any books he might like. How he began to read, gobbling up books, "hungry like a wolf," and realized he had stories to tell, too.

Linda asked if anyone had read anything by Gary Paulsen. They blurted out titles: *The River*, *The Winter Room*, what about that one with the kid who is stranded in a plane crash? Oh yeah, *Hatchet*. Linda talked about how "the seeds of these stories"—characters, settings, conflicts—came from Paulsen's life. That's the theme of the day, as it turns out: how reading helps us turn our experiences into stories.

When Linda finishes reading and the laughter and groans at Harris' electrifying conclusion subside, students pull out their notebooks. They've only got two minutes to jot down ideas—words, lists, sketches even. They could note an experience Paulsen's story reminds them of or write the stories they collected for last night's homework assignment: to ask their parents to tell them the stupidest, scariest, most dangerous, or most embarrassing thing that ever happened to them.

After this "quickwrite"—Linda's term for it—students clamor to share. There are the requisite pee stories, and then one student tells a story his dad told him. His dad grew up on a military base overseas and was playing outside one day. He thought he'd found a toy. Only it wasn't a toy. It was a hand grenade. There's a murmur of awe, some discussion about what it might be like to be a kid in a place littered by the remains of war, and then Linda talks about how the student might use that story in his own fictional writing project. He could extend it, embed it in something else, tell it from another character's point of view, or ask the *What If* question: "What if your dad hadn't realized it wasn't a toy?"

Linda points out that one of Jodi Picoult's books starts with a *What If* question: Picoult read a newspaper story about a girl conceived to provide her sick sister with bone marrow, and asked herself, "What if that girl grew up and didn't want to give her bone marrow to her sister?" That question turned into *My Sister's Keeper*. The *What If* question, Linda tells her class, is an important one for a writer.

Now they're into the real work of the class. They've each already chosen and read three books by the same author in the same genre—historical fiction, horror, science fiction, whatever they've been drawn to—and they've noticed and written about the characteristics of that genre. They're using this genre study to write a story of their own. They've got hundreds of "seeds of stories" to draw on, many of them already recorded in their notebooks.

After just twenty minutes of observing Linda's class, I've got a hundred ideas and am itching to pull out my own notebook. But I want to know how things are going for those who aren't so thrilled about school in general and English class in particular. There's a kid across the room with a stack of historical fiction on his desk, brows furrowed, looking like he's going straight from eighth grade to a 1600 on the Scholastic Aptitude Test. A lanky young man flips through a book with a picture on the cover of a giant robot lurking over high rises, a mechanical King Kong of sorts. I walk over to him.

He isn't much of a reader, he confesses, but he's become obsessed with this series. Each story involves a robotic villain and the violent takeover of a well-known city, and he's noticed that the first line always involves extreme weather. It sets the mood, he says. He reads me the first line of the book, then the first line of his own story: "It was the hottest, muggiest day on record in Dover, New Hampshire." By the end of his half page start, I'm starting to sweat despite the January chill, wondering what awaits the inhabitants of Durham's neighboring town.

Students are working on different projects with varying degrees of sophistication, but they all talk about where their ideas come from and what they're trying to accomplish and what they might do next and how other authors have done similar things. This isn't a room full of students doing school. It's a room full of readers and writers who, for all the laughter and talk of body fluids, are working seriously on their writing, inspired by their lives and their reading.

✳   ✳   ✳

But don't take my word for it. Don't even take Linda's word for it. Find out what the kids have to say about it. It's a year later, and I've just shared some of Linda's practices with the education majors in my literacy methods course, pointing out how they express the same principles about literacy and learning we've spent the semester exploring. But I'm warning my preservice teachers that good teaching is not distributing someone else's good handouts. "If the students feel it's hoop jumping, it isn't going to work. In the end, best practices and your best intentions matter less than how the children in your class experience them. To find that out, you've got to ask them."

As it comes out of my mouth, I realize I've just backed myself into an interesting corner. I've got to take my own advice. So, it's back to Linda's classroom in New Hampshire—not to watch her teach, but to talk to her students. I randomly pick fifteen of Linda's students to interview twice—in pairs or small groups—at the beginning and the end of the school year. We talk about reading and writing—what they're working on, what it means to them—and how they experience Linda's class.

While these eighth graders talk enthusiastically about various writing projects they're working on and books they're reading, the first thing that emerges most strongly from these interviews is the powerful effect of Linda's dogged insistence that *their intentions matter*. Sam kicks off the discussion of choices in reading. "Last year, we had to read a book, and we had to read it chapter by chapter." He leaves an agonizingly long pause between the words *chapter by chapter*. "And some days we would only read like four pages. But this year, when we read *The Outsiders*, I told [Mrs. Rief], 'I like to read books really fast-paced.' She said, 'If it helps you read better, and understand the book better, then go ahead and read ahead.' She lets you do what's best for you."

Andrew jumps in, "We get lots of choices in the class, which really helps because you get to write about what you want to write about, and when you get to do that, it really makes it better. You enjoy it and want to go on with it."

But it becomes clear that Linda's concern for her students' intentions isn't confined to what and how they read and write. It also permeates her responses to students' writer's-reader's notebooks, which they turn in every two weeks. Joey discusses how those responses make him feel. "It's really nice because she reads every single piece in our notebook for every student and . . . and when she comments on it, where she highlights stuff, you know that she cares about it. So that's really nice."

Then, Joey begins to grapple with how to describe the quality of Linda's responses. He is trying to articulate something complex, and his hands get involved where his words fail. "She helps us shape [our writing], but she shapes it in the way *we* want to. She's not fixing it for her, she's fixing it for us. Because she knows how we feel about writing. So she's not trying to fix the *way* we write, but . . . " At this point, Joey is speechless, gesturing wildly, and the four other boys in the room talk over each other trying to help him out. In the end, Andrew supplies an acceptable ending clause, "But, you know, improve it."

Then, Jake nails the effect of Linda's concern for their intentions. "The way that she shows us that she really cares about us makes us really care about what we're doing, so that just really motivates us. And really, like . . . I don't know, I just feel better about writing than I have in the past."

I ask Jake if he's now more likely to want to write outside of class. All five answer affirmatively, nodding vigorously. But they become most animated when Jake explains that Linda has her own notebook and writes with them. Andrew says, "It feels like she's respecting us because she's not above us."

Joey interrupts, "Some teachers in the past, they feel like, they already passed seventh grade, so they don't have to do it anymore. But Mrs. Rief, she likes to [write], and that makes us like to do it, because she's really good at it and she inspires us. So when she writes about something, we're like, 'Oh, we should write about that too.' And it really helps when she shares her own writing, because then she can reflect on it, like, from her, and it really helps us to know what she felt."

Joey is reminding us that *process matters*—that writers need to read what other writers write, but also to know what they think and feel as they do. But process matters to teachers, too. The products of Linda's teaching—her assignments, her handouts, the list of books in her classroom library, how she sets up notebooks and the number of times she collects them—aren't a five-paragraph essay formula that all teachers should follow for a proficient score on the teaching rubric. Teaching, like writing, is contextual. It's one thousand decisions made every day, in context. It's holding and honoring relationships and principles and a dogged insistence that students' intentions and experiences matter.

In the end, it is important that this book isn't a compilation of tear-out reproducibles designed to help us replicate Linda's practices. Instead, it's the most powerful gift that a master teacher can give us: the story of her thinking and feeling as she teaches. Because, to borrow Joey's words, "She can reflect on it, like, from her, and it really helps us to know what she felt." This is a book grounded in stories, because Linda's teaching is grounded in stories—her own, published authors', the students' stories—and they all inform each other. We would be wise to let Linda's story—and her students'—inform ours.

Maja Wilson is the author of *Rethinking Rubrics in Writing Assessment*, which won the NCTE James Britton Award in 2007.

ACKNOWLEDGMENTS

This book has been years in the making, each year of my teaching adding new thinking to my learning. Different kids. Different colleagues. Different challenges. What has been consistent is a community of learners that always stimulates, energizes, and, sometimes, exhausts me, yet always provokes more thought. It is with admiration and deep respect that I thank all of the following for helping me to continually recognize that our learning is never done, and this book only represents where I am at the moment.

At Oyster River Middle School:

Jay Richard, principal, and Bill Sullivan, assistant principal, who always know to ask "How can we help you?" And mean it.

The eighth grade Odyssey team (Tom Bonaccorsi, science, Nate Grove, social studies, Julia Widelski, math, Keith Savage or Jason Duff, special educators, Laura Fant and Gail Volk, aides extraordinaire, Dave Ervin, music, Beth Doran-Healy, art, Al Stuart, tech-ed, Holly Pirtle, health, and Alida Carter, advisory partner). It is built into our schedule for a Team Meeting every day—to discuss, plan, and apply all we learn from each other about kids, about curricula, about the processes of learning, and about each other.

Our team discussions center on how to help adolescents build on their strengths and overcome their weaknesses by offering them innovative opportunities that challenge their thinking, and ours. We push ourselves—what do we believe and why? Even in our disagreements we are nudged forward in our thinking and learning. It has been, and continues to be, such a rewarding and energizing journey.

Susie Renner, eighth grade Language Arts teacher on the Renaissance team, a colleague and true partner in all we do to coordinate the writing and reading for our students.

I truly appreciate the respect and trust we are given in the Oyster River School District as educators, who are always working to recognize and build on the unique qualities each child brings to the classroom.

I have been lucky to have some wonderful interns from the University of New Hampshire during my years at the middle school. Emily Geltz, now a teacher at Laconia Middle School, in New Hampshire, exceeded every expectation, becoming a colleague and partner in the classroom during the 2012–13 school year. She became a model for the students as a serious writer and reader along with them. She asked hard questions of herself and of me. With young teachers like Emily coming into the profession—deep thinkers who aren't afraid to ask the difficult questions—I have such confidence in the future of schools. I have learned so much from her, and this is a stronger book because of her.

The University of New Hampshire community:

Tom Newkirk, Louise Wrobleski, Maureen Barbieri, Tom Romano, and Penny Kittle, as well as so many other fine educators at UNH and in the Summer Literacy Institute at UNH, continue the professional conversations so vital to my growth as a teacher and learner.

When Maja Wilson and Jim Webber were doctoral students at UNH they spent a significant amount of time in my classroom, in district language arts meetings with me, and interviewing my students. It has been a gift to talk through their findings, especially things they noticed and wondered that often eluded me in the day to day happenings of the classroom.

Tom Romano, Maja Wilson, Penny Kittle, Karen Cook, and Maureen Barbieri read several initial chapters, asking pertinent questions and offering helpful suggestions that moved the writing forward. More than colleagues, they are good friends.

I love summers, not only for the necessary break from the challenges of the classroom, but for the opportunities to work with fine educators from all over the United States and throughout the world. The UNH Summer Literacy Institute, the Boothbay Retreat with Kylene Beers and Bob Probst, and a Writing Institute in the Laurentians, just outside of Montreal.

I look forward to all I learn from Kylene, Bob, Chris Crutcher, and Sara Kajder and all the wonderful educators from across the country who spend a week every summer at the Boothbay Literacy Retreat sponsored by Heinemann: writing, drawing, reading, and talking. It is relaxing and stimulating.

John and Lorraine Ryan from Montreal bring together teachers from all over Canada to work on their writing and art with me for a week each summer. They recognize the value in teachers as writers and the implications for their classrooms.

I am most grateful to my students, who truly are my best teachers. All of you have allowed me into your lives in ways that so few other people have such access. With clarity, with sincerity, with integrity, with humor, and with respect for each other, you have opened your worlds as adolescents through writing and reading, from which other kids and teachers can learn so much. You have made me laugh. You have made me cry. You have made me love what I do. *You* are the reasons I go back into the classroom year after year, and day after day. Thank you.

To my husband, George, my sons and their families, Bryan and Laura, Julia and Fiona, and Craig and Jennifer, Hunter and Harrison: for your patience, your questions, and your love through so much "teacher talk."

To Heinemann:

Your patience in waiting for this book to be finished has been extraordinary. Twelve years of "How's it coming?" since the first contract for the book was signed. And when the writing was done, your expertise given through editing, production, and marketing has been equally impressive.

Hilary Goff, you in particular, have been the glue that kept the bundles of chapters, student writing, photos, on-line resources, and permissions organized and moving forward. If you couldn't answer my questions, you knew who could.

All of you at Heinemann continue Don Graves' legacy of valuing, honoring, and taking seriously our students' voices. Special thanks to Lesa Scott, President, Vicki Boyd, Senior Vice President and Publisher, Lisa Fowler, Publisher of Professional Books, Holly Kim Price, Acquisitions Editor, Hilary Goff, Production Editor, Monica Crigler, Interior Design, Suzanne Heiser, Cover Design, Patty Adams, Production Manager, Kimberly Cahill, Product Marketing Manager, Cindy Black, Copyeditor, and Sarah Fournier, Associate Managing Editor.

INTRODUCTION

Story: At the Heart of All We Do

August 2010

I am taking a creative nonfiction writing course with Meredith Hall, the author of *Without a Map*. Each day we read and discuss short pieces from professional writers: Mark Spragg, Sandra Cisneros, Sherman Alexie, Natalia Ginzburg, Jamaica Kincaid, Frank McCourt, and many other fine authors. We write, read aloud, and discuss our own drafts. I am learning from Meredith how to build an essay from a variety of scenes, each one a montage that can stand on its own but contributes to the whole. Lee Gutkind, editor of *Keep It Real*, describes montage writing as "an interpretive duet between the writer and reader, . . . a steady closing out of one scene and the unannounced opening of the next, fluidly and confidently. . . . At each opening discovering another component of a suggested truth" (Gutkind 2008, 104–105).

On one of the days in the course, I write:

> She is wearing turquoise Bermuda shorts, a sleeveless cotton blouse, starched and ironed, and white Keds that walk her across the lawn, down the ramp, and onto the dock. She starts to untie the dinghy, then stops, turns, looks—from dock to ramp to rock wall. She recleats the boat, and walks up the ramp, across the lawn, and into the garage. Then out. In her left hand she clutches two oarlocks. The oars rest across her right shoulder, clamped against her waist with her forearm. White Keds—across the lawn, down the ramp, onto the dock.
>
> She steps into the small boat, setting her legs firmly across its width, as the dinghy rocks with her weight from side to side, scraping, creaking against wood and canvas. She lays the oars across the seats from bow to stern. She plunges each oarlock into its cradle, unwinds the rope, and shoves off. She

sets each oar in its lock. Leans forward and pulls back. Dip and pull. Dip and pull. With only the splash of wood paddle striking water, my mother dips and pulls, her feet planted firmly against the empty seat in the stern. The small rowboat weaves in and out of cabin cruisers and unmasted sailboats, a speck disappearing behind Pumpkin Island.

Inside, he maneuvers down the stairs. He is not an old man, nor a young man. He is thin. Graying hair scatters in short, damp clumps just as they were when he stepped from the shower. He has been drinking for three weeks: beer, scotch, rum, whiskey—cough syrup, vanilla extract, if he can find nothing else. He doesn't like alcohol. But once he starts, he cannot stop. Today he is trying to stop. He is wearing the beige, terrycloth robe, tied at the waist, the robe he always wears when he's trying to stop.

His bare feet read each stair as his trembling hand grasps the rail. Step down, one foot then the other. Wait. Rest. Step down, one foot then the other. Fourteen stairs. He turns in the hallway and his hand skirts the fading wallpaper—dahlias and lilies—that leads him into the kitchen, where a cup of instant coffee—strong, two scoops, a little milk, no sugar—waits. He places trembling hands on the Formica countertop, . . . and leans over the cup. His lips meet the edge of the mug, and he sucks in the warm liquid.

Outside boats turn with the tide, drifting on buoys anchored between World's End and our back porch. My mother returns, up the ramp, across the rock wall, up the stairs and across the back porch. She catches the screen door so it doesn't slam. She does not look at me, or my father, or the cup of coffee she has placed earlier on the kitchen counter. But she says, as if to both of us, as if to neither one of us, and not about the coffee—"If he takes one more drink I'm tying him to the raft and floating him out to sea."

September 2010

Howard Colter, our superintendent, closes his remarks to all the teachers in our district on the opening day of school with the following story about himself.

As a little boy, he was awkward and uncoordinated when it came to sports. His parents forced him to go to a camp out west that focused on athletics. He did not want to go, but they insisted, thinking it would be good for him. He was as miserable as he thought he would be, as the campers, all athletes, continually made fun of him.

Eventually he made friends with a little boy who had polio. They walked slowly to the river, as his friend was in leg braces. They spent one entire day fishing, catching one trout after another. He said it was the best day he had had at the camp.

On their way back from fishing they had to go past the baseball diamond. The players spotted Howard and his friend and their line filled with trout. "Whatta ya got there?" the baseball players yelled, as they walked toward the two boys. They grabbed the line. These boys proceeded to pull each fish from the line, stood at home plate, and smacked each fish like baseballs across the diamond into the dirt.

Howard and his friend watched, unable to do anything to stop them, until the boys had had their fill of entertainment and left them staring at the remains of the fish in the dirt. Howard gathered the fish, and he and his friend started back to their cabin.

On the way they passed the dining hall, where one of the cooks spotted the boys. "Whatta ya got there?" the cook asked. He listened to their story, cleaned up the trout, cooked them over an open fire, and served them to Howard and his friend for their supper. They sat at a picnic table, talking, laughing, eating. The best meal he had ever had, he said.

He ended his remarks with, "You know, we have to keep testing in its place, as only one way of understanding if kids are succeeding. There are so many other ways. If you see a little boy with a trout, cook it for him."

August 2011

I am in Val David, a small town in the Laurentian Mountains in the province of Quebec, doing a weeklong writing workshop with teachers and administrators. I ask them to think about those indelible moments of reading and writing in their own lives that left an impression on them.

Julie tells the story of passing by her three-year-old daughter, who is sitting on the floor, legs crossed, head bent into a picture book. She looked down and noticed her daughter was "lire a l'envers," reading the book, she says, not knowing quite how to translate "l'envers." "Upside down," another teacher says, when Julie looks around for help with the word. She tells us, she reached down, picked up the book, turned it right side up and handed it back to her daughter. With no hesitation her daughter flipped it back, upside down. "Mama," she said, "I'm reading in my imagination."

September 2011

My eighth-grade classroom. Jewelia writes in her writer's-reader's notebook:

> As I sat she smeared the goop on my plate. My heart sank like the Titanic. I couldn't take much more anxiety. I used my fork as a plow, pushing mashed potato mush everywhere. I spear a bite of lettuce with my fork, as the voice in my head screams "Put it down!" It sits in my mouth for a moment, the ranch dressing oozing in my mouth.

There is a small part of me that wants to just chew, swallow, chew, swallow. The majority wins though, and when I eat less, it consumes more of me. I spear another bite of salad. I guide it towards my ungrateful mouth. I'm on my second bite (two bites too many). This bite is killing me. I count how much I chew: 1, 2, 3, 4, 5, 6, 7, 8, 9, 10, swallow. It's in my stomach, it's packing on more whale blubber. I can't do this anymore. I need to run, I need to move. I can't move.

I can tell. She's watching me, but I don't look up, I won't look up. I can't see her disappointment; it will only make things worse. I swallow the lump of tears in my throat. Can't eat. Can't live here. Can't eat. Can't live with the tubes in the horrible hospital.

The only reason that they let me stay is because I'm fat enough to stay. They say 93 is stable, but they want 100. They say 93 is stable, but I want 85.

October 2011

"We have to put all those stories of kids and families out of our heads and look at the data, the numbers," says the presenter at our staff meeting. We are about to be taken through a two-hour training in how to read the data, the numbers, from the latest round of more reading assessments we are forced to give—a mandated test for having *only* 83 percent of our students score in the proficient range and above on the *New England Common Assessment Program*, our state's test under No Child Left Behind, and not high enough to make AYP (the percentage gain defined as "adequate yearly progress"). I turn to one of my colleagues and ask with my eyes, "What? Put those stories aside—just look at the numbers?"

We are given a worksheet with the acronym ORID, subtitled Focused Conversation Data Analysis. To summarize, the presenter says: This is Focused Conversation Data Analysis: I notice (Objective), I feel (Reflective), I wonder (Interpretive), I need (Decisional). (To myself, I wonder if *decisional* is even a word.)

We spend the next hour and a half examining the scores of one class of students—what we notice, how those scores make us feel, what we wonder about these scores, and what we think we need to do as a result.

The teacher who has volunteered his students' scores to be used to train the rest of us to read the data says, "Isn't it odd—the scores don't seem to show what I notice in the classroom," but no one asks him what he notices. I notice 89 percent of our kids are at or above benchmark on this test. I raise my hand.

Normally, I say little to nothing at staff meetings. I cannot help myself this day. I want to know what we want for our students that these numbers reveal to us. Where do we want them to be that can be shown by these numbers?

The presenter calls on me. "What is that, the *benchmark*?" I ask. The presenter looks surprised at my question. "It's where we want kids to be," she says. "No, I mean, what *is* the benchmark? Where do we want them to be?" She pulls her shoulders up, lifts her chin with her thumb, curls her fingers into a loose fist, and presses them into her face just below her bottom lip. "*At or above* the benchmark," she says, and turns back to her PowerPoint presentation on the screen.

I forgot. We are here to focus on the data—the numbers. I do not pursue the question.

With these five stories I have attempted a montage, a series of scenes that reveal some truths— who I am as a person, who I am as a teacher, who my students are, what I value, and what they value. If I have presented them clearly, the reader takes his or her own truths to them, and from them, even as I have my own reasons for telling these stories.

Why tell about my mother and my father? Because I loved them, no matter their failings and flaws and struggles. No matter my failings, they loved me. I want my students to know me. I want them to know my stories. I read them my drafts of writing because I also want them to know I value what I ask them to do enough to do it myself. I use my writing to show them how to respond in a productive way to help me better my writing, so they will respond to each other in the same constructive ways.

I want my students to understand that I am what I teach—a writer and a reader. I am writing along with them in the risky business of telling some truths about my personal life and my professional life. I know that if they write about those things that matter to them, they will make it the strongest writing they can, because they have stories, opinions, knowledge, and feelings that matter enough to them to write convincingly and compellingly, for themselves and for an audience beyond themselves.

I want my students to see all kinds of writing, including the memoir as essay. I use this writing as one example of looking at the craft of writing in this genre. I show them what I learned about crafting a scene, putting the camera on the character and the action. I help them through the implications and truths in the story by looking at what I chose to include and not include. What conclusions can they draw about these characters from what is there, what is not there? What questions do they have that I need to consider as I write? I show them several more scenes as I build a more complete story.

As they read and write, what do they notice about the craft of writing in any genre? What are they attempting to do, and growing stronger at, as they craft writing with intent and use the writing of so many fine writers to mentor their writing?

After reading the writing of Karen Hesse, Meg Kearney, Ann Turner, and Sharon Creech, Cece writes a personal narrative in poetry—fourteen poems so far—about a father she has never met, never seen, who shows up at their front door the year she turns nine with a kitten in his arms. "He thinks he can buy back our love with a kitten," her opening line reads.

Mike writes a two-page essay about observing his dad perform surgery—an aorta bifemoral bypass, a cesarean section, a knee surgery, and a femoral-to-femoral bypass—after his dad asked him, "Do you want to come see me cut people open?" He did.

In his writer's-reader's notebook, he made lists of the kinds of doctors present, the extensive equipment used, jottings about happenings (cesarean section: make incision to abdomen, . . . pull out womb, cut open womb, literally manhandles baby's head to pull out, baby comes sliding out in bluish color, put in heater, replace womb, sew up fascia, . . .), and drew diagrams of all of the surgeries, labeling the equipment used, the body parts, and procedures for each of the surgeries. He drafted his essay from these sketches.

The essay begins:

> If your dad came up to you and essentially said, "Do you want to come see me
> cut people open?" would you have said yes? I did. I didn't exactly know what
> I was putting myself into. It would be an experience of interest, some slight

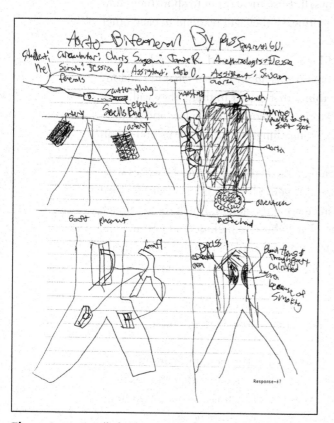 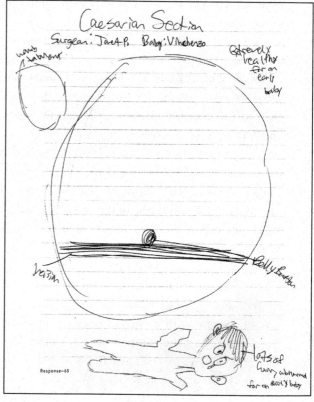

Figure Intro.1 *Mike's First Draft Sketches of Observations During Various Surgeries*

gore, perseverance, and a little bit of hands on. I also thought it would be an experience of a lifetime, so I said yes.

Surgery is important to me because it's my dad's job, and I am considering practicing medicine someday. Surgery saves people's lives and can make them a whole lot better. Surgeons must have very steady hands, smart and quick minds, and be able to not have their skin crawl at the sight of blood.

In the essay, Mike admires the characteristics of the surgeons—their knowledge of body parts, their confidence in knowing what to do when a procedure does not go exactly as planned, and their ability to work efficiently and skillfully while holding someone's life (and body parts) in their hands. Mike's dad found his son composed and intrigued throughout the surgeries, concluding that watching these operations made him even more interested in medicine in his future.

Mike's Second Draft: Caesarian Section

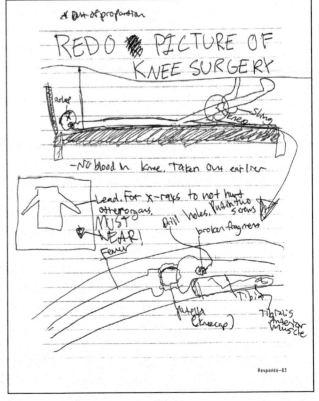

Mike's Second Draft: Knee Surgery

continues

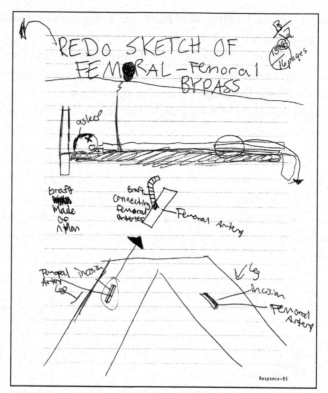

Mike's Second Draft: Femoral–Femoral Bypass

Morgan writes about her love of the beach, until her parents take the family there, sit them down in the sand, and tell them they are getting a divorce. The beach changes for Morgan and her siblings. In her second draft she begins:

> When you think about the beach, you probably picture the dazzling sapphire waves spilling onto the sun-drenched sand, wisps of happiness swirling around with the wind. The icy water engulfing your toes until they're numb. You probably remember the sun's hot kisses. But when I think about the beach, all I picture is sadness. The bright, colorful memories concealed by sorrow and confusion that ripped our family at the seams.

> *   *   *   *   *

> One . . . two . . . three minutes of complete silence pass. I glance back and forth at my parents. Why haven't they said anything? I can feel the salty wind blowing my hair.

Stories define us and nourish us—intellectually, aesthetically, imaginatively, and emotionally. Our stories, and the stories of others, teach us to be human.

I was shocked to hear a presenter tell us to "forget the stories of our students." I cannot forget Jewelia's story, as she describes pushing food around on her plate and all it implies about what is going on in her life. Even as a first draft, she knows how to effectively write a poignant, compelling scene. She slides back and forth between past and present tense. But this is first-draft writing. We will talk about being consistent with tense if she chooses to take this to a more finished draft. What is more important is that I let her know that I care as much about her, and all she is going through, as much as I want to help her continue to craft a piece of good writing that helps her negotiate her world, a piece of writing that helps her clarify her thinking and speaks to a larger audience.

I cannot help Morgan craft her story as a piece of literature until I let her know how sorry I am her entire family has had to go through this troubling time—for all of them. Since writing is helping her work through all that is still going on in her life because of this divorce, I want to help her craft the event and feeling into the strongest writing.

Now we can talk about ways of entering this story in a surprising way, to reflect the shock she and her siblings felt when they learned the truth of this trip to the beach. "What if you start with what you, and most readers, expect at the beach, and then jump right to the scene? What if you sit us down next to you on the sand?" I ask her as we talk about the writing. Through the entire piece of writing, she continues to work out her surprise, her anger, her disappointment, and her eventual understanding of this event. She will draft and redraft this writing until it clearly portrays her feelings, her story, because it matters to her.

Our emphasis *should be* on the stories. The numbers give us a look through the window into our students' strengths and weaknesses, too often as test takers, not in the context of their lives. It's in their experiences, their efforts, and actual accomplishments as writers and readers that a much wider and deeper picture is revealed. I want to invite them into the house, not just take a peek through the window.

I carry Howard's story with me into the classroom in September. I can see it, hear it, feel it. What is the truth he reveals to me in this story about this little boy and the trout? How well do I know my students? What matters to them? What has hurt them? What makes each of them different? How do I let them know I care about them? How do I help them care about and respect each other? How do I build on their strengths?

It is the stories we remember that define us as thinking, feeling human beings. Every time I look into the faces of my students, I try to remember, "If you see a little boy with a trout, cook it for him."

Ursula LeGuin told us this when she said, "The story—from Rumpelstiltskin to *War and Peace*—is one of the basic tools of the human mind for the purpose of understanding. There have been great societies that did not use the wheel, but there have been no societies that did not tell stories" (Pink 2006, 105).

Daniel Pink confirms the importance of story in our thinking in the twenty-first century, when he reminds us:

> Stories are easier to remember—because in many ways, stories are *how* we remember. "Narrative imagining—story—is the fundamental instrument of thought," writes cognitive scientist Mark Turner in his book *The Literary Mind*. "Rational capacities depend on it. It is our chief means of looking into the future, of predicting, of planning, and of explaining. . . . Most of our experience, our knowledge and our thinking is organized as stories." (Pink 2006, 101)

> Stories are important cognitive events, for they encapsulate, into one compact package, information, knowledge, context, and emotion. (Pink 2006, 103)

> Stories can provide context enriched by emotion, a deeper understanding of how we fit in and why that matters. The Conceptual Age can remind us what has always been true but rarely been acted upon—that we must listen to each other's stories and that we are each the authors of our own lives. (Pink 2006, 115)

In the education of our children, we must remember their stories and work to invite and encourage them. As Daniel Pink reminds us, it is how they remember their past and shape their future.

Children are not numbers. My teaching cannot be defined by the data of numbers alone. Numbers may be a portion of the story, but they are just that—a small piece. My teaching is defined by the stories my students tell. Stories in the classroom—that fill their portfolios and journals. Stories that tumble out of them in response to stories they hear and read. Stories in the hall, or out at recess, in the lunchroom, the locker room, or study hall. Stories of historians and scientists, musicians, and athletes. Stories of their lives that I can help them craft into essays, poetry, memoirs, letters, reviews, speeches, short stories, and so on.

Story shows that we are thinking, feeling human beings with connections and relationships to each other. When I write about those things that I believe, and think, and feel, students do also.

What have I learned, after years of teaching? I want the same things for kids that I wanted when I began teaching. I want them to like reading and writing. I want them to be the best they can be at both. I want them to know that their opinions, their beliefs, their imaginations, their voices, and their lives matter. I want them to ask big questions of themselves—who am I and where do I fit in this world? I want them to ask big questions of each other and their worlds. I want them to notice what is going on around them and imagine the ways they might solve the dilemmas and situations in which we find ourselves.

I want them to be curious and creative. I want them to see and understand the lives of others. I want them to gain empathy and understanding of just what it means to be a human being. I want them to read and write with their head and their heart.

I want them to have choices in their lives, and the better they are at reading and writing, the more choices they will have, and the more thoughtful they will be in those choices they make.

I want them to be articulate, compassionate citizens of the world who can communicate their thoughts and beliefs and feelings well to others, and who can understand and evaluate the thoughts and feelings and beliefs of others. I want them to work together cooperatively and collaboratively to solve the problems in the world. I want them to have a voice.

I want my classroom to be a place where we value stories, not just numbers. I want a place where our curiosity and creativity are valued. I want to honor Julie's three-year-old daughter, where I let my students "lire a l'envers." (Read in their imaginations.)

Benjamin Zander, conductor of the Boston Philharmonic, said that after twenty years of conducting he had a life-changing realization. "The conductor of an orchestra doesn't make a sound. . . . My picture appears on the front of the CD—but the conductor doesn't make a sound. He depends, for his power, on his ability to make other people powerful. . . . I realized, my job was to awaken possibility in other people."

He continues, "I wanted to know if I was doing that. And you know how you find out? You look at their eyes. If their eyes are shining, you know you're doing it. If their eyes are not shining, you get to ask a question . . . Who am I being, that my children's eyes are not shining?" (Zander 2008).

These are the questions I am trying to carry into my classroom when I begin again each September. Am I awakening possibilities in my students as writers so they see their voices have power—the power to make others think, or feel, or learn something?

Who am I being to *get* my students eyes shining? In what ways have I awakened possibilities in each of these students as readers, as writers, as people?

What are the questions you carry into your classroom every September? In what ways are you awakening possibilities in your students? How are you offering them choices and challenges as readers and writers?

My hope is that my students, through their writing and speaking in this book, will help answer some of those questions as you think about your students.

The Essential Questions That Frame Our Year

Choice is the focus for my students' learning and my teaching. These are the essential questions that frame the year for students and for me:

- What choices do you make as a writer and a reader? In what ways do those choices lead you to becoming a stronger writer and reader?

- What choices do writers make that you notice in your reading of their works that make their writing so strong, and that you will try in your writing?

- In real life, and in literature, what are the consequences of little to no choice in a person's life? What choices do these real people and these fictional characters make in response to their experiences? What choices do they make to nudge the world a little?

- What would you still like to do as a reader and a writer that you have not had a chance to do? What topic or issue would you like to investigate and present in a variety of ways? What choices do you make to nudge the world a little?

CHAPTER ONE

Grounding Our Choices in Our Beliefs

Everything you find in this book comes from thirty years of learning from adolescents, from thirty years of writing and reading myself (both professionally and personally, but only after I began teaching), and from thirty years of constantly questioning myself daily about the things that went well and the things that went badly. The challenges. Why did that work with one class and not the others? How can I reach this student? How do I convince all kids that reading and writing well will matter to them? From asking kids every year, "What makes writing easy for you? What makes reading easy for you? What helped you the most as a reader and writer? What could I have done differently? What could you have done differently?"

When we offer our students choices, the challenges often feel exacerbated. They choose a difficult topic. They choose a controversial book. They choose not to write. They choose not to read.

Writing and reading are not options in my classroom. I expect students to read and write. *What* they read and write is mostly up to them. My job is to help them find that writing and that reading that matters so much to them that they want to keep writing and they want to keep reading. My choices are guided by the students, who they are, and what they walk through the door of Room 201 knowing, thinking, and believing. And my choices are guided by my beliefs and experiences drawn from the past thirty years.

What You Will Find in This Book

- The beliefs that ground my teaching and the students' learning.
- How I frame the year for an abundance of writing and reading.
- The goals I have for the students, guided by the goals they have for themselves.

- The reading and writing opportunities that lead the students to deeper understandings of themselves, others, and the world around them.
- The handouts—the expectations and the guidelines—I give to students throughout the year.
- The voices of adolescents—examples of their writing, drawing, and thinking— as thoughtful readers, writers, and citizens of the world.

I do not do everything I am sharing with you every year. I have the students for forty-five to fifty minutes a day—all reading and writing—in the language arts class. The students are heterogeneously grouped with a range of abilities, including some kids who struggle with decoding words to others who are reading well the works of Malcolm Gladwell, Jane Austen, or Khaled Hosseini. I have kids who tell me they hate reading and writing and kids who tell me they love reading and writing. I try to find out what all the children are capable of doing at the beginning of the year, what has made reading and writing easy or hard for them, and I encourage, cajole, nudge, shove, and teach them to be the best they can be at reading and writing by the end of the year.

When I talk to the students about writing, I frequently remind them that they must write for themselves first. I tell them, "You have to like what you are writing. You have to have a strong desire to figure out what needs to be said and how best to say it. You have to have feelings about the subject about which you are writing. We all write for ourselves first—because we have something to say."

I am writing this book for myself. It is an attempt to organize my thinking, my planning, my materials—for my students, and for me. The kids are different every year. I can't anticipate what they already know and can do, any more than I can anticipate the experiences they come with. This year I have a young woman who only speaks Arabic or German. I have a young man who is only well enough to attend two classes a week. I have a young woman who spent the past six months in Patagonia, another who has never left New Hampshire. I have another who is homeless. What I do know is that I will try to get to know each of them to figure out what works best for each. Who are they as readers and writers, and how do they learn best? What are their stories?

You will find the what, the how, and the why of a year's planning. It's the frame that guides me, but it is flexible and malleable. Make this book yours. Take what's helpful of mine, but reconfigure, extend, change anything to fit you, your students, and your beliefs. But do think through your own beliefs.

What grounds your teaching? What do you believe about language arts, about writing, about reading? What do you do to get to know the stories of your students?

Our students want to know what's expected of them and why they are doing certain things. How they choose to do something may—and should—look different for many of our students. I want them to challenge themselves to find unique ways of representing their understandings.

For years I was comfortable with the *what*—get kids reading and writing—but I quickly realized I needed to know more. I read a lot of professional journals, took courses, went to workshops and summer institutes to figure out more of the *how*. I paid attention to the students and asked them constantly why something worked for them and why something else didn't. I asked, and still do ask, "How'd you do that?"

"Common sense" was my reasoning for the *why*. But that, too, wasn't enough. For myself I wanted to answer *why*. What beliefs did I, do I hold that ground my choices of the *what* and the *how*?

I have set the book up as a road map for designing, framing, and teaching writing and reading, with speaking and listening embedded in all that we do. What are the goals and beliefs that ground my teaching and learning? What do I want my students to be able to do? What evidence will they give me that shows they are reaching the challenges? How do I go about designing and planning the experiences they need to get there? How do I frame the classroom in ways that offer choices and challenges?

Goals for Students

I want students to:

- write and read with their head and their heart
- know that their abilities to write, read, and speak well offer them the greatest range of choices in their present and future lives
- enjoy reading, writing, speaking, and listening
- challenge and respect themselves and others as writers, readers, and speakers
- realize that their stories, beliefs, knowledge, questions, and opinions matter to themselves and to others
- know that their reading and writing are meant to help them make discoveries about themselves and connections with others by affirming, questioning, and extending their thinking
- develop into the strongest writers, readers, and speakers they can be, by showing growth from September to June.

Language Arts Goals

In all of our classrooms, we have to frame our curricular choices—what we do and how we do it—on the goals or outcomes we want for our students. Therefore, language arts goals are designed with curricular choices that are meant to enable, guide, inspire, motivate, and teach students to:

- become competent, enthusiastic, lifelong readers, writers, and speakers, who are able to understand, create, interpret, appreciate, evaluate, and critique language and literature

- develop into literate, articulate, thinking, feeling young men and women, who contribute creatively and productively to society by communicating effectively with others, by understanding the world in which they live, and by finding their places in a complex and diverse world

- become informed, clear-thinking citizens by participating actively as readers, writers, speakers, listeners, and viewers

- use language effectively to create knowledge, make meaning, challenge thinking, and build community in their lives

- reflect on, and evaluate, their own use of language

- recognize and evaluate the ways in which others use language to affect them.

Core Beliefs About Teaching and the Language Arts

What we do, and how we do it, has to be grounded in the *why*—our core beliefs about teaching and the language arts:

- Being literate and using your literacy puts you in control of your thoughts, ideas, beliefs, opinions—and life.

- Learning occurs best in a safe, stimulating, challenging environment that encourages curiosity, imagination, exploration, and risk-taking.

- Teachers form trusting relationships with students that build a community of learners when they know their students' strengths, interests, and needs and when they model and demonstrate their own writing and reading.

- Language learning is a developmental process with students progressing at varying rates and therefore necessitates a variety of materials and teaching techniques.

- Writing is a complex process through which the writer moves recursively, shifting back and forth among steps of finding ideas, rehearsing, drafting, revising, editing, and publishing.

- Conventions of language are best learned in the context of the student's writing and reading.

- We learn to read by reading and writing; we learn to write by writing and reading.

- Reading and writing draw upon the user's experiences and prior knowledge and require critical thinking and problem-solving skills.

- Students develop fluency and grow as readers, writers, and thinkers through regular, frequent, and ample *time*; through opportunities to *choose* writing topics and books; through *constructive response and suggestions* from teachers and peers; and from involvement with a variety of *good models*.
- The acts of writing, reading, and speaking are thinking processes that involve varying degrees of recall, comprehension, application, analysis, inference, synthesis, and evaluation.
- Process is as important as product.
- Using visual tools—drawing as both thinking and performance—allows and deepens students' abilities as writers and readers.

What Students Need

To become fluent writers (and readers), students need:

- real writing—for real reasons, for real audiences
- reading that engages, interests, challenges.

Students can do their best work when given:

- time
- choice
- response (toward revision, while drafting)
  - Point out what they did well.
  - Ask questions they need to consider.
  - Offer suggestions.
- *models* of fine reading and writing (both fiction and nonfiction, from professionals, their peers, and their teacher)
- *strategies* for entering into, strengthening, and extending that writing and reading
- a writer's-reader's notebook—a place to collect their thinking
- encouragement to use visual tools to show their thinking as writers and their understandings as readers.

I have the words of Tom Stoppard on the wall in my classroom.

> Words are sacred. They deserve respect. If you get the right ones, in the right order, you can nudge the world a little.

That is what I want for my students—to know their words *can nudge the world a little*. And I want the world to nudge them a bit. I want them to be thoughtful, caring citizens of the world, who are respectful, and respected, human beings. I believe that if they read critically, talk out their thinking often, and write compellingly, they can influence the thinking of others.

As I work in my own classroom, and with teachers throughout the United States and internationally, I am increasingly aware, and concerned, that kids are not being allowed, encouraged, or taught to "nudge the world." At every turn there are new sets of standards, new scripted programs, new standardized tests, new mandates that do everything in their power to standardize kids. It feels like we are moving backward, not forward, in our understandings of how learning and growth happen.

Growth happens by trying things we haven't tried before. By making mistakes and trying again. We try to solve problems through our speaking and writing. Maybe we didn't say it clearly enough, or persuasively enough. We try again. Our teaching happens when we push, guide, and teach our students how to do that.

The importance of writing was underscored for me in 1990, when I was invited to spend several weeks in the small town of Haapsalu, Estonia, teaching seventh graders. The desks and chairs were bolted to the floor. There were few supplies. Even fewer books.

On the first day, the students arrived twenty minutes early to find chairs (that I had scavenged) arranged in a circle. They were shocked. They were not accustomed to facing each other, let alone talking to each other. They were used to a teacher delivering information, and understood that their role was to parrot back that information, exactly as it was presented. No diversions. No questions. No disagreements. No imagining. Absolutely no critical or evaluative thinking. At least that they dared to voice.

They were still under Soviet rule, as they had been for fifty years. It took awhile before *this* wall began to tumble. It started with a whisper from Irinni, "Are you sure we may say what we think?" Then Tiuu, then Havel. "You want us to write what we think? Will it not be trouble?"

"It won't be trouble!" I assured them, not sure myself if that was true.

They talked and wrote. I heard their lives. Their disappointments. Their tragedies. Their wishes. Their beliefs. Their dreams. Their questions. Their ideas. They arrived thirty minutes early for class every single day and stayed later and later. No matter how hard I tried, I couldn't get to class before they did. Sitting in a circle, they waited patiently and enthusiastically, to talk and question, to think and write.

These thirteen- and fourteen-year-olds had not been allowed to voice their thoughts. Young men and women I didn't even have in the class began showing up, ostensibly to "learn English." It didn't matter what language it was. I could have spoken Swedish or Spanish or Tagalog. They wanted to talk about important issues, world issues, which mattered in their lives. They were hungry for books. They wanted to know what others thought, how others lived. They wanted to be connected to the world. They wanted a voice.

I knew then, as I know now, that if we want children to become adults who are articulate, literate, and thoughtful citizens of the world, they must learn to think deeply and widely as both readers and writers. They must talk and share their thinking. They must commit their thinking to paper, learning how to be memoirists, poets, essayists, journalists, playwrights, activists, speechwriters, novelists, critics, scientists, historians, so they and others can examine, support, debate, challenge, and then refine those beliefs, feelings, and thoughts.

Writing and reading are about using our imaginations, our understandings, our questions, our creativity, our feelings, our humanity to work through our thinking about ourselves, about others, about the world in which we live. Surely this is crucial enough to merit our attention. It is, after all, what we are about in our classrooms. In an era of test mania (in the United States, anyway) we tend to forget, or dismiss, the importance of writing and often concentrate on reading "strategies" or writing "exercises" at the expense of real writing and real reading. If we allow that, others will do our thinking, as I learned only too well in Estonia when it was under Soviet rule.

Writing is hard work. It is time-consuming. It is frightening. It is rewarding. It helps us pay attention to the world. Good writing lets writer and reader learn or think or feel something. Putting words on paper—or on the Internet—gives us voice—allows us to be heard. All the more reason to do it at every opportunity. And then to do it some more.

The best writing not only gives us voice, it is filled with voice. Tom Romano in his book *Crafting Authentic Voice* says:

> Voice is the writer's presence in a piece of writing. My bias as a writing teacher
> is to teach students to write in accessible, engaging, and irresistible voices.
> Such voices . . . have certain qualities in common:
>
> - They deliver interesting information.
> - They often employ techniques of narrative.
> - They exhibit perceptivity.
> - They offer surprising information and observations.
> - Quite often, they demonstrate a sense of humor.
>
> (Romano 2004, 24)

The best way to understand what Tom is saying is to look at the writing of several students. These are drafts of writing that went through conferences with peers and with me, asking questions and offering suggestions, to help the writer craft the strongest voice.

Student Examples of Writing
Alden: Essay

Alden studied Rick Reilly as a mentor author, reading one of his books, *The Life of Reilly*, and numerous op-ed pieces, looking at the craft of his writing. He wrote several book reviews, an analysis of all he learned from this reading, and the following persuasive essay that captures the essence of his study of Reilly's writing: writing often laced with sarcasm, but for the purpose of making a profound point in a convincing argument about the unfortunate way we value sports in this country.

> This year in the NHL was definitely one of the most memorable in a long time. This is the first year in the history of the NHL that every single goalie had a Goals Against Average (GAA) of 0.00 and no players scored any goals. Not even one. Oops, maybe I forgot to mention the fact that the NHL didn't happen this year, and that it was officially cancelled a few weeks ago, when Gary Bettman, the commissioner of the league, announced that the players association couldn't come to an agreement with the NHL about the salary cap limit.
>
> At the point of the cancellation there had been a total of 155 days missed because of the lockout, and there had been 1,161 games cancelled. During that time, the average person would have taken 3,100,00 breaths, slept for 1300 hours, watched 600 hours of television, and gone #2 about 150 times. Personally, I think the league should have been cancelled a long time ago, right around the 20th trip to the john. After canceling over 100 games, I gave up all hope and decided that the NHL had absolutely no chance of making it.
>
> But seriously, let's take a minute to stop and figure out what these people are having such a grueling debate about. The NHL proposed a rejected salary cap of $44.7 million. If the money was distributed evenly throughout the team, each player would earn somewhere in the area of 1.9 million dollars a year. 1.9 MILLION dollars! I would die for a salary like that. I'd be blowin' my nose in Benjamin's and wipin' my butt with Grant's if I was rakin' in that kind of dough! (That'd be pretty sweet, huh?) Anyways, after the players rejected that offer, they suggested a $49 million cap. With $49 million per team, each player would get about $2.1 million. Wait! What?! This entire debate has been over 0.2 million dollars! Wow!
>
> Well, at least we Americans can say that the athletes of our era aren't getting greedy. I mean, that would be just so horrible if they were so greedy as to not play for an entire year because they want $0.2 million more on

their contracts. The average player makes around $2 million. So it's great that our athletes are mature enough to play hockey instead of arguing over the measly sum of $200,000. I mean $200,000 is only like the salary of five Americans in one year. But that's nothing to the pro hockey players of our day. Adding $200,000 to their salary is only adding 10% to the total. Basically, 10% of a pro hockey player's salary is worth as much as the salary of five Americans. Gee, I sure am glad there's not a massive debate over that kind of money!

I can't wait until I get older, and I have a chance to pursue my hockey career by joining the players' association. Maybe by the time I'm there we can debate over $250,000 when each player is making about $8 million a year. That'd be great! And then everyone in the U.S. would think so highly of me, and I'd be a star!

Pssh! Who am I kidding!? The NHL is a joke! This year has probably been the most pathetic year in the history of our sports. The athletes are getting so amazingly greedy that the entire Great Wall of China would be needed to stop the landslide of greed our athletes created. If I, or any of my children, grow up to be athletes, I'll definitely make sure that our minimum salary is $20 mil and I wouldn't stand for anything less. I mean, that's not greedy or anything, is it?

Alden read Reilly deeply. He understood how Reilly presented his opinion, but in an engaging and biting way, using humor and sarcasm to leave the reader thinking about the issue presented.

Nate: Personal Narrative

Like Alden, whose opinion comes through loud and clear in this piece, Nate's final draft was filled with his presence in a piece of writing that engages the reader with humor, yet wends its way with dramatic *emotional restraint* to a startling conclusion. (Mike Winerip, Educational Columnist for the *New York Times*, used those words—*emotional restraint*—to describe Nate's writing. Mike spent the morning in my classroom, in the process of doing an article. He sat in on writing conferences. After Nate read his piece, for response from his peers, Mike leaned in and said to Nate, "You know, you have done things as a writer that many professional writers have not yet learned to do.")

Nate held the tension well throughout the piece, pulling the reader between the house and all he can get away with in the absence of his mom, and the hospital, where something serious seems to be happening.

Diagnosis

No moms, no sisters. That left me, now at the superior age of nine years old, and my dad at home. That meant eating large bowls of ice cream and watching movies on TV that mom would never allow.

My mom grabbed the keys with one hand and Anna in the other and said, "We'll be home by 8:30 at the latest, hopefully earlier," and walked out the door. That meant I had about an hour to an hour and a half to do essentially whatever I wanted.

As soon as I saw the headlights of the Honda Odyssey disappear around the corner, I ran to the couch in front of the TV and slammed on the remote button until I reached what I was looking for, Oceans 11, a movie about a bunch of criminals who were going to steal billions of dollars from a casino. A commercial started to roll, so I ran to the refrigerator to get myself a bowl of ice cream.

When I sat back down my dad walked into the room. This was the moment of truth. If my dad noticed that I was watching something that my mom would not allow, he wouldn't just make me change the channel, he would make me turn off the TV for good. He stopped in front of the TV to see what I was watching. When the commercial ended and the show started up again, my dad realized what I was watching and said, "Oh, Oceans 11? Good show!" and he plopped down on the couch next to me. It was then that I realized I was in for the night.

We had just moved to New Hampshire a week earlier, so we still didn't have a doctor. This was a problem because Anna, who was now three, was looking sick. She would not eat any dinner, the glands under her chin on the top of her throat were swollen, and she had a temperature of 102 degrees. Since we didn't have a doctor, my mom had to take her to the emergency room just for having a fever. I guess Kelsey, my six-year-old other sister, was too scared to stay at the new house without my mom, so she went, too.

After two hours of shooting, swears, and sex, it still had not occurred to me or my dad why the three females in the family had not arrived back home yet or, at least, called to let us know that they would be late. A half an hour passed of not really focusing on the movie and worrying why my mom and two sisters were missing.

My dad peeled away from the TV and started to do dad-like things for the first time. He called my mom's cell phone. No answer. Again. No answer. On the third attempt, Kelsey answered. She said that Anna was in one of the rooms and my mom was in there with her and that she had been in there for about an hour and she had no idea when she would get out. That was it. My sister had given us all the information she had, so we were just as clueless as she was.

My dad and I went back to our vegetative state for a half hour more when the phone rang. It was my mom. This time it was her voice on the phone. She was saying that the doctors did not have a clue as to what Anna had. My mom explained that she and Anna would have to ride in an ambulance to Children's Hospital of Boston, where there were better doctors and more advanced technology. My dad told me this on the way to pick up Kelsey at the emergency room.

The ride was the longest of my life. My mind raced through all of the worst possible things that could happen. My hands were clenched so tight my knuckles were bone white. I wished this were a dream.

When we arrived at the hospital, Kelsey was standing with a police officer, who informed us that my mom and Anna were on their way to Boston in an ambulance already. Kelsey was wrapped in a blanket and shivering. Her red eyes led me to the conclusion that she had been crying. It was then that I realized that this was very, very bad.

Nobody spoke on the ride back to the unpacked house. When we shut the door and locked it for the day, Kelsey broke out in tears and sobbed, "I want Mommy!" My now red-eyed dad rushed her upstairs to bed, leaving me alone, hyperventilating in the half-lit house.

The phone rang. My dad and sister were upstairs, so I answered the phone. I picked it up, cradled it in both hands, took a deep breath, held the phone to my ear, and croaked, "Yes?"

"This is the Children's Hospital of Boston. Is this the McCrone residence?"

"Yes."

"Is Matthew available?"

"No."

"Well, . . . doctors have taken tests and we have the results." I heard wails in the background, the saddest wails I have ever heard in my life, and realized they belonged to my mom. My hands started to sweat. My eyes started to cross.

"Anna has Leukemia, a cancer of the blood."

I did not know what "Leukemia" meant, but the word "cancer" was enough. I dropped the receiver as my legs buckled. My insides burst. Knives stabbed into my brain. I was left there wondering, why Anna? Why us?

Before Mike Winerip left the classroom, he asked if he could take copies of the writing from several of the students, including Nate. In a subsequent email, I asked him what he noticed in the student writing, particularly Nate's. This is how he responded:

> I reacted so strongly for several reasons. Nate displayed a storytelling ability that I've rarely seen in someone his age, along with an ability to convey emotion so powerfully, and yet with restraint, a rare talent for writers of any age.
>
> He breaks his larger drama—going from a cozy night at home to the horror of his sister's illness—into several smaller dramas. There is the story of waiting for his Mother to drive off so he can watch Oceans 11 and the tension over whether she will find out. Then there's the question of whether his Dad will scold him or join him in his sinful pleasure; then the story of why he was alone—his sister's fever—with just enough information to give the reader a vague sense of worry; the tension of what his Dad will discover as he makes the calls and at the hospital; the hospital with the awful truth—what's going on with his Mom and sister—literally hidden behind the (hospital) curtain; and the final horror of a child answering the phone and mistakenly hearing the unbearable news meant for an adult.
>
> Each story progresses seamlessly to the next through subtle foreshadowing: "We had just moved to N.H. so we didn't have a doctor." "The ride was one of the longest of my life."
>
> He uses simple language to convey great emotion—"leaving me alone, hyperventilating in the half-lit house."
>
> And finally, the curt realistic, thoroughly-believable dialogue we can't read fast enough so we can get to the end of that extraordinary phone call. We want to know exactly what Nate wants to know. The rhythm of those sentences hits one after the other, like a heart pounding: I dropped the receiver. Boom. My legs buckled. Boom. My insides burst. And finally the question that applies to his family, but has been asked by every human in this situation, why us?
>
> I edit narrative essays all the time for the *New York Times* and can sincerely say this is as good or better than many.

This is the kind of response—so insightful, so thorough, so positive—that I wish I could give, and try so hard to give, to all of my students on every piece they write. It will keep Nate writing for years. What *can* I do—be positive enough to keep them moving forward and thorough enough so they know what they did well enough to do it again.

Hannah: Poem from Illustration

On another day we were using drawing to find writing. I asked the students to draw a shoe or boot that held significance for them. I asked them to bring in that shoe or pair of shoes. Mike brought in a construction boot. Erika brought in her ballet slippers. Jackie brought in her first dress shoes—a pair of patent leather Mary Janes.

In pairs I had them explain to each other why they brought in these shoes or boots or slippers, and how they were special to them. They spent an entire class period drawing the shoe and talking with each other about the stories behind the shoe. I did not tell them they had to continue talking about the significance of the shoe, it just happened as they drew. More stories, deeper stories began to emerge as they drew. Hannah drew a riding boot.

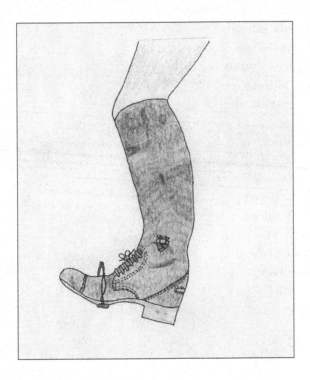

Figure 1.1 *Hannah's Drawing of Her Riding Boot*

We then looked at how other writers use pictures from which to write. Using the writing of these professional writers as a stepping-off point, we wrote. What began as a two-minute quickwrite in response to Ted Kooser's poem "Abandoned Farmhouse," which he had written in response to a piece of art, eventually became a polished piece of poetry for Hannah. In her thinking, she worked hard at making the writing say exactly what she wanted to say in the clearest, most compelling way, not just about the riding boot, but how it made her think about all she noticed about her riding coach. She drafted, redrafted, read, reread, answered questions, corrected conventions, and found great satisfaction, pride, and joy knowing her piece mattered to her and elicited response from a real audience, her classmates.

She Rode Often
(With thanks to Ted Kooser for "Abandoned Farmhouse")

She rode often
say the wrinkles
on the black leather.
She worked hard says
the dust covering the boots, one folded
and fallen over to the side. She
loved the pony says the box
of pictures and ribbons sitting
next to the boots. She quit
says the box by the trash. She
made a mistake say
the empty beer bottles
cluttering the floor. She
left quickly says the empty
apartment with the phone
ringing and the TV still on.
She's recovering says the car
parked at the barn. She's
safe say the pony's eyes
as she holds its head

and the world
with all its troubles
melts away.

Hannah told a story in her poem, conveying strong perceptions of the world, with a sense of play with language, even in the most serious of pieces. Her voice was palpable. It was convincing in conveying astonishment at the adult world, her riding coach, and the poignancy and honesty about all she notices.

Sanam: Constitution Day Essay

In response to a Constitution Day essay contest—Should the United States put into law compulsory voting for all its citizens?—sponsored by the State of New Hampshire Supreme Court and local newspapers, Sanam wrote the following essay.

Not Every Horse Must Drink

"The spirit of democracy cannot be imposed from without. It has to come from within." —Mohandas Karamhand Gandhi

"Democracy is a device that insures we shall be governed no better than we deserve." —George Bernard Shaw

I don't believe that citizens should be forced by law to vote, for ultimately, it is their choice. However, voting is an immensely important privilege. People have a chance to determine how they are governed at the city, state, and federal levels. Although the Electoral College process in presidential elections implies that every vote doesn't count, people should assume it does. The general direction of the vote is determined by each individual vote.

Voting should not be made mandatory. Forced voting will make people who don't inform themselves of issues to vote for the sake of voting, and not because they care. Care comes with political awareness. A certain level of knowledge is required for a vote to be meaningful. Although Enlightenment philosophers, like John Locke, advocated for democracy on the belief that all people had the ability to reason, I do not believe everyone in a democracy develops their innate ability to reason and attain knowledge. Mandatory voting can compound the problem of ill-informed and arbitrary choices.

Voting under compulsion results in unfairness to those who choose to vote based on reason and knowledge. Forced votes can end up being based on shallow reasons. Such votes can hurt by countering the informed vote. A candidate can end up being elected based on extraneous rather than on well thought-out reasons.

In conclusion, as Gandhi's words suggest, enforced voting itself contradicts individuals' constitutional right to freedom of expression. However, if the horse led to the water does not drink, then, as Shaw suggests, the horse should not complain of thirst.

I look for every opportunity for students to write for real reasons for a real audience beyond the classroom. Local, state, and national contests afford them the opportunity to develop and extend their voices. I asked all students to try this essay. I began by giving students several quotes that might lead their thinking to agree, and several that might lead them to disagree, with the essay question. The students wrote fast. This was first-draft thinking that gave them a place to begin. What's their position, what's their reasoning that supported their position, and what conclusions did they want to leave with the reader? We talked about what makes an engaging lead, what makes a strong impression for an ending, and how using a brief comment by knowledgeable well-known writers or thinkers is one way to introduce and reinforce your thinking.

Like any other piece of writing, students read the writing to me and to their peers for response—what was clear, and what needed clarification through questions and suggestions? All of the students wrote; not all of them chose to send their writing to the contest. Sanam did send hers. She was the statewide winner in her age group, invited to a reception at the Superior Court hosted by Chief Justice John T. Broderick, Jr. Her essay was not dismissed because it did not follow a format—it only had four paragraphs. It was honored because she provided a clear opinion in an engaging format with strong evidential reasoning.

Alden's, Nate's, Hannah's, and Sanam's writing make us think *and* feel *and* learn something. None of it is first-draft writing. They received feedback in progress, as they were writing: this is what you did well, these are the questions we have, and here is a suggestion or two that would help you further develop this piece of writing.

These students are only four of the many adolescents with whom I work daily, who learn how to develop their ideas, how to express their opinions, how to dig into their imaginations, how to develop their thinking, by learning how to manipulate words and ideas to say exactly what they mean. They learn how to use their voices. This hard work of writing gives each student deep satisfaction and pleasure because they not only clarify their own thinking, they nudge someone else's thinking.

As teachers, what we do has to be based on sound philosophical, theoretical, pedagogical, and humanitarian underpinnings. What do I believe and why? How do I shape those beliefs into sound practices in the classroom? Who are the students with whom, and from whom, I learn, to whom I teach, and for whom I care and have a responsibility?

When we ask questions of ourselves, when we think about what it is that keeps students growing or not growing as readers and writers, when we gather student work over time as evidence to support our beliefs, to confirm our suspicions and wonderings, when we continually ask the students to describe those things that help them and don't help them (and why), and when we use all this evidence to inform our instruction, we are contributing practical, meaningful, valuable, and valid information to the educational conversation. To grow as learners and teachers, we must always be researchers in our own classrooms. What I have learned frames my beliefs about writing and forms the foundation—the why—for all that I do.

Beliefs About Writing

- Writing is thinking—it is a complex, cognitive, idiosyncratic, *reading* process through which the writer moves recursively, building meaning by finding ideas, gathering information, organizing material, trying out ideas in drafts, revising and restructuring the content, editing for conventions, and publishing.

   Studies of how writers actually work show them shuffling through phases of planning, reflection, drafting, and revision, though rarely in a linear fashion. Each phase requires problem-solving and critical thinking. (National Writing Project and Nagin 2003, 10)

- Writers learn to write by writing, not by filling in worksheets or taking notes about writing. *practicum so far*

Students need to be engaged in the act of writing and reading on a continual basis. "A constant state of composition" as Don Graves so often said, so they are always thinking about writing—looking for ideas, rethinking their ideas, and noticing in their reading what writers do.

- Writing grows out of many different purposes and many different audiences; therefore, writers do their best work when they have a real reason to write for a real audience.

No one wants to write for a meaningless exercise. Writing is hard work. We want our efforts to mean something by knowing our words affect someone or something. The writer may be writing to clarify her own thinking—thus, the writing is for self first, but often, when done well, speaks to a larger audience, whether it is intentional or unintentional.

- Conventions of language are best taught in the context of writing—either with individual writers or in whole-class instruction.

   Experiments over the last fifty years have shown negligible improvements in the quality of student writing as a result of grammar instruction. Research suggests that the finer points of writing, such as punctuation and subject-verb agreement, may be learned best while students are engaged in extended writing that has the purpose of communicating a message to an audience. (Anderson et al. 1985, 22)

In my experiences as a teacher and as a writer, I have found that the more students are engaged in a piece of writing that means something to them and has an intentional audience for the writing, the more the students want to, and do, edit for the purpose of clarity for the reader.

- Writers need to be taught a repertoire of strategies for finding, starting, developing, and polishing that writing.

- Writing grows in a social context that encourages writers to share their writing with others who are taught how to give helpful feedback.

- Response to writing is most helpful when it is given in the process of drafting and shows the writer what she did well, asks questions as a serious listener, and offers suggestions that help the writer move the writing forward.

Reading his own writing aloud to a listener for feedback, questions, and suggestions allows the writer to hear his own voice and helps the writer revise and edit. Revision and editing are best taught through intentional craft lessons that may be as whole-class instruction or focused toward the individual writer.

Ideally, response through conferences is the most helpful, where the writer can read her writing to the teacher or peers to get immediate feedback. Unfortunately, large numbers of students and limited time often make a written conference, focusing on the strengths of the paper and offering a few well-placed questions and suggestions, the best we can do.

- Writing is reading. The more students write, the stronger they become as writers and readers, always asking, "Have I made my meaning clear in the simplest, most compelling ways?"

When students write, they are engaged in a recursive process of critical thinking—critical reading: Have I said clearly what I want to say? Is this well organized in developing my ideas? Have I used the sharpest, tightest, most vivid language? Does my lead capture a reader and give them a clear direction and focus? Does my writing make the reader think or feel or learn something? When kids are engaged in the process of writing something that matters to them, they do write, and they do read, thoughtfully and thoroughly.

We want students to read the same way, questioning the text. Does the author do all he can do, and how does he do it, to let the reader draw meaning from, and take meaning to, the writing?

- Meaningful assessment takes into account the process, as well as the product, always showing students what they did well, what they could do better, by suggesting and by teaching ways to improve their writing.

Evaluation should consist of understanding the process students go through as they compose a piece of writing, as well as the quality and effectiveness of the final product (content and conventions). Collecting the drafts of writing as a student composes her ideas allows the writer and the teacher to understand the process that works best for each student as she writes.

Understanding the process in which students engage to craft a piece of writing is as important as the final product. Asking students to verbalize that thinking through a process paper

("How did this writing come to be? Where did you get the idea? What did you do, and why, as you went from one draft to the next? What problems did you encounter? How well did you solve those problems?") shows teachers the multiple strategies writers use and teaches students to pay attention to that process so they become more independent as they develop skills as writers.

Evaluation should move the writer forward, helping him grow as a writer by identifying the strengths of the process and the product, as well as those elements or characteristics that need to be worked on.

- Writers do their best work when they are given *choice* about what they write and what they read, *time* to craft their writing and time to read, and *models* or examples of the finest writing from a variety of genres, professional writers, and their peers.

Writers need to care about, or be interested in, the topic they are writing about to craft the strongest piece. When writers care and are invested in their work, they write with passion and with voice. Even if they are asked to produce a particular genre, they will engage more fully in developing the best piece if they are given a choice of topics within that specific genre.

Students rethink their drafts and edit for the correct conventions when that writing matters to them. Students should be given ample opportunities to write so that choice includes selecting what pieces of writing best represent all they are capable of as writers.

Students need ample opportunities to write on a continuous basis with choices into the topics and genres that engage their interest and/or to which they can connect. When writers are engaged in the process of writing something that matters to them, for which they have their own purposes, that writing often surprises, delights, and empowers them, and therefore, they make a stronger commitment to the crafting of the writing.

Although there are times when students must write to deadline, the best writing usually develops when students are given adequate time to consider their topics, draft and redraft their ideas, and receive feedback while engaged in the process of writing. Asking students for less writing so that they have more time to develop their ideas more fully often produces stronger writing. Students need good models of writing from which to draw their understandings of writing, both from professional models, the writing of their peers, and our writing. Using others' writing to mentor one's writing is *reading as a writer*. Each genre of writing exhibits different characteristics. Showing students models from each genre (book reviews, essays, short stories, poetry, memoir, for example) allows them to step inside that genre and draw greater understanding of its inherent characteristics.

- I must be what I teach: writer, reader, speaker, listener.

When students see me struggling with a piece of writing, when I ask for and use student feedback in my writing, when they hear my drafts and final pieces, when they notice I keep a writer's-reader's notebook, they trust me as a writer who values all I ask them to do, and trust me as a listener who has some valid questions and suggestions for their writing.

When I suggest a book, they trust me as a reader, because I read books and I try to know the interests of the students. They trust me to know them and to challenge them.

More than twenty-five years ago Don Graves and Jane Hanson invited me to accompany them to the National Council of Teachers of English (NCTE) annual convention in San Antonio to give a presentation with them focused on writing. It was my first national conference. It was my first presentation. My talk centered on the research I had done on *audience in writing* in a graduate course I had taken with Don. After our presentation, I said to him, "In ten years every teacher and student in this country will be so engaged in writing, I don't know what you'll talk about." Don looked at me, shook his head, and said, not unkindly, "Linda, . . . Linda, . . . Linda. . . ."

How smart Don was, and how much I have learned and am still learning—about teaching, about kids, about writing. I still have more questions than answers. No matter how long I teach, I will never be where I want to be, nor will I get the students as far as I think they could be as writers or readers. Every year I am haunted by the same question: How do I find the time to do all I want the kids to do as readers and writers, especially in the forty-five minutes I am given with them? I have come to understand I can't do everything. But I must remember that writing and reading are processes that grow from sustained daily engagement; therefore, students must actively write and read as often as I can make that happen.

I was especially excited about all I heard at that first NCTE conference, not only from Don and Jane but from so many other teachers and researchers looking at writing. It was so different from the way I had been "taught" writing. Book reports, essays, analyses of literature were never taught. They were assigned. I did well because I took careful notes on everything *the teacher thought* and gave back exactly what he said about an issue, a piece of literature, or a topic. I gathered any supportive information from encyclopedias or critiques written by *experts*. I footnoted everything I said. I wrote neatly and edited the conventions carefully. I constructed great covers.

I can't find a single piece of writing I did, through junior high or high school, which was grounded in my thinking. I have an autobiography I wrote for a seventh-grade class that says nothing even remotely interesting. The two pages are bland, meaningless words. The cover is lovely: carefully drawn babies, obviously copied from some greeting cards. No comments or questions from the teacher, just an A+. I did very well on all my *writing*, none of which included my beliefs, feelings, discoveries, opinions, or stories. Covers counted more than thinking. "I" was never present in my writing.

There has been so much focus on literacy *as reading* over the last two decades that we have forgotten, even abandoned, writing. We have forgotten that a person can read without writing, but she cannot write without reading. If we neglect writing while focusing our attention almost exclusively on reading, it is also *at the expense of reading*. Writers are readers. If we really want to teach kids to be the strongest readers, they need to be taught how to be the strongest writers.

We need to give students ample opportunities to write often—including short, quick responses to literature on a daily basis: "What did this reading bring to mind? What did you think or feel or learn as I read? What questions came to mind? What in your own experience is similar or different? How does this make you view the world? What did you notice the author did as a writer?"

They need time to write longer pieces of wider range and depth—and time to read those pieces aloud to their peers and teachers in conference. They need choices into the topics and genres that engage their interest and to which they can connect.

Given these opportunities for engagement with their own literature as readers, they will write and read and begin to recognize and craft their strongest pieces of writing.

Hearing the writing emerge gives me such joy and satisfaction as a teacher. It gives me energy. It is what keeps me teaching—hearing the "accessible, engaging, and irresistible" writing voices as they come to be.

Putting a book in a child's hand that they love has the same effect. "Read this," they say to each other and to me. Watching kids sprawled on the floor in front of my bookshelves, handing each other books, or seeing others so engaged they don't want to leave for the next class, keeps me teaching. It keeps me constantly on the lookout for books that the most reluctant reader "can't put down."

I try to teach writing and reading in a way that encourages, allows, and fosters the voices of our students. They are our future. If we stifle their voices by offering them only inauthentic writing and reading tasks through standardized testing and preconceived, scripted programs with little knowledge of who each child is in front of us, or what that child already knows and can do, we will get what we ask for—mediocrity.

We are headed directly toward everything Don Murray warned us about when he said, "We should be seeking diversity, not proficient mediocrity." Thus the title of my 1992 book *Seeking Diversity*. I was seeking diversity then, and I am seeking it now, even more earnestly. We have to be careful that standards don't standardize our students into proficient mediocrity. I have standards, challenging standards, but they allow for the voices of the students. I want their writing to surprise me, to keep me awake, to challenge my thinking.

Students tell me the class is hard because I make them think. I actually had a young man confront me several years ago, feet planted firmly on the floor, hands shaped into fists, voice raised and shaking as he reamed me out: "I *know* what you're doing. And *you're doing it on purpose.* You're . . . *you're trying to make me think!*"

"Yes, yes, I am," I told him. "I am trying to make you think." (I tried not to smile too broadly, and I did not apologize.)

That young man was really saying to me: "Just tell me what to do, what to think, it is so much easier. Making me think is hard work."

failure

Mine is not the perfect classroom, nor am I the perfect teacher. Far from it. There are kids I can't seem to reach, and things I say and do I wish I could take back. I have failed kids and they have failed themselves. I have not worked hard enough or smart enough to reach some of them. I carry those failures like blisters that often have me limping from the classroom. But I go back again and again, trying to find the best ways to give kids choices in their lives for life.

In the beginning of this chapter, I shared my goals and beliefs. They are the foundation upon which I make curricular decisions—they are the *why* grounding the *what* and the *how* of all I do. Those goals and beliefs form the very foundation—the core—of all that I believe—and won't give up—even in a world that is trying its best, as ee cummings says, to make us like everyone else: "To be nobody but yourself in a world which is doing its best day and night to make you like everybody else means to fight the hardest battle which any human being can fight and never stop fighting."

I have spent months, years, writing this book. Some days I can sit for hours, others I do everything I can *not* to write. I realphabetize books on the shelf to my left. I make my fifth cup of coffee. I pull the dead blossoms off the hanging plant at the front door. I sweep the garage. I reorganize the food on the shelves in the freezer. I vacuum the inside of my briefcase. "Get a grip," I tell myself, "or you'll be dragging that vacuum out to the barn again to vacuum cobwebs!"

I pull all the books about writing from my shelves. I must reread them all, I think. See what others have to say that I've forgotten. I search the NCTE and International Reading Association journals for articles specifically on writing. I am encircled with piles—stacks I cannot possibly get through. In the end, it is my thinking, my experiences, my students, my teaching, my learning that will have to inform this writing about writing and reading.

As I write, I force myself to clarify my thinking. What *is* working in my classroom with respect to writing and reading? What makes it hard? What makes it easy? What questions need to be answered? What examples should I use to show what I mean? How can I explain even a fragment of all I've learned about writing and reading in the clearest, most logical way?

What are the choices I make as a teacher, to give students choices as writers and readers? How can I nudge the world a little—to remember or rethink what it means to teach, to write, to read, to learn?

I hope my teaching, my writing, my learning are affirming for you or nudge you to think about your teaching, your writing, your learning. What are the choices you make as a teacher? What are the beliefs that ground your teaching of reading and writing? How do you get your kids to nudge the world a little?

CHAPTER TWO

Getting to Know Our Students

I want to have a frame for teaching, based on the beliefs I have about learning, about the language arts, and about adolescents. Without the kids, everything else is meaningless. Therefore, I really want to get to know the students right away. How do they feel about themselves as readers and writers? What are their strengths, their weaknesses? What experiences are they bringing with them that affect their confidence and competence?

At the end of this chapter is a chart that I use as the students go through all of the activities listed here (the full chart is also on the website). Watching them gives me so much anecdotal information, often more helpful than any number scores that accompany the students on standardized tests previously taken. Take a look at the chart first; adapt mine for those things you do to get to know your students, especially if you try some of these suggestions. What's most important—we get to know our students.

I use a lot of drawing and pictures in the classroom. I believe we can often learn as much from a visual representation as from several pages dense with words. I learned about drawing as thinking from Roger Essley (2008), an artist and a writer. He has shown me convincingly how drawing stick figures and key words can convey a lot of information that can lead to a fine piece of writing. I have used drawing as thinking to have kids show me their understandings as readers as well, when they struggle to get across the same thinking through words. I will talk more about drawing as thinking in a later chapter.

In an effort to show you how much information can be conveyed in a drawing, I'll show you how the students react to "choose a book," how I react to their enthusiasm or reluctance, how I have set up the procedure for checking out books, how I take pictures for the portfolio wall, and what that portfolio wall looks like, through my sketches. I don't give these sketches to the kids; they are for you to see what we are doing. I will describe the other activities with more narrative.

We do all of the following during the first week or two of school:

Choosing a book

Checking out books

Name cards for portfolio walls

Portfolio wall

Marshmallow challenge

Poetry challenge

Covering the writer's-reader's notebooks (WRNs)

What I Learn About Each Student Chart

Choosing a Book

Figure 2.1 *Choosing a Book*

I have hundreds of books in the classroom. A lot of students are surprised when I say they can choose any book they want. I show them where the books are and how they are shelved alphabetically by last name of the author. I want to see what the students do before I recommend any. How familiar are they with books? Authors? What will they say to each other? In the past, I have noticed how much their reaction to a book drives them back to similar ones and their recommendations to each other: so sad, so scary, so funny.

For those kids with real reluctance ("Stupid!" "Boring!" etc.), I try to find a book for them, but it might take more than this first week.

Checking Out Books

I have a small filing box for each class, and a card in every book. This shows the students how to check out a book and where to file it, in case other students are looking for a specific title. I tell kids that if it takes them more than a few weeks to read a book, they probably don't love it. Bring it back. Find one to love.

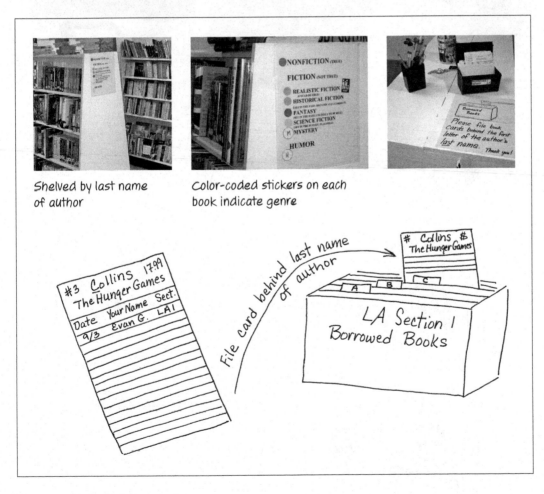

Shelved by last name of author

Color-coded stickers on each book indicate genre

Figure 2.2 *Checking Out Books*

Name Cards for Portfolio Wall

Figure 2.3 *Name Cards for Portfolio Wall*

Portfolio Wall

Figure 2.4 *Portfolio Wall Template*

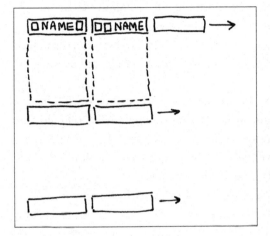

Figure 2.5 *Portfolio Wall*

Space under each name for:

- a piece of writing, or
- a book recommendation, or
- a page from the WRN (a copy, not torn out), or
- a favorite quote, or
- a favorite picture.

Benefits to all of us:

- learn about each other (interests, likes, feelings as readers and writers)
- share ideas about reading and writing.

The two previous sections should be self-explanatory. I take pictures of each student, reading and writing, mount them on name cards and set them up on a portfolio wall, where students can share their work under their name.

Marshmallow Challenge

Kylene Beers and Bob Probst introduced me—and many others—to the "marshmallow challenge" at the Boothbay Harbor Literacy Retreat more than five years ago. The marshmallow challenge is a "design exercise that encourages teams to *experience* simple but profound lessons in collaboration, innovation, and creativity." (See marshmallowchallenge.com for more information.)

The task is simple: in eighteen minutes, teams must build the tallest freestanding structure out of twenty sticks of spaghetti, one yard of masking tape, one yard of string, and one marshmallow, that needs to be on top of the structure.

I give the students these supplies in a stapled, brown paper bag. They must work in teams of three to build the tallest freestanding structure. It is amazing watching what they do and how they do it. Who takes the lead? Who is assertive? Who remains quiet? Who has the most creative ideas? Who is willing and who is not willing to be innovative? How well do the kids work together? I learn so much about them in these eighteen minutes.

After they build their structures and we measure for the tallest structures that continue to stand, I ask the students, "What ideas worked? What didn't work? What would you have done differently?" I also like to do this because I want the students to know that we learn from our mistakes. I then show the students Tom Wujec's TED Talk, where he describes how he learned the marshmallow challenge from Peter Skillman at TED several years ago. He has used the idea and describes the results of trying it with many professionals in design workshops and students. He talks about the results.

applicable to the classroom

Surprising to some, not so surprising to others, is that kindergarteners do very well because they start with the marshmallow and build prototypes to see what works. They imagine and create all kinds of design possibilities.

Isn't this what school and real learning should be about? Even as writers and readers? Being innovative and creative in the way we craft a piece of writing? Recognizing those unique and

extraordinary things that good writers do to capture our attention and give us pause to think about their ideas, their beliefs, their opinions, as we read their work? Our drafts are continual prototypes, as we revise and build our ideas until the text clearly says what we want it to say. We want children to try out new ideas, not just as architects and engineers, but as writers.

There is no single right plan that is going to solve all we face in the world and perhaps that is good enough reason to be suspicious of those who continue to promote a Common Core of State Standards to ensure our students are all alike, so they are business- and college-ready. Business-ready? Wujec tells us that the business students do the worst at this challenge because they are trained to find the single right plan. Is that what we want when we adopt the Common Core State Standards? Is that what is meant by "business-ready"?

I want far more than that for my students. I want them world-ready, to live as articulate, compassionate, thoughtful human beings who try to find creative and innovative ways to live their lives and solve some of the world's problems.

Wujec also has some interesting findings about incentives—what happened to these design teams when offered a large incentive to succeed by building the tallest structure? Offered a large incentive, every team in the design seminar failed to build *any* freestanding structure. Yet given some knowledge of angles and components of design, the success rate improved dramatically. Thinking about this in terms of writing, it makes sense to me when students are taught to notice what makes effective writing, shown how to intentionally weave those elements or techniques into their own writing, and given a real audience for their thinking (the incentive), their desire to write and their success at accomplishing some fine writing improves substantially.

Teaching kids how to work together, to collaborate, and to give constructive feedback (in the form of questions and suggestions for consideration) to each other as writers leads to stronger pieces for every student.

Helping kids to understand the metaphor that every project has a marshmallow holds true also in writing and guides them in the process of drafting. There are so many uh-oh moments

when you realize something is not working in the writing—so you reconfigure, reorganize, start again with the one sentence that does leap from the page. Try a different genre, a different focus, a different perspective. Present tense, instead of past tense. Fiction, instead of nonfiction. Poetry, instead of narrative. Third person, instead of first person. What if your last sentence became your lead? What if . . . ? Try this . . .

View the TED Talk and think about those findings garnered from this exercise in terms of questions:

What does it mean to be creative and innovative?

In what kind of situations do we actually learn something?

In what ways do we teach kids to build "prototypes" as writers and readers?

What is the nature of collaboration (each person's responsibility), and what should it do? In what ways do we teach kids to truly collaborate with each other?

When do incentives work to produce success? What are the incentives that keep kids reading and writing?

In what ways do we teach kids to cope with the "marshmallows" in their projects?

How does this marshmallow challenge relate to our beliefs about teaching reading and writing?

Better yet, talk through these questions with your students and with your colleagues. What can we discover about education and learning for our students and for ourselves from this eighteen-minute design exercise? Many sites on the Internet describe the marshmallow challenge in terms of materials, rules, and results. Two that are especially thorough are eGFI (2011) and Tom Wujec's TED Talk (2010).

Poetry Challenge

My poetry challenge is another icebreaker with so many added benefits. I collect poems that I know will speak to my kids, written by poets I admire, and on subjects that have to do with writing, reading, or adolescents' interests. I type the poems and then cut them into enough pieces so that I have one piece for each student in the class. (With four classes, this means I have four sets of poems cut into the appropriate number of stanzas depending on numbers of kids in that class.) I put the various "pieces" of each poem (varying from four or more lines) into one basket, all mixed up, then I pass the basket around and have each of the kids choose one piece.

They must read their stanzas to themselves and then walk around the room finding the other students holding the remaining pieces of their poem. I mention beforehand that students should think about the subject, the tone, the speaker, the format to help find other stanzas that seem to match. (All poems should be in the same font, same size type, and on the same color paper, to avoid matching that way.) All those students who think they belong together must sit together, read the stanzas aloud, and determine the most sensible order.

I move from table to table to make sure students are in the right groups. If not, I give them hints about looking at the topic, the tone, the perspective, the organization of lines, and I suggest they relook and see if their pieces fit; if not, they should check the other groups. I don't tell them the poet's order. They might come up with a different order that makes good sense to them. So be it. They are thinking through the words, the ideas, and their placement for the strongest meaning—in their minds. Later I show them the actual order and we talk about why that makes sense.

In these groups of three to six students (the usual number of parts for a poem), they must then read the poem aloud twice, each member of the group reading his or her part. Then, they must come up with a creative way of reading the poem aloud. Everyone in the group must have some reading role. Maybe there is a repeated line in the poem that the students could read in unison, if they have chosen, or someone has volunteered, to be the main reader. Maybe they stand with their backs to the class and turn only when they are reading a part. Maybe they all read in unison and one person reads the lead and the ending. The way they choose to present the poem should further enhance the meaning they are taking from the poem.

I give them time to practice. Based on the tone of the piece and the content, I make suggestions as I move from table to table and listen to them read. I also remind them to talk through what the poem is about and how the tone might dictate how they read it. I remind them if there are words they don't know or can't pronounce, they can ask a peer or me, or look up the words in a dictionary. You can't read something out loud if you don't understand what you are reading.

Once students at every table have finished organizing and practicing their poem, with voice and spark, I have them read the poem aloud to the whole class. (Sometimes they are *not* in the exact order in which the poet wrote them, but if the order makes sense, that's okay.) We hear all of them. We talk about each one. What did they notice about the poem? What did they like? What surprised them? What confused them? What did they think this poem was about? What lines, or something the poet did, made them think that?

I talk about what I know about these poets, and why I chose these poems. I then ask the students to each choose the one poem they like most (I have copies of the whole poems already printed up) and glue that poem into the response section of their WRN. I give them two to three minutes to respond to questions about the poem: What made them choose this one? What did they like most about it? What did the poem bring to mind for them?

This poetry challenge moves the kids around the room to read and to talk to each other. It allows me to see how the kids react with classmates they know or don't know. I see who becomes the organizer of the group, who is comfortable or uncomfortable reading, how creative they can be in their presentation, and how well they listen to each other. It allows me to mention different aspects of poetry: some tell a story, others set a scene, others ask questions. All carry strong feelings. After we are done listening to all of the poems, I ask the kids, "What did you notice about these poems? What surprised you?"

These are poems to which I think kids can connect. I choose the poems because of the topics, the wording, the style, the feeling, the surprise, the big ideas or the small ideas. I choose them because they offer something to think about—and strong feelings.

I will use these poems throughout the year for quickwrites about students' initial response to the poem from one of the lines in it or from the gist of the poem. We will look at these poems again for word choices, line breaks, enjambment, stanzas, metaphor, alliteration, repetition, perspective, point of view, verb tense, leads and endings. All decisions a poet makes as she writes.

The materials we choose to use in our classrooms could, and should, be looked at again and again, for different reasons at different times. Being familiar with writing from so many different perspectives helps the students become truly familiar with writing, with writers, and with stylistic devices. Rereading is one of the most helpful strategies we can encourage in our students that helps them reach deeper understandings. Poetry is tight writing—every word counts. It is filled with images, ideas, feelings, and so many literary, stylistic devices.

I think we could use a challenge like this with many different kinds of writing: essays written in many different ways (especially in ways other than the five-paragraph essay), op-ed pieces, book reviews, short personal narratives, perhaps even historical documents. Short pieces from which kids could talk about the content and organization, the lead and the ending. And powerful alternatives to the organization. Students begin to see that writers make intentional choices for a variety of reasons. They are reading as writers.

This poetry challenge also allows me to introduce poets with whom I would like the students to be familiar—beyond Shel Silverstein, Jack Prelutsky, and Robert Frost—the only poets my eighth graders seem to know as the year begins.

I use the following poems or other poems by many of the same poets, in any given year, sometimes the same poems in each class, other times, a variety of other poems in each class.

> "I Love the Look of Words" by Maya Angelou (in *Soul Looks Back in Wonder* [Feelings 1993])
>
> "Hockey" by Scott Blaine (in *American Sports Poems* [Knudson and Swenson 1988])
>
> "Introduction to Poetry" by Billy Collins (2001)
>
> "If I Can Stop One Heart from Breaking" by Emily Dickinson (in *Poetry for Young People: Emily Dickinson* [Bolin 1994])
>
> "Owl Pellets" by Ralph Fletcher (1994)
>
> "Nothing Gold Can Stay" by Robert Frost (1969)

"Franz Dominquez" by Mel Glenn (1982)

"By Myself" by Eloise Greenfield (1978)

"Time Somebody Told Me" by Quantedius Hall (in *You Hear Me?* [Franco 2000])

"I Dream a World" by Langston Hughes (in *Poetry for Young People: Langston Hughes* [Roessel and Rampersad 2006])

"Abandoned Farmhouse" by Ted Kooser (1985)

"The Sidewalk Racer" and "On the Skateboard" by Lillian Morrison (in *The Place My Words Are Looking For* [Janeczko 1990])

"Ode to the Lizard" by Pablo Neruda (in *The Dreamer* [Ryan 2010])

"The Rider" by Naomi Shihab Nye (1998)

"The Summer Day" by Mary Oliver (1992)

"Dog in Bed," "Bully Lessons," or "Always Take a Dog" by Joyce Sidman (2003)

"Sick" by Shel Silverstein (1974)

"Traveling Through the Dark" by William Stafford (1998)

"Swinging the River" by Charles Harper Webb (in *Preposterous* [Janeczko 1991])

"The Writer" by Richard Wilbur (1988)

This poetry challenge can also be done with picture books, such as Mem Fox's *Wilfred Gordon McDonald Partridge*. Type up the text. Cut it into as many pieces as you have students, and have them walk around and assemble the pieces until they make sense. This really helps them pay attention to order and talk through their reasoning. Like the poetry, this picture book can also lead to writing after talking about significant objects that hold memories. It is a way to find those memories.

Or even better, as kids are writing and playing with the organization of their own writing, show them how they could cut up their writing into paragraphs, give the pieces to as many students as they have pieces, and have them come up with at least two or three different organizational possibilities. After reading these different arrangements aloud, they could talk out why each one might strengthen the writing in different ways. Used several times throughout the year, the exercise itself leads students to notice and think about the various ways authors organize their writing and how that organization impacts the reading.

This reorganization is even easier to do, and visually much clearer to kids, if you are using storyboarding to tell a story, before going to words. The writer can ask a number of students to each hold one of their storyboarding cards in front of the entire class, in the order in which they told it. You can ask, "Can anyone see another way to tell this story? What if you move some of the students holding the cards around? Who would you move, and where?"

Covering the Writer-Reader Notebook (WRN)

I ask students to bring in pictures of people, places, animals, objects that matter to them. Sports, outside activities, interests in and out of school. Pictures of music groups, sayings, issues, and words that are meaningful to them. I ask them, "Show us what you care most about. Who are you? Show us through pictures and words." We then spend a class period covering the WRNs. They have to show at least five to seven different aspects of their lives. I cover the notebooks with clear contact paper, which reinforces the covers and helps them last throughout the year.

Everything that students choose to put on their cover gives me opportunities to bring up possible topics when they say they have nothing to write about. The pictures and words also help me suggest books they might like when they are stuck for something to read. I use every opportunity to get to know each student.

Figures 2.6 and 2.7 show examples of covers on students' WRNs and my cover on this year's WRN.

As I mentioned at the beginning of the chapter, I use the chart in Figure 2.8 to gather information about each student as they move through each of the previous activities. A printable version is available online. Each activity gives me anecdotal evidence about who these students are as readers, writers, learners, and how well they work collaboratively with each other, all essential to building community in a reading-writing workshop.

**Online
2.1**

Figure 2.6 *Student's WRN Covers*

Figure 2.7 *My WRN Cover*

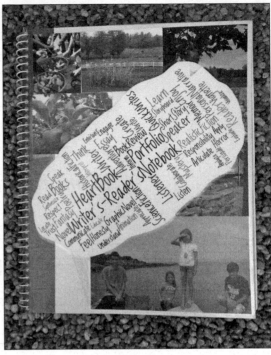

Figure 2.8 *What I Learn About Each Student*

Chart: What I learn about each student as they go through the first few weeks' activities.

Looking for:	attitude toward books knowledge of authors enthusiasm for rdg	collaboration, cooperation, creativity, imagination, leadership, planning of ideas	knowledge of poems/poets, interaction w/ peers/leadership fluency as rdrs/comfort rdg aloud	interests care of materials
Names	**Choosing Books**	**Marshmallow Challenge**	**Poetry Challenge**	**Covering WRN**

CHAPTER THREE

Planning for a Successful Year

Framing the Year in Choices

I frame the year around *choices*, posing the following yearlong questions to the students:

- What choices do you make as a writer and a reader? In what ways do those choices lead you to becoming a stronger writer and reader?

- What choices do writers make that you notice in your reading of their works that make their writing so strong and that you will try in your writing?

- In real life, and in literature, what are the consequences of little to no choice in a person's life? What choices do these real people and these fictional characters make in response to their experiences? What choices do they make to nudge the world a little?

- What would you still like to do as a reader and a writer that you have not had a chance to do? What topic or issue would you like to investigate and present in a variety of ways? What choices do you make to nudge the world a little?

As we move through the year with these questions in mind (and on a giant poster on the wall in the classroom), and as you move through this book, I hope you will see how I frame the year to give the students time, to give them choices into what they read and write, to give them constructive responses as readers and writers, and to give them models and modeling that help them move forward in their thinking and crafting of ideas. Choices within a frame. That's key.

Within that frame, there are a number of handouts I give the students and/or their parents, to let them know what I believe and how I have planned the year so the students and parents can see what is expected. Look through my handouts (available on the website). Make modifications to them to fit your beliefs and your students. Make them yours. The following sections in this chapter correspond to a handout on the website. The explanation that follows makes more sense if you download and read through the handout itself.

Curriculum Overview

Online
3.1

This is my plan for the year framed in choices. Like life, things change. We are offered opportunities that have not been planned (build an ROV—remotely operated underwater vehicle—with Navy engineers, field trips, writers or speakers in the school, etc.). We are mandated to test—for days at a stretch. My plan changes or we get behind. So be it. But I still have a plan that guides me for the year.

Teaching, at any grade level, with colleagues, with parents, with administrators—and especially with the idiosyncratic needs of our students—means we learn patience, perseverance, adaptability, flexibility, and humor. I keep reminding myself, we do what we can do in the time constraints that we have (forty-five to fifty minutes per day with each class). I am only one of many, many teachers these students will have. Instead of rushing through things, I would rather slow down and allow kids to write and read slowly and deeply, instead of quickly and widely.

Expectations in the Reading-Writing Workshop

Online
3.2

These expectations come from thirty years of asking students and noticing what I can expect from them. The structure for each week is what I try to do. I want the students to know what to expect, but always be prepared for changes.

I try to focus on writing Monday through Wednesday and focus on reading Thursday through Friday. But writing and reading are so intertwined that sometimes those distinctions are difficult to make.

Pamphlet to Parents

Online
3.3

Information on the pamphlet comes from questions parents frequently ask me each year. They want to know what I expect of the students as writers and readers, what it means to work on a team of teachers, what they can expect of their sons or daughters as readers, and any books I would recommend. This is certainly a condensed version, but parents tell me it is helpful.

During our Parent Open House at the beginning of the year, I have available copies of these three items: Curriculum Overview, Expectations in the Reading-Writing Workshop, and the Pamphlet to Parents.

In addition, I reduce the size of the Curriculum Overview and the expectations sheet to fit on the pages in the notes section of each student's WRN, so the students are clear about the year. They enter the titles of these pages on their table of contents at the front of the notes section. We review the expectations together.

Online 3.4

Overview of Expectations in the Writer's-Reader's Notebook

We use the writer's-reader's notebooks (WRNs) that eighth graders helped me design and Heinemann has published (Rief 2007b). For years, I tried different kinds of notebooks or journals with the students, each year asking what was most helpful. This is the result of years of suggestions from eighth graders.

The notebook is divided into sections: response, notes, vocabulary, and spelling. All of the handouts available for downloading on the website are published in that notebook, which can be purchased from Heinemann as a set of two books, one WRN along with a teacher guide that has nearly one hundred pages of examples from students' notebooks (Rief 2007a). This two-book package (the teacher's guide and the notebook) supplements well what I am sharing here in this book. The WRN itself can be purchased in packages of five.

However, if you don't have that notebook you can use the handouts (six pages) to set up your notebooks. Take any notebook—one that will weather the pounding of a year in and out of adolescents' lockers—and have students glue the handouts right into the notebook. That's what I did for years, before our WRNs were published.

Online 3.5

Bookmarks

I make copies of the bookmark on heavy, colored paper and ask the kids to fill the back of the bookmark with pictures or quotes that have to do with reading. Last year, I covered the back of my bookmark with pictures of students reading. The year before, I put the following quotes on mine:

"We read to know we are not alone." (C. S. Lewis)

"Writing is the making of reading." (Donald Graves)

"Reading is the making sense of writing." (Linda Rief; yes, I quote myself!)

"The man (woman) who does not read good books has no advantage over the man (woman) who can't read them." (Mark Twain)

"We create stories and paintings and music, not so much for the world as for ourselves." (Cynthia Rylant)

With the bookmark, students have suggestions for the ways they might start a response to their thinking, whether it is about the books they are reading, something they are doing, things they notice going on in the world around them, or ideas for writing. I laminate these bookmarks.

As I read a short piece to the students, either a short story or poem, editorial or essay, I have them use the bookmark starters to respond to that reading as a model for the way they might use it on their own. Especially for students who struggle with what to write and are at risk for losing these bookmarks (which is the majority of eighth graders), I have all of them glue a copy of the bookmark onto the first page in the response section of the WRN and refer to it frequently as ways to nudge their thinking.

Writer's-Reader's Survey

Online
3.6

This survey, written in the response section of the WRN, adds to the information about the students, mainly from their past experiences. Sometimes, in place of this survey, I simply ask the kids, "Who are you as a reader? Who are you as a writer?"

Student Feedback from Survey

I compile the information I gather from the surveys and share these with the students. We talk about what this means in terms of the class, especially how we can make writing and reading easier if we adhere to what they say makes it easier. I want the students to see I want their feedback and will do my best based on their honesty to help them succeed at writing and reading.

It's a good idea to post this on the wall on big sticky notes and also to reduce the size and have kids glue this into the notes section of their WRN. It's a reminder to them about what helps them as writers and readers. As we review the results, I tell them to highlight or star those things that are especially meaningful to them.

This is the latest list. Each year I compile a new list based on student feedback. Each year many of the findings are the same, but the phrasing is often a bit different; thus, it is important to make that new list so the current students recognize their wording.

Ask your students the same questions. Talk out how you will use their feedback to help them as writers and readers.

What makes writing easy?

- writing what you know, imagining what you don't
- being passionate about your writing/putting your mind (head) and feelings (heart) into it
- not being skimpy—using all your ideas
- paying attention to the world around you—being observant
- being specific and descriptive, but not too descriptive
- trying new, unique ways of writing
- being willing to revise and edit
- reading a lot, to see how other writers write
- finding readers who inspire and encourage you as a writer

What makes writing hard?

- assigned topics that don't interest the writer
- getting started, the middle, the end
- finding unique, interesting, original ideas
- sticking to the topic
- worrying about grammar, punctuation, and spelling
- trying to get it to make sense
- too much noise

Where do you get ideas for writing?

- from real-life experiences, situations, hobbies, likes/dislikes, events going on in the world
- from reading books, watching movies, listening to music
- writing
- looking at pictures
- noticing what's going on around you

What makes reading easy?

- picturing the situation, or choosing graphic novels because the pictures help you understand
- having a wide/deep vocabulary
- relating yourself to the reading
- staying interested by rereading, talking about the reading
- reading a lot to gain experience
- getting "lost" in the reading/becoming a part of the story or book
- enjoying the writing
- reading between the lines—asking yourself, what is the writer not saying?
- trying new books—that are challenging
- writing a lot—reading your own writing to yourself and out loud

What makes reading hard?

- uninteresting topic
- vocabulary that is too difficult (unknown words, unusual phrasing) and words that can't be figured out from the context
- distractions—noise, music, and so on
- assigned books

How do you choose reading?

- suggestions/recommendations from friends, family, librarians, teachers
- interesting title, cover, pictures, back summary, drawings
- known/liked author or genre
- first chapter that hooks you
- authors that show you what to do better as a writer

All of these handouts seem like a lot to organize and review with the students (and parents). I've found that the more time I prepare the kids with expectations, in a place where they can easily find information—the WRN, their portfolios (three-ring binders where they save all rough and final drafts of writing), and all around the room—the more organized they are for success.

CHAPTER FOUR

Why a Writer's-Reader's Notebook?

August 6, 1986—I read Don Murray's words.

The most valuable writing tool I have is my daybook. . . . All the writing in the daybook is a form of talking to myself, a way of thinking on paper. . . . The daybook stimulates my thinking, helps me make use of those small fragments of time that on many days is all the time I have to write. There is no sign of struggle. I'm not fighting writing. I'm playing with writing. . . . The daybook also keeps my writing muscles in condition; it lets me know what I'm concerned with making into writing; it increases my productivity . . . (it's a place) where you can do all the bad writing and bad thinking that are essential for those moments of insight that produce good writing.

(Murray 1990, 10–14)

All the things for which Don Murray used his daybook are the things I want for the students, and for me. The writer's-reader's notebook (WRN) has been crucial to the work we are doing as writers and readers. It gives students a place to be personal, individual, and real as they take notice of themselves and their world. It is their thinking for their own reasons, and it is the best tool I have ever used that allows students to develop their voices.

The Importance of the WRN

The WRN is at the core of all I expect from the kids because it allows them choice, time, and practice with regard to writing and reading. It gives me a place to learn about each of them personally and individually. It shows me who they are, their strengths, their promises, their questions, their weaknesses, so I know how to push and challenge them. It shows me what I am teaching well and what I still need to teach. Even in a classroom filled with twenty-five or more kids, this is the most important tool I have that allows me to teach to the individual, while teaching to the class.

The WRN supports my goals as a teacher, giving students a place to begin and develop their ideas as writers and readers and a place for me to see their growth. It supports my belief that kids grow as writers and readers when they have the opportunities to do an abundance of writing and reading. The WRN gets them in the habit of observing and thinking about all they notice. It supports my belief that kids' voices need to be heard as they wonder, question, argue, reason, change their minds, or affirm their thinking.

The WRN provides a structure that gives consistency in form and function for the students as learners and for me as a teacher. The structure enables them to be more productive and more thoughtful by allowing, encouraging, inviting, and teaching them to be themselves on the pages.

For many students, this is the first time they've been asked to keep a WRN. The task seems daunting, even when I explain to them that what goes into the notebook *is* wide open. And that may be why keeping a notebook is so perplexing—it is wide open, even with the structure I provide. I tell them to show me who they are as they think about themselves, they think about books and reading, they think about the world around them. What do they notice? I explain to them that they could use the notebook to:

- gather and play with ideas for writing
- record, respond, and react to nightly reading by writing or drawing
- hold on to memories (whether they feel significant or relevant, insignificant or irrelevant at the moment)
- record thoughts, observations, and questions about their immediate world, or the world at large
- question reading, writing, learning
- take out frustration, fear, anger, or sadness
- remember everything that makes them happy, makes them smile
- work out who they are by thinking about all that matters or doesn't matter to them
- keep ideas in one place so they don't lose their thinking
- establish the habits of collecting, noticing, listening, and writing
- practice writing, practice drawing, make time to play with words.

Ultimately, the purpose of this notebook for us as teachers is to see that our students are learning, changing, and deepening their thinking and insights. This is our evidence, and theirs, of growth over time.

Once we set up the WRNs (see the handouts for the WRNs in Chapter 3 on the website) I give them a packet of responses from previous years, have them read them, and ask them what they notice the students were doing in their notebooks. It helps the kids see the possibilities. Reading and noticing for themselves is always more powerful than my reading a list of everything the students did or do.

These WRNs are meant to be academic journals, the students' thinking and learning as they live, act, and grow in school and in the world. They are not diaries, places where they gush out their deepest personal feelings, hide them from younger siblings or parents, often to find their thinking a bit embarrassing as they grow and mature.

Naturally their personal lives will enter these notebooks in the same way pieces of my personal life have entered my notebooks. It's impossible to totally separate their personal beliefs and feelings as they negotiate adolescence from their thinking. I don't want them to separate their thinking and feeling. But these notebooks are meant to be centered on who they are as learners.

I make it clear to the students that I will read these notebooks, as will peers of their choice at various times. If they feel compelled to write something in the WRN that is especially personal, they can fold down the page and I won't read it. If they write something that leads me to believe they are being hurt, or they are going to harm themselves or someone else, I am obligated both legally and morally to seek more professional help for them.

More than anything else we do, the WRN is about "good faith participation" (Romano 1987). I believe students have to do a lot of writing to find their best writing. I believe writing helps them become better readers, and reading helps them become better writers. I believe they need to be readers, for the pure pleasure of a good story—without having to synthesize and analyze everything they read. I believe that talk or writing about *some* of their reading helps them unfold the layers of significance for them and from the author and that the more they read and talk about their thinking as they read, the more they will discover the craft of writing.

The more they read and write, the more they learn about themselves and the world.

This is first-draft thinking in the notebook, a one-sided conversation with themselves that I am privileged to read, while nudging their thinking with my comments, questions, and suggestions. I seldom correct their spelling or sentence structure because this is not crafted, edited writing.

Because this is a type of journal focused on their learning, and it is an essential component to the reading-writing workshop, I will, and do, read and grade all aspects of this notebook. Students also want credit for all they do. This is important work.

Examples of Students' Thinking in Their WRNs

Notice the range of books these students are reading and the sophistication of their response, especially in their thinking not just about themselves but about those things that are going on in the world around them. So much of their thinking, the depth with which they notice what is going on in the world, comes from the reading they are doing and the comparisons they are making.

The challenge: getting those kids whose WRNs are empty most of the year to read and to write. Some I eventually turn around; some, I never do. Examples from several students are on the website.

What do you notice these students are doing as both readers and writers? How does one influence the other? When given choices, what are your students reading and how are you encouraging and teaching them to read deeply?

Online
4.1–4.15

Responding to the WRNs

I read the notebooks every two weeks—but only one class section of notebooks a day. For instance, I collect one section's notebooks on Monday, another on Tuesday, and so on. I cannot do it any more often than that, although to establish the habit of reading and writing on a nightly basis, I wish I could read these notebooks at least weekly, if not daily. But I can't. When I've tried to read them weekly, it is all I do every day. I have other things to do and learn also. Every two weeks is the best I can do.

The response section carries the most weight. In the course of a week, I expect to see five half hours of reading and two to four pages filled with writing, drawing, or collecting. Evidence of reading is demonstrated through recording the date, title of whatever was read, and time spent reading. The students count up how many half hours of reading they have done during the two-week period and note that number on the last page of the writing for the two weeks. They then count the number of pages they have filled in the response section. In a two-week period, there should be ten half hours of reading and four to eight pages of writing or drawing.

This determines their *quantity* grade (time spent reading and number of pages of response). At the end of a two-week period, I add up the half hours of reading and the number of pages of writing. If they've fulfilled the expectations for two weeks, ten half hours of reading and eight pages of writing or drawing, they have earned an A for quantity.

I also give the students a *quality* grade. It is subjective, based on my belief and the students' written evidence that they are reading voraciously (for pleasure and for information); that they are thinking deeply about that reading; that they are paying attention to the world around them with all they notice, wonder, and question; and that they are drafting that thinking through writing or drawing. In other words, they are collecting thoughtful and thorough responses and reactions to all they notice—in life and in their reading. They are surprising me, teaching me, challenging me with their thinking. The quality grade is written as a check (C), a + (B), or ++ (A).

At least once during an eight-week period, I ask students to star their best thinking during a two-week period—their self-selected strongest writing or reasoning. If I believe we all need to do a lot of writing to find our best writing, then I don't need to read everything they write. Selecting their best thinking is guiding them to evaluation. Their quality grade is based on this starred page or pages.

What do all those squiggles, checks, and underlining mean on the students' pages? That I read their words and found something they said, or the way they said it, interesting. They begin to look for those squiggles and begin to realize, if they didn't get any, maybe they need to push their thinking a bit harder, that they need to be more thoughtful and thorough in all they are doing.

As an honest reader, I write notes or questions in response to things the students have written. These are similar to the way I respond to their drafts of writing: this is what you did well that I noticed, these are the questions that popped into my head as I heard or read your writing, and here's a suggestion or two that might push your thinking.

When kids are stuck for something about which to write, I can often point out sentences I've underlined, sections I've starred, questions I've asked, as places that hold real potential for expansion.

Each time I look through the notebooks I also check the reading list and put the date down the left-hand margin so I can begin to see how many books a student reads in a two-week period and what else I might recommend to them based on their rankings of books and authors. In my records, I write down the number of books and the names of authors that the student read in those two weeks.

I also check the notes, vocabulary, and spelling sections for how well the students have taken notes during the week, collected vocabulary, and/or added spelling words to the lists. I simply note this as *done* or *not done* with a check or a zero. If these sections are not done, I follow up with students to find out why they are encountering a problem with taking notes or transferring spelling to their lists. Spelling words come from individual words they are continually misspelling in their final drafts of writing, or words I give the whole class because I notice so many of them are misspelling them.

I check the vocabulary section, expecting anywhere from four to eight words (per two-week period) collected from their reading—and reading from any class or at home—or from conversations they may have. These are words they don't know at all or that they recognize but don't yet own—they are not quite sure how to use the word in their speaking or writing. I write down the number of words plus a check, +, or ++, depending on the sophistication of the words they are choosing.

Kids want to know I read their notebooks. Most of them pay more attention to my comments than they do to the grade. Some pay attention to only the grade and never take the time to read my comments or answer my questions.

I have to be very careful that my comments stay positive, even when the students appear to be doing little. Encouragement is a far greater motivator than disappointment and anger.

Still, in the rush to read one hundred or more notebooks during a week, I find myself writing things that I know have stopped their reading or writing. I have to continually remind myself to pay attention to each student as an individual and to be more thoughtful about what I say that pushes their learning forward, not stops it dead in its tracks.

Keeping a WRN for Myself

Although I wish I had written more about my personal life—being a mother, daughter, grand-mother, caregiver for children, grandparents, and eventually parents; housecleaning, folding laundry; sanding woodwork, stacking firewood, mowing the lawn—all those personal, daily pieces of our lives—I'm glad I didn't try to include everything. As an academic journal, it gives me a focus despite all the other demands on my life. By keeping it centered, I can concentrate enough to find the details in that learning and teaching. I can even trace the roots of every piece of writing I've done back to my notebooks, whether it's an article about evaluation and assessment or the disconnect between mandates and what actually is good teaching. A poem or narrative about my mother's death. The love of my grandparents. Attempts at a picture book based on what I see and hear from my grandchildren.

My personal life *has* crept into these notebooks. I can't help it. And those moments seem more prevalent. Since 1998, my grandchildren have stepped into the pages: Hunter, Harrison, Julia, and now Fiona. Their surprises with language. Their favorite books. Their first words, first drawings and first jottings. I can't keep them out. I don't want to keep them out. They are central to my life.

I notice the same phenomenon with my students. When a student truly keeps the notebook for herself, all that's important to her creeps in. Jewelia, Meegan, and Madi, anorexia nervosa. Jeff and Lou, family alcoholism. Daiyao, family punishments. Alex, treatment of animals in the world. Troy, a grandfather's Alzheimer's. Arthur, his obsession with chess. Keerthi, treatment of women, especially in third world countries. Riley, his passion for mathematics and perfection-ism. Kailey, divorce. Their WRNs are filled with their thinking about issues that matter to them.

That's my biggest goal in asking students to keep a WRN—that all that's *important* to them "creeps in," because they are paying attention to the world. That world may be close to home or may broaden out to a bigger environment. What's important is that they are noticing the world. They are making connections. They are asking questions. They are participating by thinking. They are capturing who they are at the moment. (See the examples of students' writing in their WRNs on the website.)

I often ask myself, "If there is nothing a reader wonders about in their books, are they really engaged in reading? If there is nothing a person wonders about the world, are they really engaged in living?"

Online
4.1–4.15

My hope is that the WRN becomes more than an academic journal kept by the requirement of the teacher. It is not a diary, but it does begin to hold the honest thoughts, feelings, ideas, observations, and questions of the students; it becomes "a quiet place to catch your breath and begin to write" (Fletcher 1996, 1). I want it to be a place where they are the most honest, most passionate, most thoughtful, and most thorough writers and readers they can be at these moments in their lives—ten-year-olds, or thirteen-year-olds, or sixteen-year-olds.

Focusing the WRNs with Younger Students

Liz Schmitt, a third-grade teacher at one of our district's elementary schools, has her students keep a weekly circle journal. It's simple. On Fridays she gives each student a small picture of something they were working on during the week: a math problem, a science experiment, a piece of writing, reading a book, and so on. Something at which each was engaged. (She can print twenty-four pictures on one page on her computer.) The students glue the picture in the top right corner of a page in their journal (an inexpensive black-and-white marbled composition book). Liz then gives them each a circle with lines that divide it into eight slices. In each slice she has written something they have worked on during the week. She reviews these slices with the students as a reminder of the work they did.

The students glue the circle on the top left side of the page. They then write a letter to their mom and dad describing the thing they liked doing best and what they learned during the week. Students bring the journal home on Fridays, so their mom or dad can write back during the weekend, in the journal, and students can return the notebook on Monday.

This is not only simple; it is smart. Students are recapping and reflecting on their work for the week. They are thinking through what they learned. They are writing—for a real reason to a real audience for real response.

Liz can see what the kids took from her lessons for the week. What fascinated the students? What struck them? What wonderings are they bringing to her teaching? Where is their curiosity aroused? What does she need to reinforce or go over again? What engages them as learners?

These third graders are using the language of the learning—their academic vocabulary—as they summarize what they did and what they learned. They are playing with spelling, punctuation, capitalization, grammatical constructions, and letter format as they write. They are reading, as they write, and reading the letters from mom and dad in response. It also answers the question, "How was school? What did you do this week?"

This kind of journal teaches kids to take responsibility for their own learning and for inform-ing someone else about their week. It also provides thirty-two weeks' worth of *data* (thirty-two letters) that show growth over time, all collected in one place for anyone to look at. The teacher does not have to carry these journals home every weekend and write a response to the students.

Yet, all that information is there for her to see if she needs to. She can see what the majority of kids might need to know to write a better letter. A punctuation rule she might follow up on. A grammatical error they all seem to be making. Most importantly, she can see what they are taking from the major lessons for the week. What experiences is she giving them that really make a difference in their learning lives?

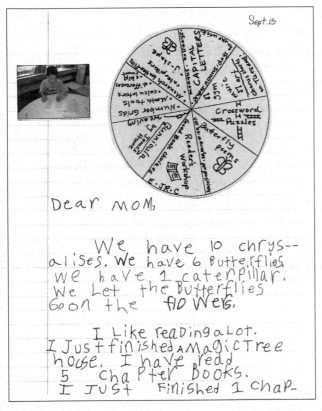
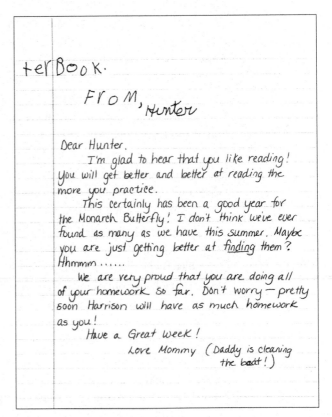

Figure 4.1 *Examples from Hunter's Third Grade Circle Journal*

My students' WRNs and their portfolios of rough and finished drafts are my data. They are the concrete evidence of what students have learned to apply in the context of reading and writing. When my daughter-in-law taught first grade, she collected a piece of writing each month, her evidence (data) on how those six-year-olds were growing as writers. We all need to collect examples of our students' work over time, as it is in the application of all that we have taught them, or hope we have taught them, that is the evidence of their growth, their learning.

Focusing the WRNs with Resistant Students

Josh comes into class day after day with little to no reading or writing in his notebook. Most of the time he doesn't bring the notebook. When I ask where it is he says, in a barely audible voice, "Look, I got football. I have practice every night and two games every weekend. I don't have time to read, or write."

I have tried for years to figure out how to make these notebooks worthwhile for all kids. I tried all kinds of ways to focus them, but none of it has worked well. Oh, kids are compliant. They try to write what they think I want, but these journals are never *theirs*.

I know Rich Kent, but I had no idea what he was doing with sports journals with college and professional teams until I sat next to him at a doctoral defense at the University of New Hampshire several months ago and we talked about his work with the National Writing Project and at the University of Maine.

Now I am reading his book, *Writing on the Bus: Using Athletic Team Notebooks and Journals to Advance Learning and Performance in Sports*, in an attempt to entice Josh, and Ben, and Cheyanne, and several other students, boys and girls, into using their WRNs as sports journals. I am pulling out some of Rich's ideas with examples from the athletes in hopes of convincing these kids that writing about their practices, what they learn from the playbooks, what they learn from their games, and what they learn from their coaches might improve their game.

I like Rich's Preseason Thoughts and Competition Analysis forms. I will give these to the kids so they have something concrete to hold onto as they write. I will offer a sports notebook as a suggestion, using Rich's examples from athletes about training, diet, games, opponents, pre- and postgame discussions, physical and mental training for the games. I'll try some of his quickwrites and guided writing prompts, using sports pictures and questions.

I'll gather the nuggets of information, especially about which athletes or teams keep blogs, trying to convince my students that this is real-life writing. I'll quote William Zinsser directly from Rich's book: "Writing organizes and clarifies our thoughts. Writing is how we think our way into a subject and make it our own. Writing enables us to find out what we know—and what we don't know—about whatever we're trying to learn" (Kent 2012, 180).

As this book goes to print, I am just bringing this idea to my most resistant readers and writers. I'll let you know how this goes.

When these WRNs are working well, I get what I ask for. Pessimism. Optimism. Likes. Dislikes. Loves. Hates. Biting, cryptic sarcasm. Joy. Anger. Frustration. Delight. Confusion. Envy. Humor. Fear. Loneliness. Surprise. Boredom. With, in, and about themselves, others, their worlds, their reading, and their writing. This is what I ask for: personal, individual, real, and so insightful.

Inside the Writer's-Reader's Notebook (Rief 2007) has an even fuller description of the WRNs and their importance in the classroom and nearly a hundred pages of examples from my students. Here, in this book, are some additional examples of what kids have written or drawn in their notebooks. I include many of these in the packet I give them to look at as they begin their reading, thinking, and writing. As part of the package of handouts on the website, I include all the information that Heinemann printed in the WRNs that we now use. I am so grateful to be done with glue sticks, scissors, and questions as to placement of the pages. But, if it helps you organize your own notebooks, use the pages. Otherwise, try our WRNs.

Online
3.1–3.6

Students' Responses to the Value of the WRN

At the end of the year, I ask the students, "In what ways are these WRNs helpful to you?"

Madi writes:

> (The WRN) allowed me to explore new ways to gather ideas and get inspiration for pieces of writing. Like when we looked at the pictures, then did a quickwrite with them. I loved that and am probably going to try that again. . . . I liked having all of my writing in one place to look back at what I wrote whether it was good or bad. It's fun to see my thoughts on books as I read them and where those thoughts took me. . . . The WRN allowed me to get an award-winning piece, "Last Goodbye?" Without the WRN no one would've read the piece. I will continue writing in a WRN because I have all my thoughts in one place and I'm able to see the change through drafts as the piece gets better.
>
> I now enjoy writing in this. It actually makes me think.

Alex B. says:

> When I have to write responses in the WRN it helps me think about the book. It helps give me a little nudge and motivation.

Kristy writes:

> In past years we wouldn't have a place to write down thoughts or ideas or poems so if I came up with an idea for a story I would either forget it or write it down somewhere then forget where. . . . This year I was pumped when I found out about the writing we had to do. I had ideas flooding through my brain. I knew characters I wanted to develop and plots I wanted to twist all because my thoughts and ideas were all in one place—here in the WRN. Even though the final draft has been handed in there is no way I'm done with it. This journal lets me scribble things down when they are pulsing through my brain. This journal has made me a better writer. . . . Since 5th grade I have wanted to be a

marine biologist but with this journal I have realized how much I love to write. I find myself describing an empty hallway I pass in terms that makes it seem like an empty abyss or a place teeming with life. . . . In a nutshell I learned this year: 1. I love to write, 2. Reading makes my writing better, 3. I can't become rich by becoming a marine biologist, and most importantly, 4. I can't imagine a future where I'm not a writer of some type.

Spencer writes:

This reader-writer notebook has revealed a part of me that I never knew existed. I remember that in fourth grade I wrote about how much I hate writing. "I will make a robot to do my writing for me. Also, if my robot gets angry I will put in a laser gun so it can blow up whoever told me to write." But this year, I discovered that I actually liked writing.

This notebook was like a curious explorer, prowling through a cave, shining a lantern on the walls, and then, suddenly, a group of bats flies out and startles him. My writing this year really surprised me. I used to have a lot of trouble converting my good ideas into words, or my opinions into pieces that were actually persuasive. But with this notebook I learned how to do those things. It was the thing that finally bridged the gap between my mind and my stationary pen.

This notebook really changed my view on reading, too. I used to only read stories for the plot line. Now, I prowl through the book looking for things like: memorable language, character description, leads, endings, etc.

I was truly surprised when I wrote "War in a Winter Wonderland." I was sitting at the table with my head in my hands, and I scoured my brain for ideas. We were responding to a piece about stars, and I finally decided to just steal a line. The line I took was something like, "We try to catch the stars with our tongues," but I had no idea where to go with that line, so I changed it to, "I tried to catch the snowflakes with my tongue." I then thought about writing about my brother, sister and me playing in the snow. I really hope this will get me an A, I thought as I handed in my Reader Writer Notebook the next day.

Well, it turns out that the piece got me lots more than an A. It was sent to Scholastic, and in February I found out that I had won a "Silver Key" for writing it. I was amazed. That piece was just my thoughts in my Reader Writer Notebook. This notebook has really brought out the best in both my reading and my writing. I am so grateful that I found it, or else I'd be sitting at my desk, blankly staring out the window, and clicking my pen, hoping to be visited by the "Genius Idea Fairy."

Lindsay says:

> If you asked me this question at the beginning of the year, I would've said whatever I could've to prevent anybody from ever using these notebooks ever again. But sometimes we need what we don't want.
>
> I always did like writing, but I never realized how much I lacked in the art of expressing myself. These notebooks helped me with that. Before I was afraid to write my thoughts on paper, so I never did. Before I would write stories about faraway adventures that had nothing to do with my life. Before I never appreciated the little things.
>
> I still remember the couple of F's I got at the beginning of the year when I didn't fill out my notebook. Or the B's I got when I didn't fill them out well enough. But I wouldn't consider myself a person who settled for mediocre, or anything below. So for most of the year, I searched for things inside my brain that I was comfortable with sharing. I like to test the waters before I dive in. So it took awhile for me to finally open up. But I'm not giving all the credit to me. I think it really was . . . this notebook that helped me. I'm grateful for that, even though I thought at the beginning of the year I never would be. Now I can write my thoughts on paper.

Lucas says:

> I hated the WRN. . . . But in the end I do not regret doing it. I feel that the reader's-writer's notebook made me a much better writer. . . . The notebook has actually shown me that I can actually write some stuff that I like.

Amy writes:

> The WRN's have helped me slow down with my reading and enjoy books a lot more than I used to. Whenever I respond to something I read I feel more connected to the book, like whenever I slow down and think real hard about what is going to happen to the characters, thinking, where is the author going with this? As I was writing "Visiting Memories" I thought of everything I read and wrote in my WRN and then I wrote down some ideas that could make the story more interesting. For instance, I wrote the beginning of the piece similar to Child of My Heart and The Silver Linings Playbook. Those two books gave little introductions and then dove right into the story.
>
> The setup of the WRN has helped me to be organized. I really love how there is a response section, a notes section, and a vocabulary section.

Alex R. says:

> I really liked how you would comment back like you were talking to me or check what you liked or give me suggestions for what I could do better. The WRN may have been a little hard to do but I always loved getting them back the next day, seeing what you wrote, my grade, and starting fresh for the next two weeks.

Libby writes:

> The writer reader notebook has helped me become a better reader and writer in so many ways. . . . I always found writing boring and felt like I had nothing to ever write about. After doing the quickwrites in class I always found that I had a topic to write about and once I started I hated to stop. I liked how we had to write about our reading and how it connects to our lives because it really helped me understand the context of the story better. I love how we had to write so much. . . . I now enjoy reading over all of my writing. . . . Having to read 10 half hours in two weeks helped me stick with reading one book and actually finishing it. Once I got into the routine of reading I loved it. . . .The notebook actually made me love to write. I'm actually going to keep writing in mine even though I won't have to pass it in any more. . . . I looked back to my first ever entry and when I thought about writing I thought: yuck! Hand cramps, don't know what to write about. Now I'm thinking fun, frees my mind, always have something to write about. I think that everyone who gets a chance to experience the WRN is lucky. They may not think so at first but in the long run it's one of the best things that you will do in your whole 8th grade year.

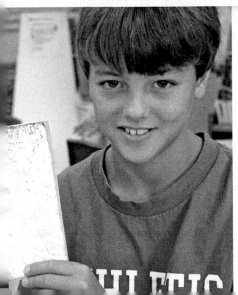

CHAPTER FIVE

Immersion in Writing (and Reading)

Given choices, kids will read and write about things they care deeply about. We allow them those choices, but not in a void. For too many years, I watched kids stare into space, telling me they had nothing to write about when I gave them time and complete free choice. They needed something to stimulate their thinking, to remind them of all the things they knew or thought or felt or believed. I've found the simple routine of doing quickwrites to be extremely effective in helping kids generate ideas and get words on paper. This first-draft response often leads to much longer, more polished pieces of writing.

Finding Writing
Quickwrites

Quickwrite, to me, means to write fast for a short amount of time, less than three minutes. It is writing to find writing, not planning or thinking through the writing before the words hit the paper. It is writing for the surprise of not knowing you were going to write what you wrote. But it is having something to see, hear, and hold on to (borrow a line and write from that line) as you try to find ideas for your own writing.

Several times a week, I put a short piece of writing on the screen (a poem, short essay, memoir, letter to an editor, journal entry, etc.), read it out loud, and ask the students to do a quickwrite in response. I specifically ask them to:

- write as quickly as they can for two to three minutes, capturing all that comes to mind in response to the work as a whole, or
- borrow a line or part of a line (one of their own choosing or a particular line that I suggest) from the work, and write off (or from) that line nonstop for two to three minutes.

Collecting the Quickwrites in a Writer's-Reader's Notebook WRN

Quickwrites begin the thinking, letting students know they do have ideas and they are competent at getting those ideas on paper. These quick, short jottings let the students see those things they didn't know they knew, or they wouldn't have known, before committing words to paper. The whole notion of this kind of writing—writing to find writing—comes from Don Murray. Don't think out the writing. Don't stop to brainstorm or plan what you want to write. Just put words on paper fast, letting the writing lead your thinking.

What I love about quickwrites is that students are often surprised by what appears on paper, and how quickly. "Wow, where did that come from?" Because they have seen examples that are short, crisp, and focused, their writing often appears that way too. It is freeing because they will often write things they didn't know they knew.

Once they feel competent at finding ideas, students begin to realize the power writing has to support them more deeply and fully as thinkers. Once they have these initial thoughts or ideas or feelings down, what happens? How do the students go beyond these initial writings? Writing is a recursive process that takes time to find, develop, resee, craft, and refine. It takes time to push these ideas toward a purpose and an audience.

My book *100 Quickwrites* (Rief 2003) is a collection of models that inspire students (said with humility and modesty) to put their own thoughts and feelings on paper. In this section, I briefly explain some of the ways my students take their initial writings to fuller, more developed pieces.

My students date their quickwrites and write them in the response section of their writer's-reader's notebook (WRN), which they are required to maintain. In addition to the quickwrites, they are writing or drawing thoughts to their required half hour of nightly reading and jotting any ideas they have for writing. The quickwrites they do several times a week count toward the two to four pages of writing I require in this response section each week. (This amount of writing is individualized and modified based on prior experiences of the students and what they and I, working together, believe makes sense to keep them growing as readers and writers. All students are not all at the same place at the same time.)

Benefit of Collecting

Keeping these initial ideas in one place, rather than on separate sheets of paper that seldom find their way back out of the bottoms of lockers, allows the students to collect them, look back on them, and reconsider their value. It also allows me to see what the students write, and nudge them toward some further thinking/writing, when I read their WRNs every two weeks. Still, this is first-draft writing and the decision to simply collect and save or develop that writing remains with the students.

supplying students w/ notebooks for quick writing. writing workshop

What can we expect students to do with these quickwrites?

- Simply collect and save them for future reference.
- Expand on them right away or later with further ideas.
- Take to peers and teachers for feedback on content.
- Resee, redraft into more polished pieces.
- Take to final drafts of best writing.

Responding to the Quickwrites

I allow students choice as to which quickwrites remain undeveloped and which ones matter enough to expand or craft further into fuller, sometimes finished pieces. If their writing is kept in one place, such as a notebook, it is easy for me to point out possibilities when I read or hear what they wrote. Quickwrites may remain undeveloped in the WRN, with neither the student choosing to say any more, nor any comments from me that might nudge their thinking. Students still get credit for this writing, even as it remains in just the notebook.

Hilda seldom developed any of her quickwrites into anything lengthier or more polished. She was thinking and playing with language every time she wrote. In a quickwrite to a winter poem, Hilda wrote:

> I'm really tired of winter poems. I know the look and feel and thoughts of snow falling around me. I know the night feeling of dirty slush and streetlights. I know that the sun abandons us earlier and earlier and the bite of cold stings into my skin. I know the warmth of a hug in the blazing chill and how empty trees scrape the sky. I know all of this. I live it. I don't need the constant reminders that this is winter.

In a two-minute response to an excerpt from *Sitti's Secrets* by Naomi Shihab Nye, Hilda wrote:

> I hate prejudices. I hate that whispered things and glances would build up so much that a girl with cinnamon skin would raise her hand and say "I wish there was no such things as homosexuality." This hurts, as the only "out" person in our middle school. I wish that we didn't have that kind of feeling in our classrooms, these pent up feelings of distance. "Gay Youth" is just a term that means people outside of our schools, our towns, our states. Wrong. We need to educate the people in our halls and classrooms that these are real people. This term that seems so distant is really people walking our streets, working in our stores. These are people you could sit with on the bus, maybe even your friends, neighbors, family.

Two weeks later, Hilda wrote quickly in response to a passage about the cutting of hair in *The Giver* by Lois Lowry:

> I remember that night, late darkness through melted windows and the weight of my hair pressing into my head more and more. This is something you've always wanted to do, I'm thinking. Why wait any longer? And I am cutting it off. Bundles of thick hair—black dye and blonde roots. I am pushing heavy black-handled scissors through my long, thick hair. I am cutting as close to my scalp as I can. I am feeling the freedom of air on my scalp. Small hairs stick on my neck and my face seems somehow distorted in the old mirror, sharp edges and divots in shortened hair.

Hilda's stance in this first quickwrite, that she doesn't want any more reminders of winter, told me she was done with this line of thinking and I decided not to push her to tell me more about all she *doesn't like* or does like, about winter poems, or understandably, about winter. I could have asked her to tell me about the season she did like most. What were the sights and sounds and smells and moments of that season? She could also have reorganized her lines as they stood to make an effective piece of poetry. Her words were saturated in strong feelings.

I could have asked her to tell me more about her own experiences with prejudice, in reference to the second quickwrite. I already knew she would when she was ready.

In the few months school has been in session, I have watched Hilda's hairstyles change dramatically—from shaved head, to Mohawk, from blonde to green to purple. Her hair fascinated me. I could have asked her to tell me more about how she changed her hair and why, but I don't. She used the quickwrites to play with her thinking and play with language. These pieces often led to deeper, much more detailed and complex pieces that bore little semblance to the quickwrites but I could see the seeds of ideas that were planted.

I gave her credit for the writing, but asked her nothing else in many of these quickwrites, as she seldom answered me. She already knew where she was headed. The quickwrites just put her in the driver's seat.

James wrote in response to "The Game" by Myra Cohn Livingstone:

> This peace of poetry reminds me of the war were going into, and how bad the out come can and probably will turn out horribly, but on a lighter note. It also reminds me all the fighting video games I have. I don't think war is the anser to anything but games like James bond and perfect dark, are my favorite games and I think as long as you can tell the difference between games and life it's ok because when you kill someone they don't just push start and start over.

I starred this entry when I read his notebook and said:

> You really see the seriousness of life situations as opposed to games. Tell me more about the difference between video games and real war. In what ways are they similar? In what ways are they different? Some people think kids can't tell the difference between video games and real life. What do you think? Do you think playing too many of these games affects kids? In what ways?

James chose not to expand on this writing, but if he had nothing else to write about of his own choice, this offered a place to ask him to consider my questions. James could have had something to say about the notion that some people believe watching too many video games leads to violent behavior. He knew the difference between real life and games and he might have had a strong opinion about that stance. It's an idea worth pursuing and my questions were meant to nudge him to consider the possibilities embedded in this initial thinking, especially the next time he found he had little to write about and needed some direction.

It's important to note that this is first-draft thinking and I seldom correct the spelling or the punctuation. Students are asked to write fast to capture their thoughts. Conventions of language don't count in this first-draft writing.

Expanding on the Quickwrite

Sometimes the students have a lot more to say and they simply continue writing on their initial idea. This can be done in their WRN or on separate sheets of paper as they expand on their thinking.

Emily, in response to "Black River" by classmate Janet, wrote:

> This reminds me of Christmas this year. There was a huge snowstorm that day, more snow than we had gotten for the whole winter last year. My best friend's family came over for Christmas dinner, battling their way through the thickening storm. We spent the afternoon eating and talking about presents, occasionally glancing outdoors at the white world outside. But once darkness had fallen we decided that we wanted to go sledding on the hill in my backyard. Realizing that neither of us had sledded since sixth grade, we became fixed on this goal. Our parents finally gave in, and we headed outside . . . [She ended the quickwrite here, but during writing time went back and added more.]
>
> The whole world was buried in snow. The dead reeds at the bottom of the slope are usually clacking in the breeze, but that night their sound was dampened by flakes. The snow was a fogged-over mirror, gently reflecting an orange light from the neighbor's house. Icy pellets falling from the smoky sky

fogged Cassie's glasses and stung my eyes. Frozen, my hands wet and numb, I mounted the sled and began to move downhill, a deep drift of snow piling in front of me.

It took several minutes for the path to smooth out. By then I was shivering with cold, ice water in my veins. But after just one run down the hill, all that was forgotten. What could be better, I now wonder, than sledding in a blizzard on Christmas night?

When I read Emily's journal for the two-week period, I underlined the lines from this quickwrite that I especially liked for their sense of sight, sound, and touch. I also liked the way she ended this with a question that needed no answer. I did not suggest to Emily to take this piece any further, as she had plenty of drafts of writing that she was already working on. This had potential should she become stuck. By underlining certain lines, both she and I knew where she might find some ideas, should she be looking.

knowing when to push students further with certain pieces

When Amy listened to the poem "Bullfrogs" by David Allen Evans (Janeczko 1982) she wrote down the line "asking for their legs" and continued with: "This made me think of Petey, a man with cerebral palsy. He could never walk and was always contained in either a bed and then when he got luckier, a wheelchair. I wonder if he ever asked for his legs, asked for strong legs, to let him walk. He had legs that bent in at the knees and were shriveled, weak and useless. I wonder if he ever wished for his legs."

Several days later in her WRN she wrote:

I enjoyed the book *Petey* (Ben Mikaelsen) for several reasons:

- It made me try to imagine my life if I could not walk or talk effectively. That would be so hard.

- It made me try to imagine never really being independent, always having to rely on someone else to care for me.

- It gave me great glimpses of the potential the human mind has, regardless of how the body works. You'll always have your thoughts, dreams, observations.

- This book deepened my respect for people with disabilities. I guess I had never stopped to think and imagine what life must be like for them.

- It also made me more conscious of how people act around others with disabilities. I will try to do as Trevor did—to get over the initial reactions I may have and not be turned off by appearances or what may seem to be a lack of intelligence, thought and life. People who can not speak may be dying to tell their stories. They may just need someone to learn their language.

Quickwrites often lingered in her mind and reentered her WRN in different forms throughout the year—a list, a poem, questions, an opinion, a letter, an essay. Every time she wrote, it was to further her thinking by taking her back or pushing her forward. I had only starred that first entry, telling her that her words were worth listening to, poignant and provocative to my thinking.

Nudging an Idea

When I read a quickwrite that I think holds potential for a lot more thinking, I might simply star or bracket that writing and jot a note in the student's journal:

> Tell me more.
>
> This is really interesting. What happened? Tell me more.
>
> This creates a vivid picture in my mind. Tell me more.
>
> You really feel strongly about that. Tell me more.

It is difficult to say exactly what questions nudge a writer further, but responding honestly and asking a student to "tell me more" shows enough interest to elicit more writing, from which even more questions and suggestions may evolve.

Ryan responded to Lindsay's poem about her grandmother by borrowing her first line, "I remember we . . ." and wrote for two minutes in his journal.

> I remember we went to the fair and you brought me on all the scary rides, and
> all the bonfires we had on the beach as we watched the day go by and how
> you told me stories, the best I've ever heard.

In my reading of his journal at the end of two weeks, I starred this quickwrite and said I liked the detail of particular events. I asked, "Who are you doing these things with? Tell me more." Because he knew he needed a final draft of writing and only had one other piece started, he read his quickwrite to a friend and ended up adding several more lines when she asked, "What else did you do together?" He wrote a second draft:

> **I Remember . . .**
>
> I remember when you took me to the fair and brought me on all the scary rides.
> And all the bonfires we had on the beach as we watched the day go by.
> And how you always told me stories, the best I've ever heard.
> And how you always offered me popsicles, saying no was just obserd.
> And when you came to my football games, you always cheered me on.
> And then you brought me home, and played catch with me on the lawn.
> And how you always cracked a joke, even at the toughest times.

And how you had so much wisdom to share, the funniest ones would rhyme.
And I remember all the plane rides home, when I only thought of you.
Thinking of the things we did, and the things that we will do.

Ryan read this draft to me and showed me how he had set up the lines and the rhyming. I pointed out again how much his love for his grandfather came through in each detail. I suggested he consider moving *and* from the second line to the end of the first line and to consider using *and* a bit more sparingly to give the eye a break—perhaps every other line and perhaps an odd number of times to give the ear a bit more variety in sound. He added *Pappy* to his title and switched the endings of lines seven and eight around to make more sense. I gave him the correct spelling for *absurd*. This became a poem he liked a lot and couldn't wait to send to his grandfather.

I nudged Katie in a similar way, with checks next to details she included in a quickwrite she did, in response to my rambling autobiography. I told the students to write their own autobiography, thinking especially of the things they did when they were little. Katie wrote:

Children run through sprinklers on a sticky summer day, you hit your first home run in T-ball with that special boy watching from the stands, sandcastles tower over small children's faces and watermelon juice dripping down your cheeks, you play hide 'n seek in clothes racks and jumping from rocks into the deep blue sea of the ocean, you listen patiently for the music of the ice cream truck.

In two minutes this is as much as she was able to write. During writing time, she added another page and a half of things children do, more likely that she did. She said she liked what she had written and asked to read the first draft to me. I repeated back to her the lines that stuck with me, the ones that were the strongest images and feelings of childhood. I suggested she think about using the present tense throughout, as if she were still living these rambling events, and that even the use of the second-person *you* would help pull the reader into the moments. I left her with a question: could she think of an ending that surprises the reader as well as surprises the child in this piece? Think about how quickly time passes.

Katie worked on the piece for several days and ended up with:

On a sticky summer day you run through sprinklers, hit your first homerun in T-ball, and build sandcastles while watermelon juice drips down your cheeks. You play hide 'n seek in clothes racks, listen patiently for the music of the ice cream truck with puffy eyes from swimming in a teal-blue public pool. You crawl through homemade blanket forts and roll huge snow balls for your first snowman. You dress up in fancy sparkling gowns and high heels three sizes too big. You draw your name in the sand and watch it wash away with the tide.

You catch fireflies in jars to light up the night, fall back into freshly fallen snow to make a snow angel. And you finally make it down your driveway without training wheels, and cannon ball into a mountain of red and orange and yellow leaves. On Christmas Eve you cuddle in front of a fireplace to see if Santa really comes. You tuck your first doll into her crib before desperately trying to blow out all five candles on your birthday cake and suddenly realize there are fourteen.

Katie liked the ending. She never took this to a final draft, as she didn't feel it was one of her stronger pieces of writing. It still had, and has, the potential to be crafted into an even stronger piece. The initial ideas are here. She might think more about the sights and sounds and smells of her childhood and reorganizing some of the details in a pattern that shows some vague connection as she moves from one recollection to the next. The ending is a wonderfully subtle way of showing the passage of time in the same way it shocks the child.

Ben wrote little throughout the year. It took him until spring to actually produce much writing. I always invite students to use quick sketches instead of writing if that comes more easily to them. Ben drew in response to my writing about being young at the ocean. I read to the students and then asked them to write about or sketch a place they loved going or hated going when they were younger. Ben drew himself at the ocean and then wrote:

(This is a) picture of me sitting on the beach watching the waves crash on the shorline like big rocks bashing against each other. I did this drawing because I think I was scared of the beach when I was little and watching every one having so much fun. I also had another problem. I was fat and very scared if I touck my sheart off I would be teased like when I'm in school.

I never heard this piece until I read Ben's WRN at the two-week point. In response I wrote:

This is a great description—the beach is not a soothing place in this memory. What scared you about the beach? The picture brought out strong feelings and words. This is beautifully written, almost poetry. Here's how you might start shaping this into a poem:

I am five.
I am sitting on the beach
Watching waves crash
On the shoreline like
Big rocks bashing
Against each other.
I am five and
I am scared . . .

Ben could not understand how to continue crafting his thinking as a poem or in any other format. He had said what he needed to say, I understood the feeling, and he was satisfied with the way he said it. He had taken great risk admitting his fear. This was a big step toward writing for him, telling the truth and reliving the experience.

Sometimes we have to let the ideas we recognize as having potential in students' work go. *letting go* We have to remember they might not see the same possibilities. It doesn't mean what they did is any less compelling.

Encouraging Students to Take Quickwrites to a Well-Developed Draft

Juliana used two quickwrite jottings to craft a piece about her great uncle's barbershop. In October she wrote a one-paragraph quickwrite in response to the poem "Barbers" from Cynthia Rylant's book *Something Permanent*. But the minute Juliana was given time to continue writing on any piece of her choice, she went right back to this piece and wrote several more pages.

Several months later I had the students respond to the passage about the cutting of hair in Lois Lowry's *The Giver*. Juliana went back to her first quickwrite. She already had a first draft of the piece in her journal. Her memories flooded back the more she wrote, and she wanted to capture as much of her thinking as quickly as possible.

I had starred and bracketed this initial piece of writing. She knew it had potential. She read it to several peers and to me to find out what worked and what she needed to expand. We pointed out the lines that let us see and hear and smell that barbershop. We asked her questions, some of which she answered. She used the passage from *The Giver* (Lowry 1994, 46) about hair as an epigraph, then she wrote:

> My great-uncle Pete has a barbershop. Every time I step into that room it's like going back in time. There is a striped barber's pole, comfy leather chairs, and black and white photos covering the walls. As my brother's hair is being cut, my father points to the people in the pictures. "That's Nana and her brothers. That's me with Mary Jean. That's one of Johnnie's paintings." Johnnie was the artist/photographer of the family. I have a huge extended family. Sometimes people will come into the shop. My father calculates in his head and then says something like, "This is your fourth cousin, twice removed," and I shake hands with this distant relative I've never seen in my life.
>
> On the wall one big painting of Johnnie's. It is of Scilla, the town from which every member of my dad's family is descended. Scilla is in Italy, at the very toe of the boot. The ocean is bright blue and all the streets are neatly lined with rows of quaint little houses roofed with red tiles. Cliffs hang over

the water and white wave caps crash on the shore. It's a beautiful painting. I never had the chance to meet Johnnie, but his paintings have inspired me to try to be an artist like he is. He drew Scilla from photographs and stories, but never from real life. If I ever go to Scilla I will sit on those cliffs and paint.

The rest of the wall is covered with a scattered arrangement of other memories. The photographs have torn corners and are all of old or deceased relatives standing in front of the old family barbershop. The men all have their hair slicked back and are wearing white crisp uniforms with old-fashioned square caps. All the women are in long dark dresses with little dogs in their arms and smiles on their faces. There are newer photographs also, of little babies, of anniversaries, and 80th birthday celebrations.

The barber's chair sits in the middle of the room on a brown rubber mat. The mirror is spotted. A cluster of spray bottles and combs and scissors in jars of green liquid are lying scattered around a small table.

My great-uncle is over ninety and has gone through several major surgeries that he was only half-expected to survive. He always wears an old camel barber shirt and brown corduroy pants. His gray hair is thin, but always combed neatly. His dark hands are freckled with sunspots and moles and they are rough and muscular from his work. He holds his plain metal barber scissors firmly in his hand, twisting his whole arm as he carves out hairstyles. He takes a break from cutting, to examine his handy work or check if the bangs are coming out even; he continues to snap his scissors, cutting through the air. Scrape, click, scrape, click.

While he goes through the motions, hair cascades to the brown rubber mat and he talks. His stories are engrossing even though I've heard them all before. There is a pattern to his speech, and wisdom to his words. He talks about things he did yesterday or seventy years ago and you can hardly tell the difference.

I fidget in the chair as he sweeps up my brother's fallen hair. He starts the story of his heart bypass surgery from a few years ago. "I was there outside the operating room on a table . . . you know the ones they wheel you around on? I'd told Aunt Mary and the kids that I loved them, and then they wheel me into the operating room and before they give me the medicine so I sleep, the doctor tells me, 'Peter, you need to understand that there are three possible outcomes of this surgery. You could just die right here on the operating table. You could end up bleeding to death, or it could turn out fine.' So I look at him and say, 'Do I get a choice?' He laughs and the other doctor says, 'I'm ready,' and I say, 'I am also.' Then the Doc says, 'I'm going to count backward from ten and then you'll fall asleep.' And then he starts counting '10 . . . 9 . . .' you know? But I'm not counting, I'm praying and asking Him to be with my family and then the next thing I know I'm awake and the doctor's telling me it went well. 'Johnny, you know,' he says to my father, 'The doctors thought I shouldn't have heart surgery at my age but Rockie—remember Rockie Lofaro, Johnny? He's a doctor now—he says, 'treat this man like he's sixty.' That's what he told them, Johnny."

My Uncle Pete has faith and selflessness I've not seen matched by anyone. He has a very trusting outlook on life. He believes God is always there to help and guide everyone, and even though that's not what I believe, in the same sense, I see that God is there for him. He is the kind of man who I can never imagine dead. He will always be there in his barber shop, cutting hair, recalling his past and saying in his typical old Italian accent, "No, Johnny . . . I couldn't . . ." with a wave of his hand, when my father offers to pay him.

In his WRN Nick wrote a quickwrite in response to my piece of writing entitled "When I was fifteen I believed . . ." I asked the students to write as quickly as they could, beginning with the phrase "I believe . . ." or "When I was (name any age) I believed . . ."

In his quickwrite Nick essentially wrote the first paragraph as it appears in this final draft. After reading this first paragraph, a question posed to him: How did he know people follow religion blindly? He wrote from his own experience and own beliefs as he crafted this writing. He added several epigraphs up front to show that he was thinking about religion from many different perspectives.

I Believe . . .

". . . and God said, 'Let there be light,' and there was light." Genesis 1:3

"God drove back the sea with a strong east wind and turned it into dry land. The waters were divided." Exodus 14:21

"God is powerful over everything." Koran IV

"I am the beginning and the middle and the end of all this is." Krishna in Bhagavad Gita 10:32

I believe that religion was created to rationalize phenomena that people didn't or don't understand. Early in history, right up through the middle ages, people followed religions blindly. They were illiterate and generally accepted that the priests were smarter than they were so they assumed that the priests must be right. The human mind naturally likes to have explanations for everything. People look to religion to find those explanations. To this day many people still follow religion blindly.

While participating in a Sunday school group at the Christian Science Church, the leader asked, "What is God?" The reply from the group seemed to be repeating some things that they memorized from a book. "God is the all powerful, the all knowing . . ." all in perfect unison. I asked, "What makes you think that?" My question was greeted with blank stares. One member of the Sunday school group, who obviously had read the Bible many times, said, "because it is said in . . ." She gave the exact location of the statement in the Bible.

Not wanting to pursue the issue any further, I said, "Never mind," and the group continued its discussion as normal. This is a more modern example of blindly following religion. This is not to say that religion is bad. Religion can be a great thing, as long as it is understood.

I believe that you should never blindly follow a person or set of beliefs. You should think for yourself and search for what you believe in. When you formulate your set of beliefs you are not bound to them. Beliefs evolve over time. By stating my current beliefs here I am not saying that I am in any way stuck with them for the rest of my life. They are constantly changing and will continue to do so.

I believe:

- There are no gods or goddesses. The idea of god was created to rationalize certain phenomena (ex. Death).

- You should never blindly follow a person or a set of beliefs.

- Humans do not own the earth; they are just guests. We should treat the earth and other people with respect.

- Everyone has the capability to do something great for the world. Many people think that they are insignificant. Only a few have realized their potential and acted upon it.

- Science and communication are the keys to understanding the world in which we live. By sharing our ideas and discoveries, we will begin to understand a lot more.

- Violence should never be a solution to anything. Governments and individuals should resolve problems peacefully. The only way to achieve this goal is for society to not recognize violence as a way of resolving a conflict.

Developing a Piece to Its Fullest Potential: Teaching Through Conferences

At the heart of moving writing forward is feedback and response—from peers and from the teacher. I ask my students at the eighth-grade level to bring two pieces of writing to final draft every four weeks. This writing that they choose *may or may not have* initially come from a quick-write. No matter where the thinking originated, whatever piece they want to take to final draft, I teach the students a particular way to respond to each other because I've learned this is the kind of response that pushes me forward as a writer.

I will talk in more depth later in this book about conferences and the kinds of possibilities I teach as minilessons with respect to rethinking the writing during the revision. But I wanted to mention conferences here also because they truly are essential in helping the writer develop his ideas.

I always share drafts of my writing before I ever ask students to respond to each others' writing. I ask the students to listen carefully to my writing as I read it to them. I give each of them a conference sheet that says:

- You can help me by _____.
- Tell me what phrases you hear that you like, or that surprise you or stick with you (that I wrote).
- What questions come to mind (as I read to you)?
- What's one suggestion you could give me (based on what help I asked for)?

This structure helps the students stay focused on the writing they are listening to and offering the kinds of comments that move the writing forward. By stating right away how the listener can help the writer, they are focused on what the writer has already perceived as the most problematic area for which she wants, and therefore welcomes, help. Listeners must write these phrases, questions, and suggestions down as they are listening to the piece read to them, so they don't forget what they are thinking.

Repeating phrases or sections back tell the writer that he was heard, that the language or construction affected the listener in some way, and these might be the areas the writer wants to preserve. As I model this, I put check marks next to the phrases the students repeat back to me.

Questions from listeners tell the writer this might be information she needs to consider adding. Is it important to add that? How many listeners had the same questions? What questions seem relevant to answer?

Suggestions should be focused on the writer's perceived areas needing help. (Did they want a stronger title? A more compelling lead? An ending that kept the listener guessing? More information about the character? More convincing arguments? Were they wondering about tense?

Or person? Or change in time? How could they make the character more believable? Would this work better as poetry or prose?)

This is the structure students must follow as they respond to each other whether the writer is sharing with the whole class, a small group, or one person. It is the structure that I have found that best helps the writer craft his ideas. Generic responses (that was good, that was interesting) are no help at all.

A large percentage of the writing students choose to take to a final draft comes from quickwrites. I take one or more of my quickwrites that I want to develop further to whole-class conferences with the students. I model several pieces like this before I ask them to take writing of theirs to a small group or before they read it to me. The students always read their own writing in a conference when they are working to revise it. I want them to be responsible for hearing their own voices as they write, revise, and edit.

Relooking at the Models

Any one of the models included in this book can be relooked at a second or third time to help the students draw some conclusions about leads, endings, line breaks, use of punctuation, titles, layers of meaning, fragments, writer's intentions, word choices, and so on.

One of the things I point out specifically to students, especially when we relook at these models and relook at their own quickwrites, is that they no longer need a line they may have borrowed. In the process of crafting an initial quickwrite to a more finished draft, they can get rid of a borrowed line that prompted the quickwrite. If they choose to keep a line from one of the models—whether it is a first line, a repeated line, an embedded line, an ending, or an epigraph—then I show them how to put that line in quotation marks to indicate it came from someone else's writing.

Don Murray says that good writing makes us think *or* feel something; the best writing makes us think *and* feel something. So many of the students whose writing is in this collection didn't think they had anything to say. Giving them another student's words to hold onto, or a professional's, until they found their own, gave them the confidence to know they could show us what they think *and* feel.

Writing and teaching writing are both hard work. Quickwrites offer an easy and manageable writing experience that helps students find their voices and develop their confidence, as they discover they do have things to say.

I am always surprised at the precision of language, level of depth and detail, and clarity of focus I hear when a student reads a three-minute quickwrite out loud. When the models for quickwrites are compelling and carefully chosen, students are able to focus closely and write clearly. But we can't forget, this is first-draft writing meant to help kids get ideas on paper. It's in the further development of these initial ideas and words, through peer and teacher conferences, that students craft lengthier, fuller, more polished pieces.

The following books are the most helpful to me as I choose pieces of literature to which the students can quickly connect. They are filled with short, compelling, thoughtful pieces that offer worthy ideas that stimulate the students' experiences and feelings. Especially at the beginning of the year, I use many of the pieces from *100 Quickwrites* (Rief 2003) because they are organized chronologically to match the curricular design of my classroom and they are autobiographical in nature, such as: "When I Was Young at the Ocean," "Rambling Autobiography," "When She Was Fifteen She Believed," "Dandelions," and "School Daze." There are also many fine pieces that I look for in poetry anthologies, from the list of books cited here, and from the Internet (Writers Almanac and American Life in Poetry). What pieces have you found especially compelling for the students you teach?

Resources for Quickwrites

Cisneros, Sandra. 1989. *The House on Mango Street.* New York: Vintage Books.

Fletcher, Ralph. 2011. *Mentor Author, Mentor Texts.* Portsmouth, NH: Heinemann.

Gendler, Ruth. 1988. *The Book of Qualities.* New York: HarperPerennial.

Graves, Donald H., and Penny Kittle. 2005. *My Quick Writes for Inside Writing.* Portsmouth, NH: Heinemann.

Heard, Georgia. 1995. *Writing Toward Home.* Portsmouth, NH: Heinemann.

Lowry, Lois. 1998. *Looking Back.* New York: Houghton-Mifflin.

Rief, Linda. 2003. *100 Quickwrites.* New York: Scholastic.

Rosenthal, Amy. 2005. *Encyclopedia of an Ordinary Life.* New York: Crown Publishers.

Quickwrites are only one way I help students find writing. Here are some other ways.

Interviewing

Explanation: In-Class Interview

One of the most valuable strategies we can give kids for gathering information is how to conduct an interview. I take my students through this particular exercise of interviewing a classmate, one they know the least about (see In-Class Interview Instructions, Online 5.1, on the website) especially effective with adolescents because they feel less intimidated writing about someone else. The listeners respond with positive comments when the writing is about them. They feel good about themselves when someone needs and wants their information. The process teaches

Online
5.1

them information-gathering and interviewing techniques they can use for any writing. It teaches them that they have things to say and unique ways of saying them.

Karen's interview contained just snippets of information, even after she focused her questions. But look at how she tied everything together when writing about Amanda:

> Have you ever felt the urge to get even? Amanda did.
>
> During the summer Amanda went to Cape Cod. One day in a restaurant there, she dumped a bottle of cream over a girl's head. "She was a little brat who we hated," was the explanation Amanda gave.
>
> Maybe the reaction was a little hot-tempered, but Amanda is a Taurus, born the Year of the Rat. She can spend plenty of time analyzing her behavior when she becomes a psychologist, or defending herself when she becomes a lawyer.
>
> Of course, if Amanda gets her one wish for "a million bucks," she won't have to work at all. She can just travel. She has already lived in Florida, Georgia, and New Hampshire.

David wrote this piece after interviewing Molly:

> ". . . ten, nine, eight, . . ." Molly crouched low over her horse Seal's neck, preparing for the start. She focused her sight between Seal's ears, at the first jump of the cross-country course that loomed ahead. ". . . seven, six, five, four, three, two, one!"
>
> Seal took a few quick steps and then broke into a fast canter. The first jump came closer and closer, and then suddenly it was behind them. The rest of the course went by just as quickly, and Molly let out a whoop as they swept through the finish line, and slowed Seal down to a walk. This was only a practice run, preparation for shows to come.
>
> Molly started riding when she was six years old, and it has been her obsession ever since she got on her first horse. She also loves swimming, singing, reading, and writing. Every time she gets an idea, Molly writes it down, as a story or a poem or a song. She wants to be a singer or a horse trainer and breeder when she grows up.
>
> Molly's most embarrassing moment was not when she was riding, but when she was seven years old doing a relay race in a swim meet. She accidentally dove into someone else's lane. Maybe that's why she likes spending time in the woods, where she can be by herself, silent and listening. She loves the autumn wind and rain. She says the wildness is "food for her soul."

Writing about others

If you asked her, Molly would tell you that if you know how to listen, you will hear things you didn't think could be heard. If you go deep enough into the woods, you may find her stretched out along the bank of a river, feet dangling in the water, listening to the sound of your footsteps, thinking about the sound of hoofbeats.

Tim took the piece Owen had written about him and extended it by adding all the problems he encounters as a gardener.

Gardening. Who does that? Retired, old ladies? Well, if old ladies were your answer, you are wrong! Though many old ladies enjoy gardening, I've been gardening since I was six years old. "I don't know whether it was the worms or the smell of the dirt, or both, . . . I just love working hard and having something to show for it—especially big stuff. Really big stuff. Really big pumpkins."

Can you imagine a home-grown pumpkin that weighed more than 200 pounds? Now that you are thinking of that over-sized pumpkin, imagine going out to check on it one afternoon and realizing that it has a slight mushy-ness to it. As the days go on, the mushier the pumpkin becomes, until finally you have to cut the pumpkin off its vine and throw it in the compost heap.

That was just one of the many problems I had this year, growing my prized pumpkin. Everything seemed to go wrong. First, I had vine-bore, then cucumber beetles, and to end off the bugs for the year, I had squash-beetles. Though that seems like a lot, it was just the beginning. It snowed the weekend I was putting the plants into the ground. There were hailstorms that chopped the leaves into tiny pieces and wind that blew the pieces in every direction.

Now I ask again, is it only old ladies who garden?

Expanding on pieces written about you

In a workshop I did with teachers, I interviewed Tricia and wrote:

Tricia's head swam with words: noun, adjective, predicate, conjunction, pronoun, as the teacher droned on. Her head bobbed. Her eyelids fluttered. Her chin dropped to her desk. Sound asleep. Again. Sound asleep in a hot river of teachers spitting out parts of speech while she slept on the desk.

"I slept through those classes because nobody ever took the time to say, 'Let's look at what you do know, so we can help with what you need to know.'" She remembers those classes as she reads *Green Eggs and Ham* and *Pat the Bunny* to her six-year-old. She remembers those classes as she holds her four-month-old to nurse. She remembers those classes when her students rush to her with books. "Ms. Poore, what do you think about this? Have you read this? It is such a cool book."

"It's too cool," she says. "Too cool." And she never worries, *Cool? Is that an adjective or an adverb?*

These pieces of writing are just drafts. They may turn into longer, more in-depth pieces, but that is the interviewer or interviewee's choice. If they choose to do that, they read the piece to me for feedback; I let them know what they did well and what questions I have, and I give them a suggestion. In conferences I am always responding to the content first; before the final draft I am helping the students edit for the conventions of writing.

Benefits of Interviewing

After the exercise, which takes one to two class periods, we talk about everything we've done. We discover we have:

- Experienced the entire writing process as a writer, reader, speaker, and listener.

Although I give students a topic by asking them to find the person in the room they know the least about, they have choice of ultimate topics by the questions they ask. When I ask them to look at the information that surprised them or they want to know more about, they are making the topic their own. They choose the focus and the format (narrative, letter, poetry, etc.) for presentation, and even decide whether they want to go public, by sharing what they have written with the whole class. At the very least, they are reading what they wrote to the person about whom they wrote.

I am always amazed at the quality of what they produce under the topic and time constraints.

We all tend to write more than we need to—the "bed-to-bed stories" Don Graves (1983) often talked about. By having the writers choose a focus for their second set of questions, I am showing them how to discard superfluous information. I am teaching them how to evaluate. (I show them by sharing what I had and my thinking as I keep or discard information.) This is similar to the same questions I ask in a conference: "You wrote about this and this and this. If you had to choose the one thing that surprised you the most or was the most important to you, what would that be?" By asking them to come up with five more questions that focus on that one area that surprised or interested them, I am showing them how to develop a topic.

Throughout the entire process of the interview they are drafting, revising, reading, speaking, and listening—to themselves and to a partner. Throughout every phase they are evaluating—making judgments about what they want to know, what is important to include, what makes sense. Watch their eyes. Watch their thinking.

- Been introduced to the kind of response and ways to get response that I reinforce throughout the year.

Over the years I've discovered that the most helpful response to me as a writer and the students has come from adapting Peter Elbow's technique in *Writing Without Teachers* (1982). Writers need to hear what the listeners (readers) heard that stuck with them, any questions that came to mind as they heard or read the writing, and a suggestion or two, best linked to what the writer wants to know how to do better.

I intentionally ask the students to find the person in the room they know the least about. If they can feel comfortable working and sharing their writing with that person, they most likely will feel comfortable with anyone else. By having the students write about their partners, it ensures positive response. The partners are not going to make derogatory remarks about the writing if it is about them.

The writers have the opportunity to revise their writing. After receiving responses, they can add, delete, reorganize information in a way that makes the most sense to them. By reading what they wrote out loud, they are hearing in ways they don't hear when they read to themselves. In conferences throughout the year I ask students to read their writing to me. Unless we run out of time, I listen to the writing. They are the best conferences because we can focus on the content and the writer can hear what she did that works well and what doesn't. Conferences (response) focus first on the content, making meaning, and last on the conventions, the editing.

- Been introduced to skills we need and reinforce throughout the year.

One of the most important skills we can teach our students is how to gather information from primary sources—real people. Whether they are gathering information from people or firsthand-account books or websites, they need to know how to formulate questions that elicit information. Yes-or-no answers give the writer little with which to work. But I want them to discover that. In this exercise, once they realize they have to write from the information they gather, they discover they have to get their partner talking. We talk out how to do that. What happens when they asked certain questions? How do they restructure their questions?

In addition to learning how to interview, they research a topic by brainstorming questions; reflect on the information by looking for surprise, finding specifics, and connecting ideas; rehearse their own voices as they hear about themselves and read their own writing; reveal what they each knew; and restructure a meaningful piece of writing for themselves and for others.

When they need to conduct research to make their writing the best it can be throughout the year, I remind them of this exercise. How do they do that? What can they do now?

■ Learned skills in context.

In one to two short class periods, I introduce the students to interviewing techniques, focus, leads, and dialogue. I model interviewing by participating in the process myself and explaining the how and why of my decisions. I show the students a variety of leads, what the leads should do, and how well they accomplish the intentions of the writer. I explain how dialogue, the voice of the speaker, is used to move the writing forward. What does the speaker say, and how does he say it, that strengthens the writing, clarifies our knowledge of the interviewee, and conveys what the writer is trying to show us about the person being interviewed? Where is the dialogue best used—in the lead, embedded in or throughout the text, or in the ending?

These are the minilessons (interviewing, focus, leads, dialogue) embedded in the exercise that become the notes I give students as reminders of all we did and how to do it again.

■ Chosen publication for our own reasons.

Do all students read their writing aloud, to the entire class? Not at all. But they must read what they wrote to the person they interviewed. I want kids to know they can trust me to believe they have responsibility for determining when their writing is ready for publication.

With this exercise, some writers feel they haven't done justice to the topic. Some aren't committed to the writing. Others simply couldn't get their partners to talk. It works for some, not for others. I used to lament my inadequacies as a writer to Don Murray, who would remind me that you have to do a lot of bad writing to get the good writing. I share that with my students. I may read my piece *because it is bad*. I want them to know writing is hard work and I often don't get it the way I want it.

This is simply an exercise, but one with lots of strategies and lessons that frame the year for writing and reading. There are so many fringe benefits as well:

■ We get to know each other. It establishes a social environment in which there is a lot of talk, laughter, and sharing. Students get to know one person in more depth, while hearing about many of their classmates in a way they normally would not.

■ I learn so much about all of the students—as learners and as young men and women. Their strengths. Their interests. Their experiences. Their ways of interacting with each other.

■ They hear a variety of voices—kids they might not normally talk to. They hear their own voices when other students read the pieces about them. They hear their own voices as writers when they read what they've written.

■ They learn that they have things to say that matter. It feels good to know someone needs and uses our words.

■ It establishes a positive, nonthreatening atmosphere in which kids feel good about each other and are willing to share because they know they don't have to.

- They become more confident as they start talking about everything they know and can do. Even in such a short time, they hear effective pieces of writing and know they can do that also.

- It reinforces the value in writing, reading, speaking, and listening when I am a participant in the same process—a model and modeling—showing the what I am doing, how I am doing it, and why I am doing it.

- It gives the students ideas for future writing: topics come from their own questions, something a partner said or wrote, or something they heard someone else write. (I often ask them, at the end of the process, to jot down any ideas that came to them as we were going through this process and to jot down the questions they wish the person who had interviewed them had asked.)

Instructions for the in-class interview and the follow-up notes I give to students to remind them how to conduct an interview are on the website.

Online
5.1

Positive–Negative Life Graph

I ask students to make two columns on a blank page in the response section of their WRN: one column labeled "Positives" and the second column labeled "Negatives."

"What are seventeen of the best things that have ever happened to you?" I ask. "These could be personal or world events," I add. "Invention of the cell phone. Winning a state hockey tournament. The birth of your little brother." With the mention of a little brother I usually hear—"Can that be in the Negative column too?" For seven minutes we list dash facts (short phrases to get them back to the memory) in the Positive column.

"What are thirteen of the worst things that have happened to you, either personally or in the world, directly or indirectly. Your dog was hit by a car. The World Trade Center was destroyed by terrorists. The birth of your little brother." For another seven minutes we list.

I do my list right in front of them—and I try to keep it to within my first eighteen years of life—school days.

Positives (17):

grew up in Hingham
tri-capt HS basketball team
summer—tide pools
Mr. Webb—favorite teacher
and so on . . .

Negatives (13):

tried to cut out my sister's tonsils
played softball
discovered dad an alcoholic
Camp Aldersgate—slugs
and so on . . .

"Look back at your list and star three of the most positive things and three of the most negative." I star the ones on my list. "Is anyone willing to read what you starred?" Hands shoot up most of the time. If not, I share first. I remind the students that something someone else has listed might remind others of a similar thing. "Jot down what you are reminded of. Add it to your list." Sometimes I ask the kids just to share their starred items with those at their table. I give them another two minutes to add anything to either list. Try for seventeen positives. Try to remember thirteen negatives. "If you don't have many negatives, you are one of the luckier persons in the world."

"Look through your lists and check those things that are most significant to you for one reason or another. They make you happy or proud, show your creativity or your talents, help you in your work or play, demonstrate you are confident, generous, loved, or they make you sad, embarrassed, angry, worried, fearful, disappointed, hurt."

After they've checked the most significant events, I have them jot down, on those lists, the age at which the event happened. I add those ages to my list: next to "tried to cut out my sister's tonsils" I write "age 6."

The students then chart the most significant positives and negatives in their lives on graph paper. They may not have seventeen and thirteen, but trying to come up with that many helps them to remember many more than if I said just to think of three.

I add positive and negative scales that run down the left side of the graph paper, +5 being the most positive of any event, and –5 being the most negative of any event. Then I add a line that runs across the page from left to right to represent their age. The distance representing each year should be the same, for instance, 5 cm = 1 year in their lives. If there is little that happened across several years, students can change the scale, giving greater space across the graph to the years when more happened.

I put a sample of a chart that was done well from a previous year on each table. At each point where the students chart an event I ask them to put at least three of the five W's (*who, what, when, where, why*) and *how*, focusing on the most important information in the limited space. I ask them to draw or find a picture that illustrates best what happened.

When I graph the time I tried to cut out my sister's tonsils as a –4 when I was age six, I draw a stick figure face with her mouth wide open and the uvula hanging down over the back of her tongue. I draw a pair of scissors in her mouth, and write: "tried to cut out sister's 'tonsils' because I wanted to be a doctor." Ultimately this becomes one of my pieces of writing because the students are so interested (flabbergasted and disgusted would be closer to their actual reactions) in what I did and why, and what happened. (The babysitter stopped me just in the nick of time.)

Just in case you, too, are interested, here's the lead to my story:

"I know how you can get a lot of ice cream," I said to my four-year-old sister. "You want to do it."

My mother had taken us to visit Barbara Adams, who had just had her tonsils out. She had a big bowl of ice cream in her lap, and her mother said that was all she could eat. We left her coloring books, crayons and a puzzle. I walked home with an idea planted in my head. I wanted to be a doctor. This would be good practice. I could cut out my sister's tonsils, despite the fact I had no idea where they were in her throat.

And so I began the story.

The point of the lifeline is to help students find those events, topics, and/or people who matter to them. By graphing the degree of impact on their lives (How positive? How negative?) the students (and I) can see how much these events mean to them. The graphs become invaluable resources for topics of writing—personal narrative, memoir, even persuasive or informational pieces. Many of the students' final pieces of writing throughout the year can be traced back to these graphs. They may not recognize this yet—but by spending time graphing, drawing, and noting dash facts with each event, they have planted the kernels of ideas.

In addition, the graphs give me invaluable visual clues into what each student's life has been like—how positive, how negative—so that I can begin to know them. The way I talk to them about these events helps them know me, and know how I will be with them. The better the students know me and trust me, the more honest they are. Do they have to include very personal negatives or positives? Not at all. Do they have to share their lists or final graphs with the whole class? Not unless they choose to.

I have noticed that the more opportunities I give students to draw, the more successful many of them are. Using stick figures and key words to convey information is not only acceptable, but encouraged. When we draw, we spend time thinking about what we are drawing. They talk to each other as they draw. They slow down. They think about how this event or person matters. They give ideas to each other, and they learn about each other. It sets a tone for the year.

I want kids to understand the process as well as the product, but I do not want the process to become the end product. If the listing alone helps them get to writing ideas, terrific. It's the spending of time graphing those events that lets many of them see even more clearly how this event matters to them. Letting others see and read their life stories gives the readers ideas and helps them get to know each other better.

We talk also about aesthetics. How can they make their graph appealing to a reader? How can they visually represent what they are saying to limit the use of words in such a small space? I simply want everything they do to be their best effort, especially if they go public—let anyone else view their work.

After the students finish their graphs, I start them thinking even more deeply about writing from them. I ask them to fold a standard eight-and-a-half-by-eleven-inch piece of paper in thirds. I have them choose three of the most memorable positive events and three of the most memorable negative events from the graphs—events or topics that surprised them, or they want to know more about, or that affected them most strongly. On one side of the paper they

Figure 5.1 Annika's Positive–Negative Life Graph

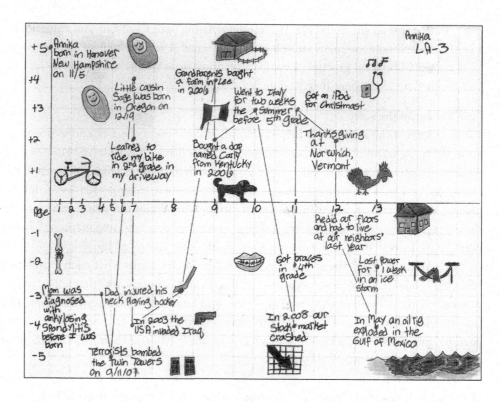

Figure 5.2 Nate's Positive–Negative Life Graph

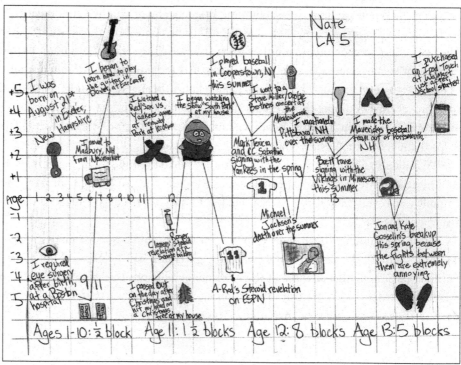

list the three positives, each one at the top of a column. On the opposite side of the paper they list the three negatives across the tops of the three columns. I give them several minutes to list under each topic or event all the words, phrases, sentences, or questions that come to mind with respect to the topic or event. We go through all six topics, giving about three minutes to each column. One of the lists may lead the student to a piece of writing, because they have something from which to write.

They can fold the paper in thirds, and tape it down one side into their WRNs, so they don't lose all the ideas and phrases that came to mind with these six events.

Throughout the year, especially when the kids are stuck, I refer them to their list or their graph, often looking at it with them. "Aidan, you said that the death of your grandfather was one of the worst things that ever happened to you. Tell me more about him. What made this so difficult?" He wrote numerous pieces about his grandfather: poetry, personal essays, and reading response that often took him to the memories of his grandfather.

Annika listed her grandparents' purchase of a farm as one of the most positive events in her life. So much of her writing came from experiences on that farm. A first draft of an event at the farm became a more polished piece of poetry several months later:

> Small pumpkins in random clusters dotted the bales of hay emitting a sweet dry smell; a barn's air freshener. Music ran from two fiddlers; a bouncing, dancing, leaping ribbon that tied together the sweet, warm, dry and crisp autumn essence that reverberated throughout the welcoming, even, yellow lighting of the barn. Some people clapped their hands to the lively beat of the music. Nothing modern, only authenticity characterized that moment and the barn seemed to sink around us, relaxing in the festive atmosphere.

Best draft:

The Pig Roast

> Small pumpkins in random clusters
> Dot hay bales
> Emitting sweet dry smells:
> A barn's freshener.
> Music runs from two fiddlers—
> A bouncing, dancing, leaping ribbon
> Tying together
> Autumn's sweet, warm, dry, crisp essence
> Reverberating through the barn's welcoming, even, yellow light.
> People clap to the music's lively beat.

Nothing modern, only authenticity
Characterizes this moment.
The barn seems to sink around us
Relaxing in the festive atmosphere.

Outside, gnarled, twisted apple wood,
Piled sloppily,
Dry and brittle like the air,
Rests by the roaster.
A pig sizzles inside,
Radiating fall's quintessential scents—
Smoky-sweet maple and apple,
Intertwined with thick, flavorful pork and wood—
      The signature smell of our annual pig roast.

From the life graph she also began thinking about age, drafting the following piece:

Fifteen

Fourteen had just become familiar;
I stopped stumbling, stuttering over the word
Hoping it was right,
Knowing it was right.
It came out awkward, choppy
From beneath the word "thirteen"
I shoveled back when people asked,
Because that wasn't right,
Not anymore.
Fourteen had just become familiar.
      Just in time for fifteen.
Fifteen that came too fast
Because fourteen had yet to leave
      And yet to come.
When did thirteen become fourteen,
And when will fourteen become fifteen?
When will I ever feel the age I am?
      And when will I ever be the age I feel?

Occasionally—more often than I like to admit—I will have a student who resists anything I ask him or her to try from the first day of school. The chart of one particular student was slapped together with everything ranked at the same level: +3. And every topic was the same: "video game, video game, video game," again and again. Not even the names of the video games. I talked to him about how clear it was that he loved video games. "Do you want to name some of the different ones you play?" I asked. "Not really," he said. "Have you been playing the same ones since age seven?" I asked. "Pretty much," he said. "Are there any you like better than others, that are more challenging, that you're playing now?" I tried. "Not really."

He kept saying nothing happened in his life and playing videogames was all he did, all afternoon and all night. "You must have had some good things happen in your life, and maybe even, but hopefully not, some bad things," I wondered. Maybe it was to get rid of me. Maybe it was to finally say something, that he added a huge black dot at the −5 point under the age of eight. It said, "Discover moms an alcoholic, because she's an idiot."

His anger was palpable, even more so, I imagined, now at fourteen. He put the pen down and stared at me, as if to say, now, now are you happy. He wouldn't, perhaps couldn't, talk about it or write about it. But I did begin to understand where his anger and bitterness came from, no matter what we were doing as readers and writers and how little he did. I understood. Pleading, begging, trying to persuade him that a strong education could change his life, I never succeeded in convincing him to read or write, at least while in eighth grade. I couldn't change things for him no matter how many choices I gave him. I still worry about him, but I could not make his home life better.

I continue to hope that, like James so many years ago, I might see this young man standing at my door someday—strong, confident, successful—apologizing for giving me such a hard time but telling me he was "listening."

In addition to using the graphs for students' lives, graphing the positives and negatives in a character's life from books they are reading is helpful in showing students how to gather and analyze those events or people that motivate a character's actions and reactions.

For many students, being able to see their lives visually helps them make meaning in what they see. For most students, charting the events in their lives helps them realize they do have experiences to write about and that the experiences are memorable to them for the emotions they hold and their relationships to others.

Likes–Dislikes Chart

Some years I do a variation of the Positive–Negative Life Graph and ask the students to construct a chart of their likes and dislikes. They make two columns on the first blank page in the response section of their WRN. In the middle of the two columns I give them some ideas of things they might like or dislike. The list looks like this:

Like/Love	**Dislike/Hate**
(make you happy, comfortable, etc.)	(make you sad, uncomfortable, etc.)

Sights

Sounds

Tastes

Touch

Things

Fears

Weather

Chores

Events

Feelings

Qualities

People Who

Online
5.2

We spend at least fifteen minutes filling out as much as we can on these lists. I tell the kids to number those things in order of most to least liked and most to least disliked. I give the students a chart (on the website), if they want it, and ask them to draw a picture and some key words to represent those items they listed. Again, as in constructing the Positive–Negative Life Graphs, they talk as they draw and write.

They tell stories connected to many of their items. Using the senses as categories also leads the students to think a bit more poetically. Just being able to use the chart as ideas for writing gives me one more thing to talk about with kids. Simply asking when they first remember loving the sound of skate blades across the ice, or what happened when they realized how dangerous sudden thunder and lightning storms can be, or what things made them list fear as the feeling they dislike the most. It is just another way to get students thinking about those things that help them find writing ideas when I ask, "What are the strongest memories associated with each of your categories?"

Writing and Reading Memories

Online
5.3–5.4

I want to know what experiences the students have had with reading and writing prior to this year. What kept them reading? What stopped their writing? I want them to know what I experienced through school and at home as a reader and writer that either stopped me or inspired me. I want to create those conditions that help move them forward. So, we have to know what those conditions are.

I show them my Reading Memories Chart and my Writing Memories Chart. I explain how I listed K–12 in two columns, of In School and Out of School, so we can see where that reading and writing flourished or where it floundered. I show them how I wrote only a phrase next to each grade level as a reminder of the fuller memory. I tell a writing memory, and I show them a reading memory. I point to one specific entry on my chart.

Figure 5.3
Annemarie's
Likes–Dislikes Chart

Figure 5.4
Charlie's
Likes–Dislikes Chart

We talk about why this memory sticks with me and why it's memorable. After talking through these memories, I have students make their own columns (In School and Out of School) and lists (K–7). I give them eight to ten minutes to think of reading and writing memories at each grade level, positive or negative. What kept them reading, kept them writing? What stopped them reading, stopped them writing? Just put a phrase—a dash fact—that will take them back to the memory later.

When kids complain that they can't remember much, I remind them that my charts contain a lot of blank lines. It's okay to leave something blank.

After they have listed all they can think of, I have them put a star next to the most vivid reading memory and a star next to the most vivid writing memory. "Turn and talk to the person next to you and tell them the story behind the phrase that you starred." After taking two to three minutes each to tell the story behind the phrase, I give the students time to write.

Typical of this first draft quickwrite, Madi wrote from her Third Grade, Out of School reading memory that she starred: *Mom read The Hobbit.*

She wrote:

> Short hobbits, gold, silver, heroes, dragons, darkness, Golom, the ring. These fantasies are turned into reality in my mind as my mom spins out the story. I love this, I say to myself. This is so real. More real than anything I've known. My cat curled up on my pillow, the rain drumming on the tin roof of our house. I'm supposed to be in Jefferson, NH but instead I'm millions of miles, hundreds of years away, captured in the land of books and imagination. This is where I belong.

In response to her starred writing memory—poem for mom's wedding—Madi wrote:

> I'm almost shaking. I tell myself that there's no reason to be nervous, no one will be judging me. But I'm sweaty nonetheless, and it's not from the August heat. Mom's smile is enough to make me remember why I'm doing all this, for her. I start to read. This is what I've been waiting for I realize, this is my moment. This poem I hold in my hands is "the best I've ever written," so I've been told, or that anyone else has read.

Yasmine's extended reading memory (worked on beyond the quickwrite) is not as positive:

> So many books. The book cases tower over me. Not that I'm tall. I'm one of the shortest ones in the class. The teacher tells me I have to pick from one shelf. Other kids don't have to. Why can't I pick from the other shelves? I wonder. They can pick from whatever shelf they want to. I can't.

I've already read all the interesting books, and some of the not so interesting ones too. What else can I read? Surely the teacher won't make me read a boring book. I'll just see if I can find some better books to read. If I can't, I'll go right back to the shelf from which I'm supposed to pick.

I drift along the other books until I see a familiar title, If You Give a Mouse a Cookie. It's one of my favorites. I read it all the time; it's a great story. So I sit down to read. "If you give a mouse a cookie . . ." I'm about halfway through the book when the teacher interrupts. "What are you reading?" she asks. "If You Give a Mouse a Cookie," I answer innocently. "Is that from the shelf I told you to read from?"

"No, but . . ."

"No buts. I told you to read from that shelf. Pick a different book," she tells me. "You can't read that book yet. You have to start with easier books."

"But I can read it! Listen, 'If you give a mouse a cookie, then you'll have to give him some milk to go with it . . .'"

"You can't read it. You've just memorized it."

"Yes, I can! I'm reading it now. I haven't memorized it."

"Yes, you have. Now go and pick another book from your section," she says sternly.

Now I realize why I can't read from the other shelves. The teacher doesn't think I'm smart enough. She thinks I can't read as well as the other kids. I'm afraid I might get in trouble, so I go back to my shelf. I try to pay attention in class, but I can't forget how my teacher has wrongly accused me. I am as smart as they are, I tell myself. The problem is, I'm not so sure anymore.

We talk out many of these memories and what they mean for us, especially *this* year in *this* classroom. We talk about how much we love playing as writers, using our imaginations to create characters and stories and settings. How much we love being read to, especially when someone reads with the voices of the characters. How I will never tell them they must pick from a certain shelf. If a book is too hard, they can decide to switch to another. Maybe the book is hard, but if they are really interested, they can stick with it, or let it go for the time being. I will trust them as readers and writers to determine what keeps them reading and what keeps them writing.

We go back to my two memory charts. I show them all my blanks. I have few memories of reading or writing, especially in school. I don't want their charts to look like that. I want them to leave this classroom liking, or still liking, reading and writing, I want them to be the strongest readers and writers they can be in the limited time we have. I want them to be proud of all they will do as readers and writers. Those are my goals. My goal is to not get in their way.

I tell the kids about one of my worst, but eventually, best experiences in graduate school. I had to choose five readers for my master's thesis. Other students warned me about one professor, saying he never found anything positive in their writing. I didn't listen. I enjoyed his class and asked if he would be one of my readers. He agreed.

For two years I researched the importance of audience in writing. I received positive feedback from the other four readers—pointing out the strongest sections of the thesis, asking good questions that would help me build on those points, and offering a suggestion or two for strengthening my findings and the implications.

I stood on the opposite side of the desk of the fifth reader, the professor I had been warned about. He threw my thesis, several hundred pages, across his desk. As it slid toward me I grabbed it before it fell to the floor. "Garbage," he said. "Do it over!"

I left his office—devastated. His comments not only did nothing to help me, but even worse, they totally stopped me from writing and made me forget all the positive comments and questions I had been given by the other four readers. I couldn't work on the thesis for another six months. His negative comment stopped me cold.

"I will never do that to you and your writing," I tell my eighth graders. "It is not helpful. I will try my best to notice what you do well and ask questions and offer suggestions that move your writing forward." So why was this one of my best experiences? Because it taught me what never to do as a responder to anyone's writing, and it reinforced how devastating that kind of response can be.

The blank charts that are included on the website with all the other handouts list memories all the way through graduate school—perfect for use with teachers. Naturally you would end the charts based on the grade level of your students.

What would your Reading and Writing Memories charts look like? As you construct your own, think of the implications for your students in your classroom. What kept you reading and kept you writing, and how do you make sure those conditions exist in your teaching?

Online 5.5–5.6

Writer's-Reader's Poster

Because I really want these students to get to know each other, especially as readers and writers, I ask them each to construct a Writer's-Reader's Poster that includes so much of the writing we have been working on these first few weeks.

Each piece selected for the poster is revised (they read the pieces to me, and I tell them what they have done well, ask questions that come to mind, give them some suggestions) and edited, while students work on the layout to determine how and where the writing fits. I show the kids how to justify their work (make the words even on both the left and right margins of the writing) so their pieces fit more easily in the column format of the poster.

I have included excerpts from a variety of students' posters of each of the different kinds of writing I expect, so you have some examples to show your students as they construct their own posters.

Best Piece of Writing Over the Last Several Years

"Now take a step out," instructed Matt from so far away that I could barely hear him. My whole body began shaking again and my mouth turned very dry at just the thought of it. I could hear the laughter of the other kids down below. "Just wait," I told them angrily under my breath, "you won't be laughing when you're up here."

Very timidly I loosened my grip on the vertical pole and took a step out onto the thin log. I could feel the faces of everyone watching my back, waiting for the mistakes I might make. They seemed almost as frightened as I was."

Juliana, seventh grade, excerpt from "Merrowvista"

Reading Memory

"Read us more! Read us more!" my sister and I begged as we hopped onto the plaid comforter and lay down next to Mom. "Okay, a little," she smiled. Then she opened our copy of Little House of the Prairie, the paperback with orange and cream checkerboard around the edges. Then she took us back in time and we felt sorry for Jack, their bulldog, who had to run behind the horse-drawn wagon the whole trip, and with her words we were riding through the grasslands on a covered wagon. The woods around our house were so different from the prairie in the story. Every night mom would read a couple of chapters, and Hannah and I would be on either side of her, dreaming of Indians, cowboys, prairie hens, long wagon rides and rivers full of fish. Hannah and I loved hearing about a place and time so different from ours, and we thought it was perfect that there were two sisters, just like us. I can see it in my mind now, the white room, the big bed, mom in the middle of us like a human hotdog. Her voice made the words lift off the page and warm up the room, making the dark outside the window seem brighter. We got through the whole book eventually, but I still remember being lost in joy in the long brown, waving prairie grass with Mom and Hannah.

Jane

Reading Memory

My hands grasped my brother's but our arms didn't come anywhere close to encircling the giant standing before us. Standing over 300 feet tall, the Redwood is exactly what I had been looking forward to seeing. Only two months before I had read about national parks full of natural beauties. What once was only a far-off dream, had become a reality. I was finally in the Redwood Forest.

It was hard to believe that I was actually here at last looking at the tall trees Four Against the Odds had spoken of. That book had sent me and my family off on a six-month cross-country trip that would become the biggest time marker of my life.

Devin

Autobiographical Pieces

I was born in Berlin, Germany just before the wall came down. I used to roller-skate over to the brook where I fed the ducks stale oyster crackers that I thought smelled bad. I can remember the look on my brother's face after he took a bite of soap because I told him it was a chocolate bar. The taste and smell of fresh-baked cookies still triggers a memory in my mind of making cookies with my Nana when I first moved to America. The feel of fear and excitement on the first day of kindergarten is still fresh in my mind, knowing that I didn't know a soul in the country except my family. That tingly feeling that ran through my body the first time my crush told me that I was his crush too is still a great memory. I can also remember the devastation that I felt the day my Mum told me that my dad had filed for divorce.

Amelia, "Rambling Autobiography"

I am from the vast cornfields of Illinois that go on for miles, waving in the wind like the ocean I had never seen. I am from the day I moved, leaving everyone I knew behind, not yet ready to take on a whole new life. I am from the Christmas tree farm, my arms covered with pinesap after working in the trees for hours. . . . I am from cold Sunday mornings, skipping church to go to stick and puck at the snowy Jackson's Landing, working to make my game that little bit better. . . . I am from my little sister Anna, born with Down's Syndrome, then, as if it wasn't enough, diagnosed with leukemia and still alive to tell her story, if she were able to talk well enough.

Nate, "Where I'm From . . ."

I was born on the 10th of May, a Mother's Day present, though my birth certificate says the 11th. I have traveled far, to places I don't remember. I've lost a cat to a speeding car. I have hated people I've never met. I have seen things I want to forget and things I will try to keep with me always. I have cried and laughed in the same second. I have eaten warm cookies and cold milk. I have stayed up all night just to conk out at 7 am. I have smelled lilacs in the spring and the ocean in the summer. I have held a featherless baby bird in my hand and watched it slip away from the world. I have eaten a banana every morning for four years and skied down a mountain so fast that the bitter wind stung my whole body. I've been afraid of life and death and the dark. I've gone for a month without seeing my mom. I've jumped off a bridge and made sushi. I've had six middle names and been called many others. I've been proud and ashamed, hopeful and helpless. I've told secrets and kept many more.

Juliana, "Rambling Autobiography"

FAVORITE BOOKS
(Examples of excerpts from these books from several posters)

Rosie's Three Favorite Books

The Hitchhiker's Guide to the Galaxy by Douglas Adams

Far out in the uncharted backwaters of the unfashionable end of the Western Spiral arm of the galaxy lies a small unregarded yellow sun. Orbiting this at a distance of roughly ninety-eight million miles is an utterly insignificant little blue-green planet whose ape-descended life forms are so amazingly primitive that they still think digital watches are a pretty neat idea.

Pride and Prejudice by Jane Austen

It is a truth universally acknowledged, that a single man in possession of a good fortune, must be in want of a good wife. However little known the feelings or views of such a man may be on his first entering a neighborhood, this truth is so well fixed in the minds of the surrounding families, that he is considered the rightful property of some one or other of their daughters.

I'm a Stranger Here Myself by Bill Bryson

Forgive me if I seem a tad effusive, but it is impossible to describe a spectacle this grand without babbling. Even the great naturalist Donald Culross Peattie, a man whose prose is so dry you could use it to mop spills, totally lost his head when he tried to convey the wonder of a New England autumn.

Alex's Two Favorite Books

The DaVinci Code by Dan Brown

Just below Saunire's breastbone, a bloody smear marked the spot where the bullet had pierced his flesh. The wound had bled surprisingly little, leaving only a small pool of blackened blood.

Saunire's left index finger was also bloody, apparently having been dipped into the wound to create the most unsettling aspect of his own macabre deathbed; using his own blood as ink, and employing his own naked abdomen as a canvas, Saunire had drawn a simple symbol on his flesh—five straight lines that intersected to form a five-pointed star.

The pentacle.

Act of Valor by Tom Clancy

Live your life that the fear of death never enters your heart. Trouble no one about his religion. Respect others in their views and demand they respect yours. Love your life, perfect your life, and beautify all things in your life. Seek to make your life long and of service to your people. When your time comes to die, be not like those whose hearts are filled with fear of death, so that when their time comes they weep and pray for a little more time to live their lives over again in a different way. Sing your death song, and die like a hero going home.

Rose's Three Favorite Books

War Horse by Michael Morpurgo

In the heat of the sun and the dust it was tedious and strenuous work that quickly took of our excess weight and began to sap our strength once more. The cart was always too heavy for us to pull because they insisted at the railroad on filling it up with as many shells as possible in spite of Friedrich's protestations. They simply laughed at him and ignored him, and piled on the shells.

Divergent by Veronica Roth

She is tall enough to swing her leg over the railing. Her foot shakes. She puts her toe on the ledge as she lifts her other leg over. Facing us, she wipes her hands on her pants and holds onto the railing so hard her knuckles turn white. Then she takes one foot off the ledge. And the other. I see her face between the bars of the barrier, determined, her lips pressed together.

The Hunger Games by Suzanne Collins

"It's time for the drawing," Effie Trinket says, as she always does. "Ladies first!" and crosses to the glass ball with the girls' names. She reaches in, digs her hand deep into the ball, and pulls out a slip of paper. The crowd draws in a collective breath and then you can hear a pin drop, and I'm feeling nauseous and so desperately hoping that it's not me, that it's not me, that it's not me.

Effie Trinket crosses back to the podium, smoothes out the slip of paper, and reads out the name in a clear voice. And it's not me.

It's Primrose Everdeen.

Many of the students turned some of their first-draft quickwrites—the shorter pieces that were used on their Writer's-Reader's Poster—into longer, more in-depth pieces of writing, such as Fiona's two pieces that follow. Each started with a simple phrase written next to a grade level that grew to a three-minute quickwrite, then grew to a more extended, fuller piece that told a whole story.

Writing Memory: The Six Pages of Friendship

Some best friends weave friendship bracelets. Some best friends build fairy houses. But not me and my third grade best friend—no, we wrote the grisly tales of Cornelia Blackt (not "Blacked" as we so proudly pointed out to anyone who would listen) and her partner in crime, Geisha Hauntly Grey.

For years we told the stories of their lives, everything from vampires attacking them on Halloween to their learning about avoiding evil ghosts in school. Every free writing period was spent whispering, giggling and scribbling down "chapters" behind the bookshelves, sitting in the cold of dripping snow boots and leaky water bottles. Our once sharp, crisp crayons, turned to ground-down nubs that streaked across scrap paper, our drawings on one side, a short article on Independence Day that had been cast off from a fourth grade teacher on the other.

I was Cornelia. She was Geisha. Together, the two survived the cruelest boarding school we could ever imagine, skeletons in the coatroom, fiendish monsters, and all sorts of perils we secretly wished we could face. Of course, we never got more than a few pages down. Half the fun was coming up with the stories, but since our typing and penmanship skills hadn't developed at all, most of the stories were in our heads. What survived were pieces of fat-lined paper, crayon scrawled on yellow scrap paper and a "plot line." We wished so desperately to be writers, but not just any old writers, who would tell predictable tales with good guys and bad guys and happy endings. We wanted to bring something so new to the table that not even Steven King (whoever that was, we'd overheard our parents talking one night after a trip to the library together one night) would be able to top it. We wanted to make something new and wild and just a tiny bit unethical—something that would shock and amaze the readers of America, and at the center of it all would be us, the prodigy third grade writers.

Sometimes we'd flip through chapter books, writing down publisher's names, fiddling through all the possibilities of where we could have our book published. Scholastic? No. They'd make us change it for a younger audience (though we were only eight and nine, we considered ourselves young adult readers). Delta? No, we'd have to change it there too. Young Yearling Books? Of course not. Every place (so, in total, about five) we found, we figured they would want us to make some kind of edit.

But you just couldn't edit what we'd made. You couldn't spell check the hours we'd spent under the bunk bed, talking about how we should put in the whole werewolf chase scene. You couldn't count the number of pages we'd spent hours on drawing. You couldn't put a price on what we'd made together. Because the childish, poorly written lives of the two weirdest people to ever exist were more than a book. They were the symbol of me and my best friend's friendship.

Fiona

Reading Memory: The Life That Needed Living

In the summer between first and second grade, I found the book I just knew I was destined to read—*The Princess Diaries*.

How perfect! Finally, a book about a realistic princess. She had the profession I'd been dreaming of for years, and didn't even have to lift a finger to get it. Living proof that I too, could grow up to be royalty. I pored over the first three books in my cozy nook between our wide windows and maroon sofa, my little seven-year-old hands turning yellowing pages until my knees had carpet prints in them from kneeling so long, and the spiders that had scuttled for cover came out of hiding (at which point, of course, I would cause a big scene and make one of my brothers squish them).

Every little thing about those big, long, real chapter books had me in a trance. The girls in the book were so big, double my age! They lived in such an amazing city—New York, the center of the whole world (I was sure of this, though I'd never been there before. But from the way they were describing it, it made sense to my tiny first grade brain that surely it must be a cool city).

And every single one of them lived such exciting lives! Not just the princess, but the other characters, too! Her friends were either rich or geniuses or musicians, somehow managing to get into light, easy-to-solve perils every day. They lived in huge apartments on the best side of town and watched TV shows I'd never even heard of, and, to be perfectly honest, might not even exist. They went on exotic vacations to places I didn't know were real! Was Florida part of China, or Mexico? Was Spain a city or a country? I wished desperately I could have one of their lives—or all of them combined.

Sadly, this little royal heaven had to come to an end. As I got further into the series, I got more and more in over my head with new terms and words I'd never heard before. My mother finally put her foot down and took the marvelous, glorious tales of the New Yorkers away when I asked her what French kissing was, promptly snatching the open book out of my hands and saying I could read them again when I was "older."

But, when "older" came, I decided that no, I did not like the series, not at all. Because the author butchered the books by dragging them on and on and on, silly plot line after silly plot line, and eventually ended up having the princess actually not be a princess (turns out her family was "elected" and had been formed from some kind of dictatorship for years. I'm fuzzy on the details since I skimmed through this part and promptly returned it to the school library the moment I found out).

And thus is the tale of my first big, long, real chapter book. Once a magnificent story of a princess living in Manhattan turned, over many years, into a mangled scramble of books that clearly never would have an ending or an explanation (much like *Lost*, which I was also disappointed in, after I found out that it was all going nowhere). However, I did continue to read Meg Cabot's stories, all of which seemed to have a lot in common. In fact, all of them seemed to follow the same idea as The Princess Diaries—girl gets some kind of fame, girl doesn't want it, girl gets the boy, girl has a happily ever after (and somehow manages to lose her "unwanted" fame in the midst of the somewhat cheesy plot).

Of course, I probably shouldn't complain, because all these stories provided hours of entertainment in my fifth grade year. And in that cramped little spot in between the windows and sofa, my safe little cranny of princess wonder.

Fiona

Online
5.5.–5.6

The instructions for making this Writer's-Reader's Poster, and the Evaluation Sheet once the posters are done, are included in the handouts on the website. We hang the posters in the hall. I give the evaluation sheet to each student, with the instructions "Hand this sheet to someone you trust to give your poster a careful read. That person of your choice will be evaluating your poster." I talk for a few minutes about what makes a careful "read" of the poster. We grab pens, the sheet, and head out into the hall to read students' posters.

On another day, I send students into the hall with the instructions, "Find at least five books you would like to read based on the recommendations of several of your peers,

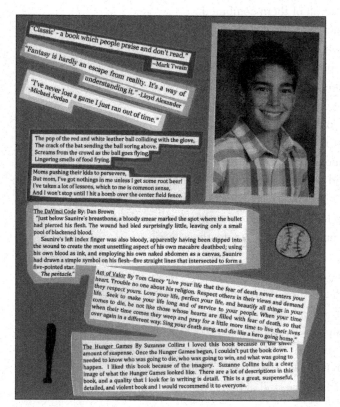

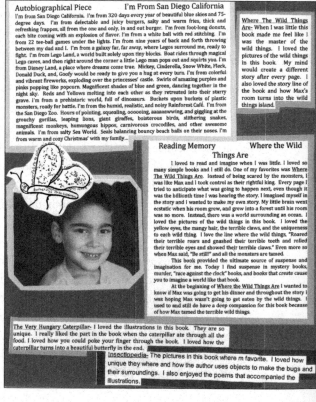

Figure 5.5 *Alex's Writer's-Reader's Poster*

whom you trust as readers. Write those titles down on the Books I Want to Read list in your WRN."

I am very picky about the size and layout of these posters because we are going to cut them in half once they come down after several months on the wall. They will become the front and back covers for their portfolios. Only eight-by-eleven-inch paper will fit into the clear pockets of these three-ring binders used as portfolios.

In addition to the handouts for these posters, I have included the completed posters of two students, Alex and Jane. I hope they will be helpful to show your students as models for these posters. I hang these, along with several others, in my room so kids can see an example of a finished product as they draft their own.

Often I will see other students, teachers, or administrators stopping to read these posters as they walk through the hallways. Jay, our principal, says, "I love these posters. I learn so much about the kids." I try my best to also get these finished and on the walls for our Parent Open House, as the parents love to see what their sons and daughters and their friends have to say about reading and writing.

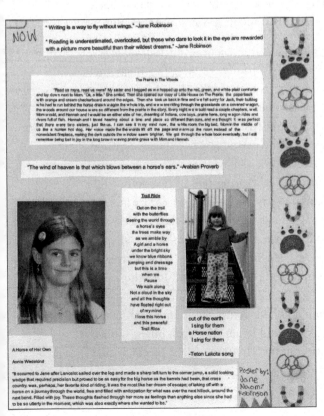
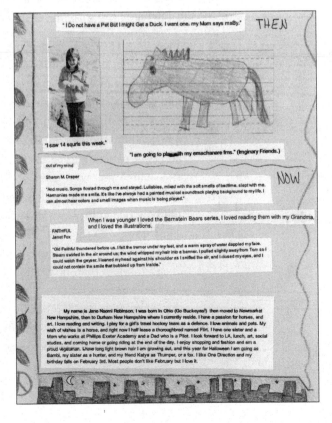

Figure 5.6 *Jane's Writer's-Reader's Poster*

Mapping the Neighborhood

In his book *Marshfield Dreams,* Ralph Fletcher has a map of his neighborhood where he grew up. I share this map with my students, along with reading one of the stories in the book. I like all the stories but I especially like "Marshfield," "Statue," and "Funeral."

After reading one of his stories aloud, I show the students his map again, helping them notice the places on the map from which the stories emerged. I ask them to draw a map of their neighborhood, or somewhere else where they spend a lot of time, and love being or going. A grandparents' house. A summer cottage. A city block. A place they used to live. A summer camp. In the same way that stories are remembered as they draw their Positive–Negative Life Graph, I know stories will emerge as they draw their maps.

I show them my neighborhood maps, the one where I lived until about third grade. And then the map of the neighborhood where I spent most of my life, from third grade through college. In the first map, where I lived at 16 Causeway Road, I began to remember more about Mr. Avery's big summer house, the tide pool where I spent most of my summer days, and the back porch, where I tried to cut out what I thought were my sister's tonsils.

The memories came to me more vividly as I drew. This map led me to write more about the tonsil episode, but also many others, including remembering my mom and dad making piccalilli in the tiny kitchen. I will share this first draft with my students as we find writing this September.

> Piccalilli. They are making piccalilli. I see this scene even today—like a Norman Rockwell painting on the cover of a *Saturday Evening Post* magazine. The counter in the back hall sags under the weight of green tomatoes, onions, and peppers. The spicy smell of a vinegar brine swimming with peppercorns, celery seed, mustard seed, and cloves, permeates the tiny kitchen as it boils in a huge aluminum pot on the small stove. The mason jars have been sterilized and wait patiently to be filled. My dad carries armloads of vegetables to the sink where my mom cores and cuts. He is wearing one of her cotton bib aprons. The one with yellow and pink flowers and ruffled edges. I watch as the bow tied at his waist disappears again and again around the corner as he steps down into the back room to fill his arms and the apron he has shaped into a sling with more green tomatoes. He steps up as he returns, moves closer to mom than he has to, carefully dumping an armload into the small kitchen sink.
>
> They nudge each other, my mom and dad, gently bump into each other, purposely brush against each other, smile and laugh with each other, as they move from counter to sink to stove to counter. They are making piccalilli, and

they hardly seem to notice my little sister and me, barely four and six, playing with paper dolls on the linoleum floor in the corner, only feet from them. They are making piccalilli, and the kitchen is warm, and my sister and I are safe with plastic scissors as we cover cardboard cutouts with paper cowboy hats and jackets and polka-dotted skirts.

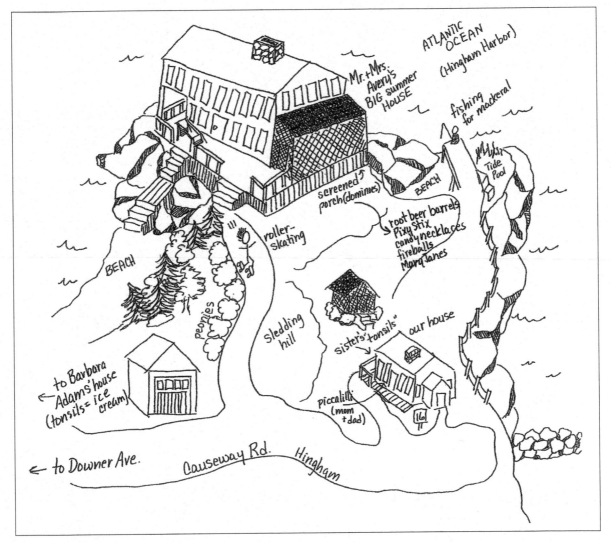

Figure 5.7 *My Neighborhood Map*

There are things I like, and other things I don't like about this vignette. I am anxious to share it with my students to hear what stays with them, what questions they have, and what their suggestions might be for the places that don't feel quite right to me.

We will draw maps to find writing in the memories that matter.

What does your neighborhood map look like? Your students' neighborhood maps? What are the stories that emerge from the drawing?

CHAPTER SIX

Immersion in Reading (and Writing)

Finding Reading

> I bring my experience and best imagination to the writing of a story. The reader brings his experience and his best imagination to the reading of that story.
>
> (Chris Crutcher, Boothbay Literacy Retreat, 2013)

In the Spirit of Ass Kicking!

In her book *Educating Esme*, Esme Raji Codell tells about reading aloud to her fifth graders every day after lunch. On this particular day, she is reading the book *The Hundred Dresses* by Eleanor Estes. When she's done reading Ashworth asks if he can tell her a secret, the way the poor little girl carried her own secret of having only drawings of a hundred dresses. He shows her how he has half a finger missing and asks to tell the class. Ashworth shows he's missing half a finger and asks not to be teased. There is a hum, then silence.

> Finally, Billy called out, "I'll kick the ass of anyone who makes fun of you!"
> "Yeah, me too!" said Kirk.
> "Yeah, Ash! You just tell us if anyone from another class messes with you, we'll beat their ass up and down!"
> Yeah, yeah, yeah! The class became united in the spirit of ass-kicking. Ashworth sighed and smiled at me. The power of literature! (Codell 1999, 34)

I want my students to read and respond to reading *in the spirit of ass kicking*. I want them to think and feel and react as deeply, as passionately, as powerfully as Ashworth and Billy and Kirk and the rest of the class did—because the story touched them as human beings. It is why Eleanor Estes told the story in the first place.

I want them to read to realize they are not alone. I want them to be able to step into worlds they can only imagine or could never imagine. I want them to learn and think and feel their worlds and other worlds.

I also want them to write well. And the most prevalent writing advice from most writers is: Read! Read! Read!

But *wanting* our students to read passionately, and *getting* them to, is not as easy as handing a child a book. Yet it is not as difficult as the world of politicians and journalists, some publishers, and most testing companies would lead us to believe. Nor is it as punitive as labeling books with Lexiles and telling kids they can only read from certain shelves. Nor as nonsensical as having kids answer computerized questions about books and calling them "experts" or "gifted" for answering efferent questions that don't matter.

We have to know books and we have to know our kids. I want them to read on their own, and I want all of us to read together.

My History as a Reader

It is the end of August and I have a week before school begins again. I am frantically trying to clean the house, prepare for a graduate course I've agreed to teach at a local university, and get things ready for the first few weeks of school. Each time I pass the book *In the Fall* by Jeffrey Lent I am so tempted to drop everything else and find out what is happening between Foster and Mebane. I am in the last one hundred pages of this three-generation epic novel recommended to me by Hephzibah Roskelly, a friend who teaches at the University of North Carolina in Greensboro. I have been reading slowly because I don't want it to end, but I am anxious to find out what has made Mebane so evil and what has happened so many years back that has affected a family generation after generation.

But I feel tremendous guilt. I have no time to read. There is too much to do for me to take the few hours to just sit and read. I have been indoctrinated in the notion that reading for pleasure is a waste of time if I am not "doing something with it." I am not going to read this book to my eighth graders, and the only thing I may do is recommend it to friends and write to Hepsy to talk to her about it. I have written lots of comments about "evil" in the margins and underlined passages I want to talk about.

I can't stand it any longer. I shut off the vacuum and take the book out to the back deck. I can't get over the feeling I am doing something clandestine, even illegal. Still, I have to find out what happened. I open the book and read.

My reading was not this way growing up. No one read books to me. Yet once I started school, I knew somehow that smart people read books, and there were no books in my house. This is what I do remember about reading.

> The log cabin came from Grossman's, bought for my four-year-old sister. Dad sets it up between the lilac and blueberry bushes. At ten years of age I am too big for it right from the start. I have to bend down to get through the doorway. But I love that log cabin, and I try to make it mine when my sister abandons it to the backyard. I set up two small chrome chairs side by side and cover them with an old afghan as a couch. I put an Allied Van Lines moving box in the opposite corner. My table. My space is full.
>
> I spread the box with a royal blue cloth, set a jelly jar filled with lilacs in the middle, light the candle I have taken from the house, stretch my legs across my couch, and open the Nancy Drew mystery. Where did I get this book? Do I know that books live in libraries? Did I walk myself to that imposing yellow building on Main Street?
>
> I don't remember a single story—what the mystery was, or how Nancy Drew solved it. I do remember the smell of lilacs and the rain splashing down on the log roof, while I remained dry inside my space. I was alone— and smart—because smart people read books, and there were few books in my house. The only literature was the *Reader's Digest* on top of the wicker hamper in the bathroom, next to Dad's ashtray, his Camel cigarettes, and the organdy curtains that always smelled of smoke despite a breeze. Here in my log cabin I was smart, as smart as Debbie and Pam and Charlie, who were all in the Robins Reading Group. Here in my log cabin no one laughed when I stumbled over words. Here I was alone with Nancy Drew and she had the problems to solve, not me.

What can we learn from our own history as readers?

I was seldom read to, knew few books and authors, and did not know how to find books growing up. Through high school I read CliffNotes because I believed I wouldn't know the answers to the constant tests simply by reading the book. I don't want these things to happen for kids.

I have been trying to catch up for years. One day Corbe came into class and asked me, "Have you read *The Crucible*?" I said no, I had not. "Have you seen the play?" Again, no. Hands on hips and a bit reticent she asked, "Who hired you?" Other kids jumped to my defense. "She's just catching up," they said. "Remember she told us no one showed her books when she was growing up."

Students expect us to be what we teach, readers and writers, and they have every right to. If I want to know what readers and writers do, I have to do these things myself.

Fill in the chart on Reading Memories for yourself in Chapter 5. Look at those things that kept you reading and those things that stopped you reading. Think about the implications for your own classroom. What do you do that keeps kids reading or stops kids reading that you can see reflected from your own experiences as a reader?

An Aunt's Story About Reading with Her Nephews

Several years ago, I was in Nebraska doing a workshop. I read a newspaper article written by a copy editor of the local paper. Vicki Reynolds spent a week during the summer while her nephews were visiting reading the Harry Potter books to them at night. Her nephews fell in love with the books and loved the nightly reading. Her eleven-year-old nephew loved the books so much he read them over and over again.

A month into the school year, Reynolds received a letter from her sister, telling her not to send any more Harry Potter books. Her son was reading the books to the detriment of his reading class. He was receiving a C– for reading, specifically because of the worksheets he had to fill out after reading short stories from a textbook. Reynolds continues that "this is not a dumb kid. He scores in the top 1 percent nationwide on those standardized tests. . . . And he loves to read. He devours books. He checks books out by the armload from the library. And he has a C– in reading. Go figure." Reynolds goes on to say she will abide by her sister's request. She felt tremendous guilt for introducing her nephews to these stories.

How truly sad, and absurd, I think. "Guilt" for introducing her nephews to books that they love reading?! What's the purpose of a reading class if it isn't to get kids reading?

What can we learn from Vicki Reynolds, her nephews, and Harry Potter?

This may be one of the biggest challenges we face as teachers. We are torn constantly between those things we know real readers do and test mandates demanding reading programs that depend on worksheets and one-word answers. We know that's not real reading.

What if the reading teacher in this case had asked her students, "What do you read on your own outside of school? What would you recommend to your peers as must reads?" What if she put that list up? What if she asked the kids to bring those books to school to read a favorite passage or do a book talk? What if she used books and short articles the kids are interested in to teach them reading strategies? What if she let them read books of their own choice at least one of her class periods? It would tell the kids she values them as readers, and ironically, values what readers do. From Reynolds' nephew we know that real reading has to be really reading.

From her sister we know that parents trust us as teachers to help kids become proficient, fluent readers. They trust us to know how that happens. As teachers we have to think about those things we ask students to do and thoughtfully critique what we believe students are getting from that work.

From the millions of kids across the globe who are reading books that are heavier than they are, we can learn that perhaps kids know a lot more about reading than they've been willing to divulge, or have been able to, through the standardized tests and worksheets that they are forced to endure, supposedly to monitor their reading successes.

A Bit of Historical Background on Giving Students Choice

How many articles and books based on research and experience do we have to study to believe that letting kids choose what they want to read gets them reading? My favorites, which cite a multitude of research studies to support their experiences and beliefs, are the following:

Nancie Atwell's *In the Middle* (1987) and *The Reading Zone* (2007)

Kelly Gallagher's *Readicide* (2009)

Joan Schroeder Kindig's *Choosing to Read* (2012)

Penny Kittle's *Book Love* (2013)

Donalyn Miller's *The Book Whisperer* (2009)

Tom Newkirk's *The Art of Slow Reading* (2012)

Anna Quindlen's *How Reading Changed My Life* (1998)

David Ulin's *The Lost Art of Reading* (2010)

Dennie Palmer Wolf's *Reading Reconsidered* (1988)

Let's step back a little farther. In the third edition of *Literature for Today's Young Adults*, Donelson and Nilsen report on a research study by George W. Norvell in 1946.

> By 1940, reading interest studies were fixtures in educational journals, and increasingly they did not merely report findings but interpreted results and questioned the literature used in schools. In 1946, Norvell reported, "Our data shows clearly that much literary material being used in our schools is too mature, too subtle, too erudite to permit its enjoyment by the majority of secondary-school pupils." Norvell arrived at six implications for secondary schools: material that is assigned as a whole class should be appealing to adolescents; there should be ample time and commitment given to allowing adolescents to read materials that appeal to them as individuals; teachers should choose materials which appeal to adolescents, and not just themselves as adults; three-quarters of the selections now used in classrooms should be replaced with more engaging materials; in particular, attention should be given to selecting materials that have appeal to boys; and to quote the study directly "to increase reading skill, promote the reading habit, and produce a generation of book-lovers, there is no factor so powerful as interest."

Let's go back even farther, to September 1937, to an article written by Ruth C. Schoonover titled "The Negaunee Reading Experiment," in which she says

> Requiring pupils to read books, some of which were boresome, distasteful, or too difficult, established an unnatural situation which failed, in many respects, to accomplish the desired results. Too many completed their required reading perfunctorily, then either read nothing more or else turned to trashy books and magazines.
>
> In many instances the exposure to good literature failed to "take." Requiring pupils to read good books does not necessarily instill in them the desire for good books, especially if the books are not properly adapted to pupil abilities and interests.

They instituted change—by filling classrooms with three hundred single copies of new books. They let kids choose what they wanted to read. The effects were immediate. In 1928–29, students read an average of fifteen books. In 1929–30, the average went up to twenty-nine books per student. By 1930–31, students read an average of fifty-five books each.

This was 1937, for goodness sake! The list goes on and on, right through 2014! Do so few of us read professionally? How much evidence do we need, and for how many generations, to believe that choosing our own reading makes us into readers? Interest matters in reading, in the same way it does in writing. If kids have a desire to read a story for the pleasure of that story, or to read nonfiction for the pleasure of the story and information, they will read. They will read difficult books that challenge them intellectually and emotionally.

We have to stop letting testing companies tell us that Dibels and Lexiles and programs like Accelerated Reader, and endless testing, will make our kids better readers. They don't. These testing companies know numbers well. What are their numbers? *Millions*. They are making *millions* of dollars. And so long as they can continue to convince the federal government to tie school funding to their numbers (their programs and tests), our kids will continue to lose as readers and writers, while these testing companies continue to fill their pockets with the *data* of extraordinarily high numbers—high numbers of dollars.

Reading Books of Their Own Choice

We are only a week into school. Nearly every one of my ninety students has chosen a book to read. Ninety kids. Ninety different books. When I handed them an index card and asked them to write down the number of books they had read in the previous year—"Be honest," I said. "I really want to know," I was not surprised when they held up the cards for all of us to see. Some had written *2*, others *80*, or *150*, but the average was about twelve. My challenge, finding books for those kids who admitted to reading only two, and keeping those kids who read fifty or more in books.

Megan, who recently moved here from another state, came up after class, barely whispering. She could not find a book, despite the fact I have at least two thousand books in my room. She said, "I noticed that none of your books have Lexile numbers on them. How do I choose a book?"

I took a deep breath. I reminded myself that this was *not* the student's fault. Yes, and it is a fault. I was trying to imagine John Kennedy or Anna Quindlen or even Bill Gates choosing what to read by Lexile numbers.

I explained that none of my books have Lexile numbers. "They have colored stickers, indicating genre, and they are shelved alphabetically by the last name of the author, just in case you know some authors you like. And they have great covers that might entice you in enough to pull the book from the shelf. Choose one by the title, or author, or cover. Then read the first few pages to see if the style and topic interest you. Matter of fact, if you look at the sign-out card in each book, the ones that have lots of names because they've been taken out the most—that's a good indicator of how good the book is. Another telltale sign—the book is falling apart it's been read so many times. If it looks brand-new, that's because it is brand-new."

"I had a Lexile number at my school, and that was the shelf I had to choose from. I didn't like the books on that shelf but I wasn't allowed to take from the other shelves. So . . . I'm really allowed to choose a book that I like?" she asked.

"Sweetheart, you can take any book you like off these shelves. We even have a library that has lots more books and you can borrow from the high school collection if you can't find the book here . . . and we can call the Library of Congress if . . ." (Whoa, calm down, I tell myself. Even though confining kids to Lexile numbers makes me crazy!) "You are a reader, not a Lexile number in this school, not in this classroom.

"I heard you say you liked realistic stories—have you ever read *Where the Heart Is* or *The Secret Life of Bees* or *The Fault in Our Stars*? Try one of these."

Thursday and Friday I focus on reading. Thursday we usually read a short piece together: an essay, a short story, a personal narrative, several pieces of poetry, an article—something that I want us to read and talk about together. Friday I usually do a book talk at the beginning of class, and then we read. I want to see kids reading in front of me so I can make sure they are really engaged with a book. If not, I can help them find a good book. I expect them to have a book with them every Friday. We must make time in our classrooms to read.

We read the book of our choice for thirty of the fifty minutes. My reading says to the students, there is nothing more important that I, or you, could be doing.

I have students who do not take advantage of this reading day. I see no pages turn. It is my job to find out more about these kids and find the book that will turn them to reading. I must have tried a dozen books to find one Sarah would like and actually read. I watched her eyes drift off the page again and again every Friday. Her writer's-reader's notebook (WRN) had no reading listed and no response to any reading. It took several months, but the book that finally turned her was *Thirteen Reasons Why* by Jay Asher. She came in smiling one morning. "You will *not* believe this but I read waiting to get picked up from soccer. I read before I did any homework. I read. I read a *book*. I can't believe it."

My standing homework assignment is to read for thirty minutes a night, four nights a week. In class reading on Friday counts as their fifth half hour. Their reading. Their choice. For pleasure. For information. For another class. Just read and record in their WRNs what they read and for how long. I keep a reading list and I keep a WRN—my observations about reading, my ideas for writing, and my thinking about the world—those things I want to remember around me. Sometimes it's about books. Sometimes it's not. I ask the same of the students. Keep a WRN—the ideas that they don't want to forget. (See Chapter 4 for the kinds of things students notice about books and reading in the WRNs.)

Book Recommendations

I find books through the recommendations of friends who know me and know what I like, or might like. Maureen Barbieri, my best friend, costs me a lot of money every year. She reads constantly. She reads deeply. She knows me. Every time she mentions a book I write it down on my list of must-reads. I have never been disappointed. Penny Kittle is another reader who I completely trust. Of course, the eighth graders bring me books or titles constantly. Books rotate on and off my desk like a turnstile on the subway. Kids ask permission for them before I can even see which titles have been added to the pile.

When students see me reading, they trust me as a reader. When I allow them to choose what they read for themselves most of the time in my classroom, they know I trust them as readers. The trust is reciprocal. When I choose a read-aloud that might interest all of them, they're willing to try it.

We recommend books to each other by posting lists by the bookshelves. We construct personal posters (see Reader's-Writer's Poster instructions on the website) that show who we are as readers and writers and mount these all around the room and hallways so we can learn from and share with each other.

Online 5.5

I cover the wall in the entryway to the classroom with the book recommendations of last year's students. At the end of the previous year, I asked kids to recommend a book to next year's class and to include the following in their recommendations:

- a color copy of the book cover
- a short summary of the book
- a passage so we can hear the style of the writing
- their reasons for recommending the book.

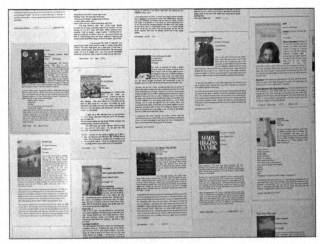

During the year, I ask the kids to use the same format for recommending books to each other. (See Short Book Review Template handout on the website.) They can also use this same format for book talks as it's the essential information we want to hear.

We then tape these book reviews/recommendations to the front of their lockers. All up and down the hallway kids see book recommendations. When they say they don't know what to read, I can say, "Who do you trust as a reader? Go see what book is on the door to his or her locker."

Online 6.1

Examples of Short Reviews

Throughout the year, I ask kids to jot down the best book they've read so far and, briefly, why it was so good. I post these recommendations near the bookshelves. Here's the first few pages of our latest list (the number in parentheses is the number of eighth graders who recommended that book):

Recommended Books by Last Year's Eighth Graders

Night—Elie Wiesel (nonfiction) (eleven students recommended)

While reading, I was totally in shock of how horrible and gruesome the things that happened were. The author says he survived for a reason . . . to record what happened . . ., how important it is for us to never let something like the Holocaust happen again.

Kelsey

This book was one of the best and most memorable I read all year. It was a tragic book that is incredibly sad because it was real and this happened to thousands of innocent people just because Hitler didn't like them and wanted to create a master race. This book totally changed what I thought of the Holocaust. . . . It's nauseating what Hitler did . . . it's an important issue that we should remember . . . not to sit back and watch something like this happen without doing anything.

Jessica

The Hunger Games—Suzanne Collins (science fiction) (eight students recommended)

. . . a new way to look at what the future of the world could become if we're not careful. Such a world could never be in store for the US. Or could it? Violence is all around us, on TV, the Internet, in sports, in schools, in streets . . . The more we see something, the more it becomes okay in our minds. When will it go so far that violence is accepted for the entertainment of others? *Hunger Games* really made me question our society and what it is slowly but surely coming to.

Kelsey

I was amazed at the strange things they did, and how brutal and terrible it sounded, but what made me feel even worse was the fact that all of this sounds a lot like what our world around us is today. Reality shows, World War II, the Middle East, and what I have learned about the Congo all revolve around either putting people through hideous events for the amusement of others, . . . I find it chilling.

Nate

The Boy in the Striped Pajamas—John Boyne (historical fiction) (five students recommended)

. . . from the perspective of a little boy . . . Most of the time Bruno's biggest problem is that he didn't like his house, or that he was bored. It was ironic . . . that these were his biggest problems while he lived right next door to Auschwitz. . . . It made me realize that no matter how long we spend learning about, talking about, and reading about the Holocaust, none of us will ever, ever, ever . . . know the true horrors that went on there. Because in some way or another, we are all Bruno. All we know is what is apparent to us, because we aren't there firsthand. He thought he was the great explorer and he knew everything in the world, but there was still so much for him to learn.

(Branwyn)

The Giver—Lois Lowry (science fiction) (four students recommended)

The idea of a world where bad things are eliminated sounded like a good idea. But then, . . . there were some major flaws. The idea of making everyone similar would usurp everyone's individual rights, almost leaving them vulnerable to one different, clever, and evil mind that could decide to control these people to do their bidding, just like how the Third Reich came to power. It's amazing that even creating a perfect society could become so terrible and horrific, if certain events transpired.

Nate

. . . made me truly appreciate the really simple things that inhabit my everyday life: color, feelings, freedom, weather, landscape, animals . . .

Kelsey

Harvesting the Heart; The Tenth Circle; My Sister's Keeper— Jodi Picoult (realistic fiction) (three students recommended)

This book broke my habit of choosing books that really didn't interest me, and got me into finding other books I really loved. In *The Tenth Circle* a girl accuses her ex-boyfriend of raping her, but questions stir as to whether he really did it or if she made it up as revenge for him breaking up with her. This book really looks close into father-daughter relationships and what a father will do to protect his little girl.

Kelsey

In My Hands—Irene Gut Opdyke (memoir) (three students recommended)

A gripping account of the Holocaust. It showed the side of a resistor, a side not heavily told. It made me remember that everyone has the power to change a life. And though it may hurt you, you should always do the right thing.

Izzy

Impulse; Glass; Burned; Crank; Identical—Ellen Hopkins (realistic fiction in poetry) (three students recommended)

. . . I felt like I should tell all of my friends to read this (*Crank*), no matter how hard it was to read at times. I may find it interesting because of my fascination of the horrors of the drug issue in the US.

Kelly

This book (*Crank*) made me think about all the bad things that could happen to you while using any dangerous drug, and that it is never a good idea to do this to your body. These things are reality . . . not only for people who you sadly expect to do things like that, but also good kids who can be easily influenced and persuaded into doing things they normally wouldn't. It also left me thinking, everybody has two sides to them—one side that's good and innocent, and then the darker side that likes to rebel. In everybody there is some of both; it's just a matter of what side you let control you that matters.

Jessica

(*Identical*) I am interested in the subject of abuse—it is like a form of horror in literature, along with drugs. This novel definitely raised my awareness of it, and I would recommend it to all mature teens.

Kelly

Speak; Wintergirls—Laura Halse Anderson (realistic fiction) (two students recommended)

Wintergirls is one of the best books I have ever read. . . . The layout and text of the story puts you inside Lia's thoughts, and shows you everything from her main thoughts, to what she's thinking in the back of her head. The story is really raw, and real. It doesn't sugarcoat anything, and it says plainly all the thoughts that all the other books I've read like this only imply.

Branwyn

Stitches—David Small (memoir—graphic novel) (two students recommended)

This is by far the scariest book I ever read. The way Small drew the figures in his life, his parents, grandmother, and doctors, is frightening. They are dark, mean-eyed people, always looking down on (him).

Haley

Learning to Swim—Ann Turner (memoir in poetry) (two students recommended)

In an innocent time when she should have been enjoying her childhood and summer, Turner was being sexually abused by a neighborhood boy. Her poems not only show how scared she was, but also how she overcame it.

Haley

Cirque du Freak series; Demonata series—Darren Shan (fantasy/horror)

Lord Loss (Demonata series), a gruesome book about demons, left me wanting to read the next book in the series. Shan is not scared to tell you about some of the most blood-thirsty, jaw-dropping demons that you will ever read about. The book is not for the faint of heart, as he puts in every detail about every gruesome death. Once you get past the blood and guts it is quite fun to read. It is not one of those books that you have to read halfway through to get to the good stuff, instead it pulls you in from the first page all the way to the end.

Gus

Infinite Jest—David Foster Wallace (realistic fiction)

In a sprawling, wild, super-hyped magnum opus, David Foster Wallace fulfills the promise of his precocious novel *The Broom of the System*. Equal parts philosophical quest and screwball comedy, *Infinite Jest* bends every rule of fiction, features a huge cast and multilevel narrative, and questions essential elements of American culture—our entertainments, our addictions, our relationships, our pleasures, our abilities to define ourselves. (Taken directly from Amazon.com review, found at http://www.amazon.com/Infinite-Jest-David-Foster-Wallace /dp/0316066524.)

This novel changed my way of thinking and my life. I still believe, like a wounded myrmidon clutching his captain, that this man can be placed in the same company of any writer—Jack Kerouac, Toni Morrison, etc.—and this book is the voice of a lightning bolt disguised as a stoner Midwesterner.

Dan

Catcher in the Rye—J.D. Salinger (realistic fiction)

It's still very much a street-novel today. There is an outright rawness of the soul that few books really have.

Dan

You Remind Me of You—Eoin Corrigan (novel in poetry)

This book left a large impression on me. It showed how a teenager's life can completely change with only one bad mistake. This book reminded me that I am lucky to live the life I lead.

Cece

Before I Die—Jenny Downham (realistic fiction)

. . . cancer. I was expecting this to be one of the saddest books I had ever read. Instead, the book wasn't trying to raise awareness of the horrors of cancer—it was a wake-up call to celebrate life, because you never know when it will be taken from you in an instant.

Kelly

The Blind Side—Michael Lewis (nonfiction)

You would think that a boy, who is poor, has a drug-addicted mother, had no education, lives in the ghetto, and has run away from several foster homes would never rebound. But Michael Oher has made it, and he is such a humble man . . . He made me completely retire the idea of self-pity. I have a great life, and there is no way that I should ever be complaining when I know what he had battled through.

Nate

The Road—Cormac McCarthy (science fiction)

Striking. Amazing. Not deep. It was very up front and real. None of the characters had names. That made it not just relatable, but familiar. These people could be anyone. It was brutal and cold. It didn't have heart. It had spirit. It carried endurance. It carried hope and life and chance. I loved it.

Catherine

Lord of the Rings—J. R. R. Tolkien (fantasy)

More amazing than the first time I read it. It is breathtaking. It is a world of wonder, of beauty, riddled with foul things, as all worlds are. But in this place, despite the hate, despite the true evil, there is respect. There is compassion. There is love, for life and friends. In LOTR you remember the people. You remember Samwise Gamgee. You see him, live his moment, as he watches his master crawling up the slopes of Mt. Doom and tenderly picks him up and carries him, as he said he would. You remember Frodo. His pain, his endurance, his will that could not be bent until the very end. The bond he shared with Sam, the love they had for each other, gratefulness. The tears that fell. The weight that was lifted. Frodo left for Valinor. And over time, Samwise joined him. Makes me cry.

Catherine

Book Talks

Penny Kittle describes the essentials of book talks in *Book Love* (2013). Her words, in bold, are followed by my words.

> **Hold the book.** Let the kids see the cover, see the thickness.
>
> **Know the Book.** I have been trying to catch up as a reader ever since I began teaching and admitted to kids I hadn't read a book for pleasure before I began teaching. If I haven't read the book, I have at least read reviews from trusted sources (online blogs such as Vicki Vinton's http://tomakeaprairie.wordpress.com, Teri Lesesne's professornana.livejournal.com/, or Nancie Atwell's "Kids Recommend" on her school's site, The Center for Teaching and Learning in Edgecomb, Maine), and admit that to the students. I share my thinking as I read or what the reviewer had to say.
>
> I also try to note anything unusual about the style or format of the book, or anything unusual about the author. Writer's Almanac sends poetry daily to its followers and includes interesting tidbits of information about authors and historical events for that day.
>
> **Read a short passage.** Often the style and tone of a character or narrator will sell a book to the students. I read it with as much feeling as I think the author is trying to convey. I know ahead of time what I want to read and I have practiced it. (In her Foreword to this book, Maya relates the day I read a section from *Harris and Me* to the students. I had five copies of that book. All gone in the first-period class after I read that passage.) Too many times I have tried to read a passage without preparing

it, and either forgot the passage contained words I stumbled through or was too embarrassed to read out loud. I lost the kids fumbling through the book talk. Like all lessons, the book talk needs to be prepared.

Keep records. Like Penny, I have a list on the wall that shows what books we've talked about, with the author's name. This helps the kids find the books on the shelves. I have tried to organize my books by topic, as Penny does, but we can never figure out exactly what the one topic is and how to come up with all those bins for every category. Shelving by last name of author, with colored stickers indicating genre, is the best I can do.

Accept help. Look at what my students had to say in the list a few pages back. Read what they wrote about the book. Better yet, get your students to give the book talks after you've modeled them in a variety of ways. Ask students to bring in reviews they read or prepare a book talk once they start raving about a book.

Remember how important you are. Kids watch everything we do. When we are excited about a book or an author, the excitement spreads.

There is a page in their WRN that says: *Books I Want to Read.* As you give book talks tell the kids to write down those titles that appeal to them, so they will know what to look for as soon as they finish a book.

Responding to Reading

Look through all the places in this book I have responded to my students in their WRNs. I try to follow a similar format as I respond to their reading as I do on a piece of writing. I underline, star, or put check marks next to things they say that really interest me—with no rhyme or reason as to why a star or a check—or phrasing that is memorable in some way for its wording or content. I ask questions meant to extend their thinking. I expect answers because the questions are based on my curiosity, wanting to know more.

Letters About Literature

I want to mention an excellent contest, Letters About Literature, sponsored by the Library of Congress. Just go onto their website under the Library of Congress: Letters About Literature (www.read.gov/letters). The contest asks kids to write a letter to an author of a book, a play, a poem, or a speech, telling the author how the work changed their lives in some way. (I'm not sure our kids have actually had their lives changed by a book, but they have definitely read books that have changed their thinking about themselves, others, or some aspect of the world, which is what I ask them to write about and which blends well with my interpretation of the intent of the contest question.)

This is actually the kind of writing (a personal essay that provides a convincing argument about the impact of a piece of writing on a reader) I wish my students did all the time—it shows the power of literature and the personal connections that are the reasons anyone reads in the first place. The site has examples of the winning letters from all previous years and across the states and many lesson plans for how to introduce your students to this kind of writing about reading. The contest offers them choice, models, and techniques for how to describe honestly the effects of an author's writing on their lives.

As in all of the student writing, their letters are treated as rough drafts that they read to peers and to me for response and feedback. I ask all of my students to try these letters. They draft, redraft, edit, and reread. We decide as a class which ones touched us as readers and should be sent to the contest. I encourage any and all students to send their letters if they feel comfortable doing that.

In 2012 Isabelle Todd was the New Hampshire Level II winner from our class for her letter to Natasha Friend, and Sydney Spencer was the 2008 NH Level II winner for her letter to Carolyn Mackler. In 2006 Kylee Drugan-Eppich's letter was selected as the NH Level II winner and the runner-up in the national competition. Hers is a good example for your students, although many other letters can also be found on the Letters About Literature website, either from your state library or the Library of Congress.

Dear Jenni Schaefer,

I'm not really sure how it started, but I remember looking in the mirror one day and hating what I saw. I saw an imperfect body looking back at me. As a runner, I thought that if I was thinner, I would be faster. So in January, 2005, I began to starve myself, and continued through June. But it didn't completely stop there. By then my pants barely held onto my bony hips, and my shirts hung loosely around my curled in shoulders. My parents were worried, yet I denied everything. My mom finally confronted me about how thin I was getting and how little I was eating, so I gave in.

Once I started talking, I couldn't stop. I cried, and cried. I cried for the pain I had gone through, and I cried out of relief, because I knew that my pain was going to end. I talked about how I thought I would be noticed if I was thin. I talked about how this voice inside my head told me what to do, and I never dared to disobey. I thought that the voice would bring me to a point in life where I would always be happy, because I was thin. I told my mom everything, and I finally realized that I was scared of what I was doing to myself. I was scared of the voice inside my head. I wanted to stop letting it control me. I know my mom didn't really understand what I was going through at the time, but she really tried. And I knew that she was someone I could count on to help me.

Your book, *Life Without Ed*, helped me through a really hard time in my life. My year long battle with anorexia was difficult and painful. You helped me separate myself from my eating disorder. I learned like you did to call this monster *Ed*, using the acronym for "eating disorder," E.D. It helped me realize that it wasn't me beating myself up over food. It was *Ed*. Sometimes I wish I had never admitted to my parents that I was starving myself to become thin. But I immediately recognized that voice as *Ed's*. After I had established that, I began to see what kind of person I really was. I realized I wasn't the person whose only goal was to become emaciated. I wanted to live, and *Ed* wanted me to starve myself to death. I want to become an Olympic runner, and I know that *he* wouldn't make that possible.

Things became better, but very slowly. I would start eating again, then *Ed* would pop in his two cents, and all of a sudden *he* was in charge. *He* always promised me that I would be happy once I was thin, but all I would be was irritable, cold, and sad. I was cold ALL THE TIME. I couldn't focus well either. Just reading a book, I would start a paragraph, read a couple of sentences, and then my mind would slip away. Then I would have to read those same sentences over again.

I hated that life. I hated being controlled by *Ed*. So that's why I read your book, as a recommendation from my therapist. It changed my life so much, and it changed the way I look at myself now. I think that if I hadn't read it, I wouldn't believe the things my doctors told me. All I would be in is denial. And all that *Ed* has done is deny me the happiness of living. You helped me divorce him after the months we were married, and I want to thank you for that. Now I know that I'm not the only teenage girl who suffers from this horrible eating disorder.

I am very far into recovery, and can't see going back to that monster you and I call *Ed*. You have helped me leave the most controlling and abusive *person* I've ever known. No teenage or grownup woman deserves to be cheated out of life. Since I've declared my independence from my eating disorder, I have had so many dreams that I know I wouldn't be able to achieve if *Ed* was still in charge of my life.

Thank you.

Sincerely,

Kylee Drugan-Eppich

Reading Together: Whole Class
Shorter Pieces

I used to worry about taking too much time to read whole novels aloud with the students. So I cut back from four a year to two a year. I then worried about not taking enough time to read more novels aloud. Ah, you thought I was going to say I added the two back in. No, I stopped worrying about not reading so many long works when I began paying attention to how many shorter works we do read together and talk about. Here's a list of the books from which we read short pieces, longer pieces, and sometimes the entire book, in addition to the short one-page pieces used for quickwrites (poetry, op-ed pieces, excerpts from novels).

When we read something together on Thursdays, these are the pieces I usually use, for both quickwrites ("What does this piece bring to mind for you?") and discussions about content or craft. The particular books listed here are the ones from which I gather stories that often lead the students to personal narratives, memoir, poetry, and opinion pieces for their own writing, but are also beautifully written for discussions about content and craft.

> *The House on Mango Street*: Sandra Cisneros ("The House on Mango Street," "Hairs," "My Name," "Bums in the Attic," and portions of "The Monkey Garden")
>
> *Woman Hollering Creek*: Sandra Cisneros ("Eleven" and "Salvador Late or Early")
>
> *Writing Toward Home*: Georgia Heard
>
> *Knucklehead*: Jon Scieszka
>
> *Guys Write for Guys Read*: Jon Scieszka (So many stories in here; choose the ones you love. I especially like: "The Follower" by Jack Gantos, from "On Writing" by Stephen King, "Funny You Should Ask" by Rick Reilly, and " 'O' Foods" by Chris Crutcher—although Crutcher's piece had me laughing out loud, I cannot read it aloud to kids for obvious reasons you'll see if you read it.)
>
> *Guys Read—Funny Business*: Jon Scieszka ("Your Question for Author Here" by Kate DiCamillo and Jon Scieszka is my favorite.)
>
> *Guys Read—The Sports Pages*: Jon Scieszka (Even reading Jon Scieszka's introduction about the sports he and his five brothers used to play is worth reading to kids, and asking, "So, what do you and your siblings and/or peers compete in . . . ?")
>
> *The Book of Qualities*: Ruth Gendler (This book, recommended to me by Tom Romano, is terrific for quickwrites. The pieces are short and vivid with tight language. Using two to three together, in comparison or in contrast to each other, gives kids some succinct models of personification.)

First French Kiss: Adam Bagdasarian ("Mount Cinder," "Little League," "Popularity," and "Going Steady")

Encyclopedia of an Ordinary Life: Amy Krouse Rosenthal (Penny Kittle recommended this book for short, unique, and unusual ways of looking at and describing one's personal world. So many short pieces can be read from this book for quickwrites or as suggestions to students—try your own alphabetical rambling of things that make you who you are: what surprises you, perplexes you, interests you?)

Every Living Thing: Cynthia Rylant ("Slower Than the Rest," "Stray," "A Bad Road for Cats")

A Couple of Kooks: Cynthia Rylant

But I'll Be Back Again: Cynthia Rylant

The Secret of Me: Meg Kearney (Many students use this for their study of poetry as novel. I pull out three to five poems to read to them to show progression of story—and as quickwrites that bring their own stories to mind.)

Love That Dog: Sharon Creech

We always read even these short pieces as story theatre. (I read all of *Love That Dog* to the students.) I make some copies and hand them out so the students can see the words as we read. I highlight the speaking parts for each character, giving the part to a student to read while I read the narrator. The kids like to read this way. It gives the characters voice and brings the story to life. I try to give many students parts throughout the year.

During our author/genre study and social justice studies, we read many more short stories, poetry collections, memoir pieces, graphic novel excerpts, book reviews, editorials, and persuasive essays. Throughout the year, we are writing and reading with abundance.

What books have you gathered that you use with your students to get them thinking about genre, content, and craft?

Close Readings of Writing

How do we give close readings to these pieces? Let's look at a couple of examples: *Love That Dog*, "Your Question for Author Here," "Popularity," and "Eleven."

Love That Dog by Sharon Creech

I read the entire book aloud. As I read I stop at several junctures and say, "What does this imply that Jack thinks about writing, or about reading, or about poetry, or about himself as a writer? Hmm—let's write that down. Would someone volunteer to jot these things down as I read?"

Once I finish reading, I show the students a copy of Jack's last poem from which they do a quickwrite—all that it brings to mind for them. I show them the other poems mentioned in the book and we talk about what we notice about these poems. We then look at the differences in the crafting of each, and talk about the simplicity or complexity that each affords us as readers.

I give them some background information about William Carlos Williams so we can talk about "The Red Wheelbarrow" with some background knowledge. I want them to know he was a doctor who loved writing poetry. But he wanted it to be accessible to everyone, not just scholars. So often as he went on his rounds visiting patients, he wrote about the things he noticed that were important to us. This poem works well as a write-around. Give a copy of the poem to each student and have them annotate it. What do they understand, not understand? What do they think a line means? What do they notice about words, phrasing, arrangement—anything? After three minutes, they pass their paper to the person on their right. That person reads their comments and writes anything that extends the thinking of the previous reader. And so on around the table. Then we discuss our findings. I sit at a table and write with the students. Having written conversations lets kids push each others' thinking, and then they have more courage to talk about all they noticed.

We talk about Robert Frost and his writing. I give them the entire poem "The Tyger" by William Blake (Koch 1985, 61) and have them annotate it (What are you thinking? What are your questions as you read?) before we talk about this poem of address. Or I do the written conversation with this poem. I change things up depending on what I know about the students and what works best for them.

When there is time, I show the students the book *Speak! Children's Book Illustrators Brag About Their Dogs* and ask them to try a drawing of their own dog or other pet with a short anecdote (the word *anecdote* always throws them into a tizzy!) about the animal (in their WRN).

Last, we gather their thinking on the following questions to summarize what they noticed about this book and the poetry. I ask them:

- What would be helpful to remember about writing poetry?
- What would be helpful to remember about reading poetry?
- What would be helpful to remember about writing in general?
- What ideas did you get for writing from reading this book?

"Your Question for Author Here" by Kate DiCamillo and Jon Scieszka from *Guys Read—Funny Business*

I make enough copies of the story for each student in the class. I ask a student who reads well, with clarity and voice, to read the letters from Joe Jones. I read the letters from Mrs. O'Toople.

I give the students the definitions of the following words, writing them on the board so they are in front of them as we read: *perfunctory, symmetry, digress, elusive, quid pro quo, minié ball, empathy, vis-à-vis, nefarious, suffice, confine, waxing gibbous,* and *incarcerated.*

I tell students to put check marks in the margins next to anything they notice the letter writers are showing each other about reading or writing. We read the letters while students follow along with a copy in front of them.

After we read, we take out our WRNs. I give the following instructions:

> Describe as completely as you can anything this piece of writing brings to mind for you. Think about all that Mrs. O'Toople taught Joe through her letters and how she did that—especially about books, and about writing. Turn and talk with a person near you. Use the check marks you made on the writing as we read the story to guide your talk. Let's list some of those things she taught him, and how she did that.

We list those things that kids believe Mrs. O'Toople taught Joe and how they know that from the story itself, things Mrs. O'Toople said or did. This sends them back into the story for evidence of how they know that, using the check marks they put in the margins.

The next day I give them a copy of the notes we took (a summary from all classes), and we talk through what these notes might mean to them as readers and writers.

Online
6.3

Notes from "Your Question for Author Here" (from *Guys Read—Funny Business*)

- On books: A good book makes me feel as if I have been found, understood, seen . . . .
- On writing:
  - Every book I write helps me to understand myself better and to love the world more.
  - A writer is imaginative.
  - A writer is curious.
  - A writer is interested in the things and people of the world.
  - A writer does his or her research.

I share the line from the story: "You know that you are a writer if you like the sound of rain on the roof." I ask them, "How do you know you are a writer . . . ?"

> You know that you are a writer if you hold a minié ball in your hand and wonder about its story.
>
>> What I Have
>> Civil War Bullet
>> The story of someone's life
>> Hides in my sock drawer

What's in *your* sock drawer?

(What are you saving somewhere for some reason?)

(What's the story behind the item? Why do you keep it?)

(What's the story you can imagine for that item?)

In your WRN write as quickly as you can in response to one of those two questions: How do you know you are a writer? Or, what's in your sock drawer?

As a side note, I love this story not only for all it has to show us about reading and writing but also for the vocabulary used. Just as I have the students occasionally draw their understandings of words from short stories or novels we read together, these are great words to illustrate with drawings. And to use in their writing or speaking.

The first time I read this I mentioned to the students: "These are great words. Try to use them in your speaking and writing." Immediately a student said, "You know, Mrs. Rief, you are gaining a bit of a nefarious reputation for the amount of reading and writing you expect of us." I responded: "Well, if you didn't approach the work so perfunctorily I wouldn't have to expect so much."

"Oh, quid pro quo!" another student piped in. "Suffice it to say," said yet another student, "that I think we digress."

I love eighth graders! (Most of the time!)

"Popularity" by Adam Bagdasarian

Here are the instructions I give the students.

I'm going to read the story "Popularity" by Adam Bagdasarian aloud to you. Four students have parts to read, which are already highlighted. Everyone should follow along.

If there are words you don't know or can't figure out from the context as we read, put a check next to them in the margin so you can find them after reading the story. One word that you might not know is *adulation* (page 45), which means "excessive admiration" (" all you have to do is round the bases and wait for the world's adulation").

After reading the story, I would like you to answer the following questions in the response section of your WRN:

1. Draw four squares on the first blank page (in the response section of your WRN)—then using stick figures and key words, draw the scene I drew here, and add three more key scenes from this story to the other three squares. Use black pen or dark pencil, and color to each scene. (Fill the page with the four storyboard squares.)

Figure 6.1 *Storyboard Format Used for "Popularity"*

2. What does this story bring to mind for you? What were you thinking as we read it?

3. In what ways have you ever been made to feel invisible? *Or,* you have seen others make someone else feel invisible? *Or,* you have made someone else feel invisible? (Describe what was done and said.)

4. What do you think is meant by the last line? And what in your own experience makes you agree or disagree with that? "And I did not trust one of them, because I knew then that I was standing on sand and was only a yellow shirt and pair of pants away from the oak trees where the two Allans were still looking for four-leaf clovers."

5. What are the characteristics that make this story good writing?

If you don't *own* the following words (know them well enough to use them in your speaking and writing), write them in your vocabulary section with enough of the sentence each word is in to make sense of the word. Then, define the word.

bewilder(ed) (page 45)

devolve (page 45)

monarchy (page 45)

resign (page 45)

prestige (page 45)

belittle (page 45)

recede (page 45)

trepidation (page 46)

destiny (page 46)

innuendo (page 46)

jester (page 46)

assure (page 46)

prominent (page 46)

align (page 47)

anonymity (page 47)

devastate(d) (page 48)

aspiration(s) (page 48)

condemn(ed) (page 48)

obscurity (page 48)

nonentity (page 49)

transformation (page 49)

After we read the story, I have the students discuss at their tables the other three scenes they think are most significant, and then ask them to draw those scenes. In talking through the scenes they are thinking through the questions that follow—often using the words *invisible* and *humiliation* in their discussion. I ask the kids to write their thinking in response to the remainder of the questions by themselves.

I think we need to give students opportunities to address the ideas in a story and what in their own experience this brought to mind, by themselves. There are many times they are asked to do that in testing situations. It does not hurt to let them practice this occasionally. We read, talk, draw, and write in response to this story and often many others.

Building on their thinking comes in sharing what they wrote after the writing, which is what we do. (See Figure 6.2.)

Figure 6.2 Madi's Responses to "Popularity"

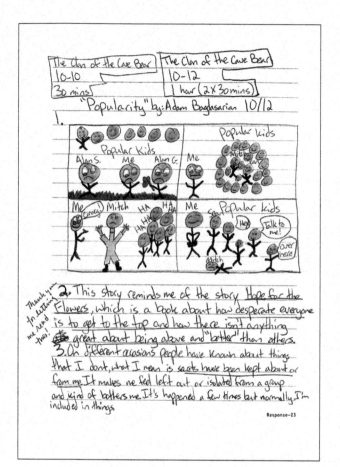

2. This story reminds me of the story Hope for the Flowers, which is a book about how desperate everyone is to get to the top and how there isn't anything great about being above and "better" than others. *(Thank you for letting me read this!)*

3. On different occasions people have known about things that I don't, what I mean is secrets have been kept about or from me. It makes me feel left out or isolated from a group and kind of bothers me. It's happened a few times but normally I'm included in things

Response—23

4. I think this last line really wraps up the story, and is pretty powerful too. I think it proves a point that I believe is very true, popular people are always out to get each other, so is anyone who wants to be "on top." But the truth is there is no happiness or joy to be found there, being "better" than others does not come with a reward.

5. This story is a good piece of writing because it captures the need constantly present in school childrens' minds. Being popular is such a concern for so many kids, and as is demonstrated by the last line, the "popular gang" are not really your friends if you're one of them, but your competitors. In this story, the main character understood and participated in the race for popularity, and he realized that other people must be hurt or fought for position. This story was good because it really caught the essence of popularity, it was well written.

3 (continued). They dress in the best clothes, they date the jocks, these popular ones. Their "friends" worship them, and then call them awful things behind their backs. They live for status and only drink diet sodas and eat low-calorie foods. Their cheerleaders, wanna be models. They have long, lean legs and no stomachs. Their laughs are superficial, fake and high pitched. They walk with expertise care, swinging their hips and swaggering past flaunting underdogs. This is their kingdom, they are the rulers. This is public school.

Response—24

That is such a sad statement! *Is that really true?*

"Eleven" by Sandra Cisneros

Several years ago Roger Essley taught me *drawing as thinking* (using stick figures and key words to represent your thinking), as opposed to *drawing as performance* (creating a piece of art) as a way for kids to share their thinking as writers. I had been searching for ways to help those kids who had such difficulty getting their ideas onto paper, and I found that once they were encouraged to draw their thinking and knew that we meant stick figures and key words, they were able to convey their ideas much more easily. Written in the format of drawing as thinking, Figure 6.3 shows what I learned from Roger about *drawing to write*.

Figure 6.3 *Storyboard: Drawing to Write*

In Roger's book *Visual Tools for Differentiating Reading and Writing Instruction* (2008), I tell about my findings with kids using this kind of drawing. I believe Roger's book is a seminal work that should be read by all teachers. As adults we use visual tools every day, yet we dismiss the importance of drawing early on in elementary school, confining and identifying all that kids know and can do through words only. Are we disabling many kids from showing what they know when we discourage the use of visual tools?

I began thinking about visual tools as a way into deeper reading. In *Visual Tools* (Essley 2008), I talk about how I used this strategy to help kids reveal their writing ideas, but also as a way to gather notes about characters for analysis when reading more complicated texts such as *Romeo and Juliet* or when viewing movies, such as *The Wave*. As you see in my previous description of delving into the story "Popularity," we use drawing to get at the essence of that story. We can use drawing for getting at other aspects of story, particularly the differences between the happening, the feeling, and the idea an author seems to be conveying.

I think it is easier for kids to understand the phrasing "the idea behind a story," instead of "the theme." It is the "So what?" of the story, but "So what?" sounds dismissive and coarse. As adult readers and moviegoers we ask what the idea is behind the book or the idea behind the movie. Kids get that.

As we read the story "Eleven," again with students reading speaking parts from the various characters as I read the narrator, I ask the students to put a check mark next to any phrase that creates an image for them as we read. After we read, I tell the students not to be concerned with the check marks just yet, but instead, to retell the story by drawing the happenings—stick figures, key words. Kelsey drew the art in Figure 6.4.

Figure 6.4 *Kelsey's Storyboard of "Eleven"*

After students draw their storyboards, I have them label this summary as "the happenings." I ask them to write "the feelings" in the story underneath "the happenings" and to draw an arrow to any box that shows feelings, labeling the arrow as to what the feelings are. They write *excitement, happiness, humiliation, embarrassment, sadness* on many of the arrows. (This is a good place to talk about the difference between *embarrassment*—something that you do to yourself—and *humiliation*—something that someone else does to you.)

They understand the happenings and the feelings in the story, but they struggle with the idea of the story. The significance. What is Cisneros trying to get across? What do you think she is trying to show? What are her intentions? This has to be more than a story of a thoughtless teacher humiliating a little girl by insisting this disgusting sweater that "smells of cottage cheese" must belong to her. What do you think Cisneros might be trying to get across to a reader about who we are as human beings?

Blank faces. Silence. I think this is a simple story and the idea is clear, but it's obvious to me that the students don't think it is so clear.

"Let's look back at the story," I suggest. "Look at the phrases you put a check mark next to. In a simple drawing, capture the image you saw in your head as we read, and write the phrase that made you see that beside the drawing." After the kids are done drawing, I tape those images on the board and we look at the most frequent phrases and drawings (see Figure 6.5).

> Because the way you grow old is kind of like an onion, or like the rings inside a tree trunk . . . only today I wish I didn't have only eleven years rattling inside me like pennies in a tin Band-Aid box. (Cisneros 1991, 6–7)

Figure 6.5 *Drawings of the Phrases from "Eleven"*

I ask the students, "What do you make of that, her metaphors that growing old is like an onion or rings on a tree or those stacking Russian dolls that fit one inside the other? Is there anything else you notice about her phrasing or choice of words?" Someone invariably notices the repetition of "ten, nine, eight, seven, six, five, four, three, two, and one." If they don't, I mention, "Did anyone notice how many times she repeated all the ages she carries inside her? What do you think of that?"

If no one talks, which happens, because adolescents care more about what their peers think of them than of being right or wrong, I ask them to take out their WRNs and write what they think Cisneros is trying to get at about all of us as human beings. We write for three minutes. I ask them to pass their notebooks to the person on their right. The person who receives the notebook reads the previous person's thinking and responds to the thinking or questions. We go all around the table, each person writing, responding to the previous person, until the notebook gets back to its original owner. This write-around (my word if it has to be named) is simply a written conversation that gives all kids time to think, to see what their peers are thinking, and to consider and reconsider that thinking.

Once they get their notebooks back, they find it a lot easier to talk out what the thinking was at their table. With all of this information we recap what we read and understood:

> **The summary.** A *summary* is the happenings in a story, usually made stronger because of some tension that exists between characters. In one sentence how might students summarize this story? (After several tries we end up with, "Rachel, an eleven-year-old, wants to have a great birthday, but her teacher humiliates her by insisting a disgusting sweater is hers and ruins her day.")

> **The feelings.** What are the feelings in the story: excitement, embarrassment, humiliation, powerlessness, thoughtlessness. . . . (This is where I say, "Have any of you ever felt any of these same feelings?" Every hand goes up, including mine. I tell them, "Take two to three minutes and describe a time when you felt humiliated, or embarrassed, or powerless—either about yourselves, or someone else you know, or some situation in the world where others might have felt like this.")

> **The significance.** Students conclude after talking it out or writing it out in a written conversation that the significance (the point or idea) is that Cisneros seems to be saying that no matter what age we are, we carry all those feelings inside as if we were three or five, no matter how old we are, and if we were older (102) we might know what to say when someone treats us unfairly.

It takes a simple story sometimes for students to be able to go back into it again and again to tease out the idea of the piece. First and foremost, I want kids to bring their own experiences, feelings, and imaginations to a piece of literature—a play, a short story, a poem, an editorial, a memoir—but I also want them to be able to think out an idea that the writer may have been trying to get at based on the context and the way the story is crafted.

We talk about what makes an effective story, going back to our compilation of characteristics of a good piece of writing. Here is what we come up with most often:

Lead—dives right into the story, with each birthday we are still 10, 9, 8, and so on.

Focus—she sets the camera on one scene, in the classroom.

Tension—Rachel wants a wonderful birthday, and it's ruined by a thoughtless teacher who just wants to get on with the math lesson.

Feelings—excitement (her birthday) changes to humiliation (trying to move the sweater off the desk with the ruler) to sadness (wishing the day was far away like a runaway balloon).

Vivid wording (use of metaphors):

> age—like layers of onion, tree trunk, wooden dolls
>
> —rattles inside like pennies in a tin band-aid box
>
> birthday—wants it to be far away like a runaway balloon
>
> sweater—stretched collar and sleeves like a jump rope
>
> —sits like a big red mountain on the desk
>
> —hangs over edge of desk like a waterfall
>
> —clown sweater arms, smells like cottage cheese

It may be a simple story, but it has so much to teach kids when we spend some time with it. If I want kids to write with intent, we have to read with intent. Still, I always want to watch the students carefully to see if they are still engaged with all we are reading, writing, talking about. Or if am I losing them. This is where we have to use our common sense, our best knowledge of adolescents, and all we know about reading and writing to decide how deep and how wide we can go with our analysis of a piece of literature.

CHAPTER SEVEN

Essentials in the Reading-Writing Workshop

Conferences

Earlier in the book, I talked about Meredith Hall, the author of *Without a Map*, and the professor in a course I took recently at the University of New Hampshire (UNH) about writing creative nonfiction. Meredith had one conference with each of us during the two-week class. It could not have been more helpful. She had read the writing ahead of the conference, noted with checks or comments the areas that worked well and why, jotted questions, and had a couple of suggestions. Her suggestions were coupled with possibilities about how I might accomplish these changes or additions. Her most helpful comments were questions. What did I notice in the writing? What was I trying to accomplish? What were my intentions? We had a conversation about what I was trying to do, how well I had done it, and what I might consider to strengthen the writing with intent.

The conversation lasted less than twenty minutes. I left it inspired to revise and with ideas as to how I might accomplish those intentions. But she left the decisions up to me. That's what our conversations—our conferences—with kids should do: inspire them to keep writing, leaving them with some ideas of how to do that, but leaving it up to them.

Ruth Hubbard, a professor at Lewis and Clark in Portland, Oregon, and the mother of two of my former students, sent me comments her five-year-old twin grandchildren had in reaction to comments from their teacher about their writing. Jacob rebelled when his teacher said he had to write a sentence (not connected to anything he was doing) each night. His mom, Meg, a former eighth grader of mine, told him that was okay as long as he wrote his teacher a note and explained why he did not want to do that. Jacob wrote: "Ms. Sanches, I am not rite eny mor sentissis, becuds I rite books."

Jacob's sister Molly received the following note from her kindergarten teacher: "Great job Molly. You may want to use: First, Then, Next, Finally" on a piece of her writing. Molly's response: "No Thanks."

Jacob already understands the serious work of a writer and what contributes to the growth of that work. Molly understands that she has the final say as to how she constructs her writing. Both understand the power of intentions and response.

I have anywhere from twenty to twenty-five kids in a class in any given year. I cannot get to all of the students during the week, even when I focus on writing Monday through Wednesday. In the best of circumstances, having kids read their writing to me is the most helpful. I can hear their intentions often through their voices, as well as in the actual writing. To accomplish this, I have to have kids read their writing during studies, after school if they are willing, or at lunch/recess. Otherwise, they have to give me a copy for a written conference. On their papers I put checks or stars next to those passages that stay with me, or a strong lead or ending, or dialogue that is realistic and moves the writing forward. All the features of a piece of writing that make it memorable. I write questions right where they arise in me as a reader. I make suggestions based on what the writer says she needs.

A few years ago, Doug Kaufman spent an entire year in my classroom researching his wonderings about conferences for his doctoral dissertation. His yearlong study became a book: *Conferences and Conversations: Listening to the Literate Classroom* (2000).

Doug's observations, meticulous recordings and transcripts, and questions pushed my thinking so hard that I could finally see and hear myself as I interacted with students over their writing. It is a privilege we are often denied when we are alone in our classrooms. It is a perspective too difficult to see well by ourselves. This is a brief summary of our findings:

- Understand that conferences are more complicated than we thought.

  I have to know the student, what kind of information helps her, know how far to push her, know if I can push her, know what her relationship is with the kids around her, know how much of a relationship I've built with her. There is no list that can tell you succinctly and cleanly what can be done in a conference.

- Listen to and learn from students.

  Each child tells us what he needs to know to push the writing forward. We have to listen hard, have to really think, really focus on the child and what he says every time we go into a conference. We have to shut out the rest of the room, and that is really hard.

  I was surprised to realize that students even watch my body language in a conference. I tend not to look directly at them as they read their writing, so that I can really focus on the listening. Many students said this told them they had to use words to get across their meaning. They couldn't use facial expressions or body language to express their intentions.

I have a harder time listening to students who are resistant to writing. I have to learn to be more open and listen more patiently to find that spark of interest. Each student's need in a writing conference is so different that I often have to change my way of listening and thinking in a matter of seconds.

- Base conferences on the wants and needs of the student.

No matter how much I want a student to do something in a piece of writing, if she doesn't already see it for herself, she's not going to move forward with the information I give her. If she does use the information or suggestion, without knowing why or wanting it for herself, then she's just giving me the piece of writing she thinks I want from her. It isn't her writing anymore.

I also learned, if a student says to me, "I really need help with this lead," then I shouldn't tell him about the ending. When I stick with what I know works, which is the question, "How can I help you?" then the conference helps the writer move forward.

- Understand that students' needs are as idiosyncratic as they are.

Every student comes to a conference with a different want or need. I have to listen carefully to address each unique need on an individual basis. There is no list of set questions or suggestions that works for all writers.

- Let students know that we value them as individuals.

For some students the conference is most important only because they need someone with whom they can talk. Other kids, who are not comfortable with themselves academically, see me only as a writer and reader and feel less comfortable. I need to build rapport with them to let them know that I value what they have to say also. They need to know someone is listening.

- Shorter conferences are more productive.

The most important things are said in the first minute or two of a conference. If a student doesn't understand the questions or suggestions at the very beginning, and can't tell me what she needs from me, then the conference is not very helpful. More is not necessarily better. Kids are usually only enthused about one piece or willing to cope with one problem at a time. Once I've given them information that they can really use, then I have to leave and let them use it.

- Dominate the conversation less, and have more happen when we leave.

The conference works best when I step out of the way of the student. I am always contributing information, experience, suggestions, and encouragement, but things work best when kids say, "I did this myself." My job is to act as a sounding board to their own words, giving comments and suggestions that turn the decisions and thinking back to them.

- Have students who share similar interests sit together for richer conversations and writing.

Balance

I don't think conferences work really well when I mix students up too heterogeneously. If they are interested in mountain biking or science fiction or Emily Dickinson, when they get together they seem to get more out of the conversation and support one another's writing in more productive ways. When there is a comfort level that is still academically driven, conversations become more informal, yet this talk leads to more effective work.

- When giving students suggestions, give them examples of what we mean.

If I say, "What if you try a question for your ending?" or "What if you try the present tense instead of the past tense?" I can't just walk away. I have to show them an example. Even the most academically confident kids really like seeing models and need specific examples.

- We have to read and write with our students.

The more I share my own writing—how I find ideas, the false starts, the problems I run into, the techniques or strategies I use to clarify my ideas, the topics that are most meaningful to me—the more I learn about writing and the more the students trust my comments to them in conference.

I model helpful response by reading a draft of my writing to the students while they have a conference sheet in front of them. I explain the sections of the conference sheet, which can be found on the website with other handouts. I tell them what I need help with. I read my writing. I ask what they liked, what they heard, or what stayed with them. I ask what questions popped into their heads as listeners. I ask if they have any suggestions based on what I need to do better. I write down all they tell me, projected on the board at the front of the room. I put check marks at the phrases or sentences that stayed with them, and I write the questions they ask and the suggestions they give me. I show them what I might do with their feedback.

I consider the places with lots of checks or underlining as sections to keep.

I decide if their questions are important to answer, and where to answer them.

I consider their suggestions.

Online
7.1

I model my writing at least once and ask for a student volunteer in front of the whole class, before I put them in response groups of three to five random students. I try to have these response groups every two weeks. The students have a conference sheet in front of them to guide their response, but I have found that giving each a package of sticky notes on which to write that response is more helpful to the writer. The conference sheet becomes a guide for what to write on the sticky notes. I explain this in more detail on the handout of conference notes on the website.

Conferences focus on the content, not the conventions. It is the reason I prefer the students always read their writing out loud to their listeners. The students and I can focus on the content, when we aren't looking at the missing punctuation or spelling errors or illegible handwriting. An added benefit is that I often see the writer revising and editing as he reads because he has not made his writing clear enough. The voice a student hears in his head when he reads to himself is very different from the voice he hears when he reads aloud.

I remind students again and again that editing is about the mechanics, the standard conventions used to *give directions to the reader* as to how the writer wants her piece read. Authors can't accompany their work—so we have conventional spelling and punctuation to tell the reader how they want their words read.

All writing does not need to be edited. There is no reason to edit any writing that is not going to be taken to a finished draft. In the words of Don Murray, "You have to do a lot of bad writing to get the good writing." Kids don't need to take all of their writing to final drafts, and they don't need to edit any of it until they have made the content of their writing the best it can be. Then we edit. Editing for conventions before the piece has anything worth saying is a waste of time.

As the kids get better at giving helpful responses to each other, I show them how they can also give written conferences. Writers come in with a piece of writing, preferably with no more than three pages typed, double-spaced. I give each student a different-color, thin magic marker. A group of students hand their writing around the circle of four to five kids at a table. The readers do what I do: mark memorable wording with checks or underlining, questions where they arose, and a suggestion based on the writer's intentions or need for help. The writing goes completely around the table, everyone reading each other's pieces and commenting. When students gets their draft back, it is filled with ideas for revising, not corrections. Different-color pens tell the writer the places where readers agreed. If all the readers have the same questions and similar places where they are underlining, the writer needs to really take those responses seriously.

Lots of checks and underlining tell the writer to consider keeping those sections. Other places where no one commented might have to be reconsidered for inclusion. Questions help the writer add or clarify information. Did everybody wonder the same thing? Definitely worth considering by the writer. Each person who comments also puts his initials at the end of the writing in the same-color pen so the writer can follow up if she has any questions.

Figure 7.1 shows the first page of a picture book I am trying to write, with student comments written all over it. It is a written conference, and gives me lots of advice. Because of time constraints—about forty-five minutes a day—I am doing more of these written conferences later in the year, once the students understand the structure of response.

As I read the students' comments, I realize they understand the process we have set up for responding—underlining those phrases that stick with them and asking questions that come to them as good readers. I will try to keep those underlined phrases as I revise and I will consider the importance of each question. My readers really want to know who Emily is and why the grandfather hasn't seen her for so long. I answer those questions in subsequent pages, but am I holding the reader off too long and should I answer those questions sooner? All good questions that will guide me as I revise.

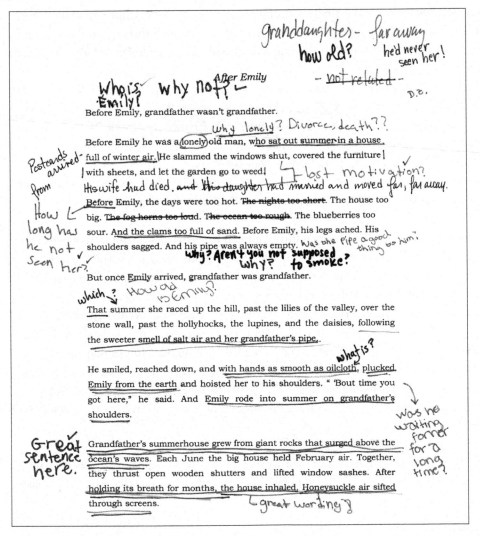

Figure 7.1 *First Page of After Emily with Student Feedback*

To reiterate my structure for conferences:

- whole-class model with my writing (with conference sheet and shared out loud)
- whole-class model with a student volunteer's writing (with conference sheet and shared out loud)
- written conferences (I take a copy of the student's writing to read. I write response on the writing in the same format as the conference sheet.)
- response groups (three to five random students I put together, using conference sheet as a model for response on sticky notes)
- write-around conferences (writing handed around the table where all readers respond in the same format as the conference sheet, but with colored markers).

Before students can go to a final draft of a piece of writing, they must read it to me or give it to me for a written conference, and they have to read it to three peers for response. All sticky notes must be attached to the rough draft with the final draft once they are ready to hand it in.

Our teaching happens in conferences. Assigning a topic, then putting a grade on it with a comment like "Nice!" or "Interesting!" is no help to the writer. If we want our students to be successful writers, we have to find the time to confer and give them feedback. Not an easy task, but essential to their growth. We need to decide how we use our time and what we get rid of that is not helpful to the writing and reading of our students.

When we have response groups or write-around conferences, I always sit in on one group, as it helps me hear more writing, and I can again guide the students in their responses.

My oldest grandson is in ninth grade this year in an English class taught by a one-year substitute while the regular teacher is on leave. The class did one piece of personal narrative the first few months of the year. There were no conferences and limited response to a first draft. When the teacher handed the writing back to my grandson, about rescuing an animal that surely would have died without his intervention, the teacher apologized as he welled up with tears and said, "I'm sorry. This piece is so moving and vivid it makes me tear up." He handed the piece to my grandson. No comments. A smiley face coupled with an 86. Hunter had no idea what he had done well or not done well to merit that number. Where did it come from? His only comment to me as he was telling me about the teacher's response was, "Seems to me, if your writing makes the teacher cry, you should get some kind of bonus or extra credit." Agreed. And a bit more, I thought.

It's in the response to students and their writing that the teaching happens. This is where I let them know what they did well ("Keep doing this!") and the questions that I have ("Consider answering these to more fully develop the piece with needed information.") and a suggestion ("This is what makes writing more effective. Try some of this in your writing.").

How do you find the time to confer and respond to student writing? If you don't think you have the time, what can you get rid of that does not help the students grow stronger as writers? What kind of response from you helps them the most as they move from draft to draft?

Describing the Characteristics of Effective Writing

Early in the year, after the kids have written some first drafts but before they take any substantial pieces of writing to a final draft, I have them read twenty pieces of writing from former students. This began as a question years ago in a research course I was taking with Don Graves. I wondered how good students were at identifying the effectiveness of a piece of writing. If they can identify the qualities, can they recognize those characteristics in their own writing? If their writing is lacking in these qualities, are they able to revise their writing in recognition of what makes an effective piece? What role does audience play in the desire to develop a strong piece of writing?

With these questions in mind, I gave the twenty pieces of writing to hundreds of teachers and thousands of students over the last twenty years. What I found did not surprise me: students who write are as proficient at recognizing and describing the qualities of effective writing as often as teachers, and often are even able to do it better than a lot of teachers.

The study answered a lot of my questions. The most beneficial aspect of reading these twenty pieces, however, was discovering that the students had a far greater understanding of the qualities of effective writing, because they had ownership in figuring out what those qualities were, and then applying them to their own writing.

I have been in too many classrooms with a poster on the wall of the Six Traits, or Six Traits Plus One, or Seven Traits Minus Two (a bit of sarcasm here) and found, upon asking the kids what the poster was about, that they had no idea and made no connections with the poster and their writing. Don't misunderstand me. They are good traits. But kids don't know where they came from.

Not only can kids recognize effective writing, but they can describe the qualities, and they do begin to think about their own writing in terms of these characteristics. I began to see, and still do see, students look at their writing more reflectively by identifying what makes it strong or weak after we have done this exercise.

The kids who have the most trouble reading and recognizing good writing carry biases with them into the piece because of topic or genre or mechanics. They have few audiences in mind for their writing, especially themselves. They don't know what makes effective writing, and they don't know how to make it themselves.

I will explain what I ask the kids to do with these twenty pieces, and how it helps them, but I want to mention right here that those kids who don't know how to recognize or craft effective writing need the most help in conferences and have to be spread out in response groups. (How would I identify the kind of help they need? First, they have to believe they have something worth saying and that someone else wants to hear it. Why write if no one cares what you think?)

They also need to rub shoulders with those who are good at using what they learn from this exercise; therefore, just as I like heterogeneous grouping, I like mixing academic levels up. These kids in particular need to be placed with other kids from whom they can learn—as writers and responders.

Reading Twenty Pieces of Writing

I have gathered writing from past students, enough years back that no current students would recognize the writing. Start by gathering writing from your own students—fifteen to twenty pieces—in a variety of genres and at varying levels of effectiveness. None should be longer than two typed pages. Until you have these pieces I recommend using writing samples given as models from state testing sites. Once you have writing samples, try this exercise.

At what point in the school year is this?

First Day

- I plan on the exercise taking at least two, maybe three, class periods.

- I make enough packets of the pieces so every student has his own packet.

- I tell students they can spread out anywhere—the room, the hall, wherever, just so long as I can see them from my room.

- They cannot talk with anyone as they read.

- They should put the pieces into four piles: 4 = strongest writing, 3 = strong writing, 2 = weak writing, and 1 = the weakest, at least in comparison to the twenty pieces here.

- I tell them the students who wrote these believed they were final drafts.

- I tell students that lines on the pages mean I could not read the writing, as I typed them exactly as they are for readability.

- I don't tell students what criteria to use for their rankings, as that's the point.

- When they are done reading all twenty pieces and have them in piles, the students are to write down the number and title (or topic) of each piece into the appropriate box.

- When they are completely done reading and ranking, students should relook at all the pieces in the 4 pile, if they have any there, and list the criteria they used to put them in the "most effective" pile.

- They must then reassemble the packets of twenty pieces in order, and clip them together.

- Students hand me their tally sheets and the criteria listed for ranking pieces in the 4 category. (I keep these because I don't want them to lose them between my classroom door and tomorrow.)
- Just this part takes an entire forty-five-minute period.
- All four of my classes do this.

Second Day

- I hand back students' tally and criteria sheets.
- Before we talk about any criteria, I list on the board all the pieces that anyone ranked as a 4, and all the pieces anyone ranked as a 1. I have them just tell me orally the numbers or the titles of the pieces ranked 4 or 1. I tell them we will talk about these pieces and their rankings later.
- At their tables, students share their criteria for ranking any pieces in the 4 category.
- Students choose one person to act as the secretary, and come up with the five strongest reasons on which they all agree for ranking a piece in the 4 category. I go right around the room asking them to share those criteria, which I also write on the board. Each time a table of students has the same criterion, I put a check next to it, to begin to see what criteria carry the most weight.
- I do this for all of my classes.
- I then talk about the various pieces of writing I use. Some of the pieces won Scholastic Writing Awards. Some won state essay or poetry contests. Some were the first pieces the student had ever written that was more than a paragraph long.
- I take all the criteria they mention, tally them up in order of importance (based on how many students mentioned each one), and type up a list of the characteristics of effective writing that I give to students to glue into the notes section of their writer's-reader's notebooks (WRNs) the next day.

This list of characteristics each year looks very much like the criteria the students gave me twenty years ago. It tells me they are still good at recognizing strong writing. It tells me they can articulate those characteristics. Unless the students tell me something dramatically different from other years, I keep the list essentially the same but add their wording to various categories. I also say, "None of you mentioned this, but I think it is important, and I added it to your list." The important thing is, they read these pieces of writing carefully and thoughtfully and have a voice in developing the traits. It is not a poster sitting on the wall from a distant publisher that is meaningless to them.

I go back to the entire list on the wall from each class, putting up each piece for them to see again, and I remind them of the content. We talk about what they recognized the writer did well and any areas where they might ask questions or give suggestions. I try to keep even the suggestions as questions, phrased as a "What if?" that puts the onus back on the writer.

Online 7.3

I am including this year's list, titled Characteristics of Effective Writing, for you on the website. But don't give it to your students. What they come up with tells you where they are as writers. It tells you what they value and what experiences they have had. Your instruction can then be designed around their experiences and their knowledge.

I tell the students some things about some of these pieces of writing because it impacts how I shape the class. With all of the pieces we can talk about the qualities students recognize as inherent in each piece. We can also ask for questions—what do they want to know more about that would help the writer improve the writing? Each piece is worth discussing to reinforce helpful feedback and response.

A few students totally dismiss any qualities in the writing and rank them according to likes and dislikes of topic or genre. If they like dirt bikes or skiing, those are ranked high. They are disgusted with a graphic description of a student playing dentist with a coat hanger in his mouth, therefore it is ranked low. Or, they like disgusting things, therefore it is ranked high. They don't like poetry, so any poetry pieces ranked low. We talk about likes and dislikes of genre or topic as not being fair to the writer.

I remind them that there are many books they said they did not like, but that doesn't mean it is bad writing. I don't enjoy fantasy, but that doesn't mean I think Christopher Paolini's books, or J. R. R. Tolkien's, or J. K. Rowling's, are bad writing.

When I respond or they respond to other students' writing, we want to make sure we give the writer a fair read or fair listen. I tell the students not to indicate where they ranked a piece (I will know, but the entire class does not need to know), but I want to tell them about a few pieces and the writers so they can think about their own rankings.

Several pieces I use won national Scholastic writing awards. One not only won an award, but the piece was published in a Scholastic magazine and the writer was invited to New York to meet the Scholastic editors. Several years ago a beautifully descriptive piece was used in the state of New Hampshire as the model piece to which to compare all eighth-grade writing. Another piece is the first piece, and longest, that this young man wrote for the first several months of the year. Another piece that feels like a personal narrative is completely fictitious. The author was invited to have it published in a national magazine for adolescents if she took out a rather bawdy joke. She declined.

I want students to realize that writing is subjective, even when we try to identify certain criteria inherent in the piece. However, if we recognize our own biases toward subject or genre, we can give writing a fair read.

We also realize, looking at our list of 4s and 1s, that it is more difficult to identify effective writing (a much larger range of pieces found their way into the 4 category that many other readers did not agree with) than it is to identify ineffective writing (that list is nearly unanimous in agreement with every reader).

Before we wrap up this exercise, I ask students to look at their latest piece and consider where it would be ranked and why. What have they done well? What might they still need to do?

Some years I also have additional copies of pieces ranked in the 3 and 2 categories. I hand out a copy of a different piece to each student and say, "If you were having a write-around conference with this student, what would you check or underline that is memorable wording, what questions would you ask, and what's one suggestion you might offer the writer?" This is a good exercise to do with your students before you try write-around conferences with them because the writer is absent. On the other hand, it is not good to do because the writer is absent. It is an exercise in teaching the kids how to respond, but meaningless as far as valuable to a writer, who isn't there and can't revise the writing.

If you don't do this already, begin to save the writing of your students, so that you have a packet of a range of writing from your classroom from which your students can collect their own criteria. In the meantime, use models from state writing assessment samples to help your students develop their own criteria for effective writing. *[handwritten margin note: Save Students' writing]*

The characteristics we list here are meant for writing in general. What should any effective piece of writing do—whether essay, poem, short story, review? There are still characteristics inherent in particular kinds of writing. We read lots of examples of these to understand what a particular kind of writing includes: an essay or book review has to have your opinion and a short summary, without giving away crucial information; a short story usually has one conflict and one or two main characters; a persuasive piece has to give evidence to convince the reader of the writer's opinion. And so on. I will discuss ways of getting at more particular kinds of writing in subsequent chapters.

Revising Writing

> Revision is like a second chance because it lets you discover what you were trying to say all along. (Susan Goodman in Messner [2011, 12])

I also love Katherine Paterson's words, "I love revision. Where else can spilled milk be turned into ice cream?"

I don't have a list of minilessons for getting to the ice cream. But I do have a list of ideas about revision that includes those things I talk about most often with students. What helps students most with their writing:

- writing conferences ("This is what you did well. These are the questions that pop into my head as you read, or I read, your writing. A suggestion you might consider, phrased as 'What if . . .?'"), always keeping in mind that response to writing is idiosyncratic and is driven by the writer's intentions. (Writing conferences were discussed in more detail at the beginning of this chapter.)

- writing myself

- showing students how to return to the WRN

- collecting the writing we admire from professionals

- using specific ideas of writers and educators, such as Nancie Atwell, Ralph Fletcher, Georgia Heard, Barry Lane, Kate Messner, and William Zinsser, to further enhance revision through individual conferences or whole-class instruction.

Writing Myself

In writing courses that I have taken I have learned again and again by having teachers tell me first what I did well, questions they had, and several direct suggestions—the conference format I have incorporated into my own classroom. I have also learned specifics from the following teachers.

Meredith Hall: Set the camera on the scene. Envision what a movie director would try to show in that scene and give us the details as the camera moves through the scene. (Example: The first montage in the Introduction to this book—my mother rowing out into Hingham Harbor as my dad descends the stairs in the house.)

Becky Rule: What if . . . ? When giving a suggestion, frame it as "What if?" What if the last sentence became the first sentence? What if the writer used first person instead of third person? What if the piece was written in the present tense instead of the past tense? What if the form was a letter instead of a narrative? "What if?" puts the onus back on the writer, while giving a suggestion as a "try this."

Gary Lindberg: Read like a writer. Positive feedback keeps a writer writing. I took an American Short Story course many years ago with Gary, who taught me to read like a writer, notice what the writers do, and try to emulate that style. We read and wrote every day. One night I read John Cheever's "Country Husband" (Pickering 1978, 98–112). That day had been chaotic: driving sons to soccer games all over the seacoast, hockey practices later in the evening, the open box of Kentucky Fried Chicken on the kitchen counter as "dinner," grabbed on the way through while changing practice equipment, taking my husband to the airport for a business trip, reading student WRNs that I couldn't finish at school.

I wrote about my day in a Cheever-like style. Two days later as Gary was reading through the stack of one-pagers, I watched him as he laughed uproariously through one of the papers. I thought, I wish I could write like that. He stood up, walked toward me, handed me the writing and said, "Do you write fiction? This is hilarious." That one comment has stayed with me and kept me writing for years.

Don Graves: Let the writer maintain control of his or her writing with "Tell me more . . ." Because I was late for the first graduate course I took toward certification and a master's degree, the only chair empty in the circle of chairs in the room was next to the professor. I went into that class expecting to take notes about writing. I did not expect to do what the professor said next: "Well, let's write." The sound of scratching pens filled the room. I wrote about loading my husband's brand-new car with wallboard from a recent renovation and nearly sending the car careening over a steep, muddy precipice at the Durham dump. After writing for thirty minutes the professor said, "Turn and read what you wrote to the person next to you." I had to read mine to the professor, Don Graves. I had no idea who he was. He laughed in all the places I meant it to be funny. He said, "Tell me more . . ." and asked me lots of questions. We wrote some more. I had never written so much.

It is Don sitting on my shoulder every day in the classroom as I talk with kids about their writing: "You read it to me. I will listen hard and respond honestly. Tell me more."

Showing Students How to Return to Their WRNs

I show the students often how to look back in the WRNs to find writing ideas and also how to take an initial idea and build on it. This year I had an intern from UNH, Emily Geltz, spend the entire year with me. It was such a pleasure to co-teach with her. She is smart, confident, and imaginative. She loves learning and genuinely likes kids. She noticed that kids had a lot of questions about how to write poetry, and she took the notion of returning to their WRNs to craft some of that first-draft writing into a more polished piece of writing, specifically poetry. "Let's give it a try," she said.

Earlier in the year as we were reading *The Outsiders*, we did a quickwrite in response to the word *panic*. We said, "Personify *panic*. Write for two minutes. What does panic feel like? Look like? Do?" On this day Emily explained to the students that she had tried to write poetry but wasn't having much luck with it. Then she realized how much writing she had in her WRN, and she wondered if there was a piece in it with a strong emotion tied to the writing that she might be able to turn into poetry.

She showed the students several pages of writing she had found and circled strong words in red. She talked through her reasons for rejecting that writing for the moment. When she arrived at the page shown in Figure 7.2, written in response to *panic*, she stopped, asked the kids to notice how many strong words she had circled in red, and described how that had made her look more carefully at this page for possibilities. She explained that panic is such a strong feeling and this event, even after five years, held such strong emotions that she might be able to shape the moment into poetry.

She put the page on the screen for the kids to see, showed them the words circled in red, and then began underlining her strongest phrases in blue pen. She picked up a purple pen and explained she was looking for a sentence or phrase that seemed to be the pulse of the writing, the place where your heart beats a little faster, one of the most important lines.

Figure 7.2 *Emily's Page of Writing*

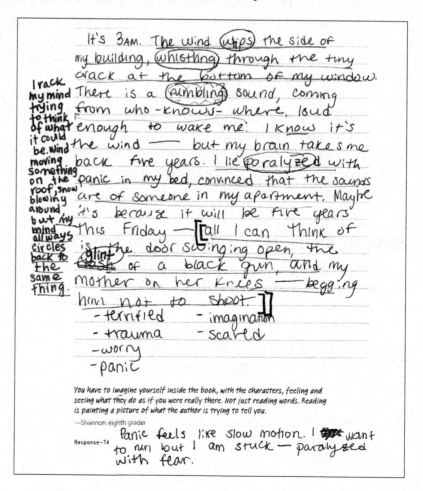

She began revising her words by choosing the strongest to shape into a poem. "It's important to remember that poems don't waste words," she said. "I'm trying to take the best words out of what I've already written to create a poem, so I go straight to my first underlined and circled words. I'm not going to use every single word I've underlined. I'm making choices as a writer, as a poet. What sounds the best? I'm intentionally choosing short lines for the pulse of the poem for emphasis. This line 'My mother on her knees, the glint of the gun pointing at her head, begging him not to shoot,' that's where my heart stopped. That was the moment of panic."

Emily wrote:

Wind whips

Whistling through
The tiny cracks in my window
Rumbling sounds

My mind always circles back
To the same thing
Paralyzed with panic

The door swinging open
The glint of the gun
My mother on her knees

Begging him
Not
To shoot

Quick write

Personify "panic" → poem about "panic"

Writer's · Reader's Notebook

Of course, everyone wanted to know what happened, what was this about, before they could even turn to their own possibilities. Five years to the day, which is why she could not get this event off her mind, they were robbed at gunpoint at home. She heard a commotion downstairs and came down to this scene. The robber did not see her. She ran up to her closet and called 911. The robber escaped from the house with all he could carry, did not harm her mom, and was eventually caught and imprisoned. Still, the sight of her mom on her knees is an indelible moment engraved in her memory.

Emily reminds the students to notice that every word in this poem was already in her quickwrite, she just reshaped it into poetry. She then turns it over to them to do what she did: flip through their WRNs finding places with strong words—words that are active or help us see, hear, taste, smell something—and circle them. Stop on a page that seems to carry a strong emotion, underline the phrases that show that, then bracket the pulse of the piece. Try poetry.

It may work; it may not. She told the students, "Your ideas are already in your notebooks. Many can be shaped into poetry, or any other genre that best captures the feeling."

Taking students back into their WRNs and showing them the process we go through to find and revise (resee) writing is immensely helpful to them, as often they don't recognize all they have captured in that first-draft thinking.

Collecting the Writing We Admire from Professionals

If you look back at the section on characteristics of effective writing, you'll notice that we list leads, endings, memorable wording that interests or appeals to the reader because of realistic, believable characters and unique ways of presenting ideas. Those are the categories I use to focus our attention as we develop stronger writing. It is why we pay attention to the things professional writers do as we read and collect what we notice that they do. I want kids paying attention to what writers do all year, not just during the author-genre study when we study authors as mentors.

What I have found that helps students best is to put several giant sticky notes on the wall of the classroom, each one labeled differently, and let the kids begin to fill them up as they read (the names in parentheses are the students who found the writing):

Most Compelling Titles (With Equally Interesting Writing)

Thirteen Reasons Why by Jay Asher

The Hunger Games by Suzanne Collins

Dancing on the Edge by Han Nolan

The Outliers by Malcolm Gladwell

The Crazy Horse Electric Game by Chris Crutcher

Stuck in Neutral by Terry Trueman

Tentacles by Roland Smith

Strongest Leads

There's a man buried in your kitchen. He's right in the stack of newspapers there, about three weeks down, a headline one day, a one-graph follow-up the next, a nobody since. His name is Ken Fox. He went to a race at Michigan speedway on July 26th and was torn in half by a tire that flew into the stands, and they didn't even stop the freaking race.

(Joey; from "Next Time Stop the Freaking Race" by Rick Reilly)

When I wake up, the other side of the bed is cold. My fingers stretch out, seeking Prim's warmth but finding only the rough canvas cover of the mattress. She must have had bad dreams and climbed in with our mother. Of course, she did. This is the day of the reaping.

(Jason, Forrest; from *The Hunger Games* by Suzanne Collins)

Benny Imura was appalled to learn that the apocalypse came with homework.

(Ryan; from *Dust and Decay* by Jonathan Maberry)

I hope you're ready because I'm about to tell you the story of my life. More specifically, why my life ended. And if you're listening to these tapes, you're one of the reasons why.

(Kennon; from *Thirteen Reasons Why* by Jay Asher)

I'm surrounded by thousands of words. Maybe millions. Cathedral. Mayonnaise. Pomegranate. Mississippi. Neapolitan. Hippopotamus. Silky. Terrifying. Iridescent. Tickle. Sneeze. Wish. Worry. Words have always swirled around me like snowflakes. Each one delicate and different, each one melting untouched in my hands. Deep within me, words pile up in huge drifts.

(Noah; from *Out of My Mind* by Sharon Draper)

It was one of those moments when Brian felt as if baseball was close enough for him to reach out and touch. Like his hands were around the handle of a bat. Or like he was on the mound, his fingers making sure the seams on the ball felt just right. . . . One of those moments when he could close his eyes and imagine he was a big-leaguer himself. . . . One of those moments, really, when he realized why his dad loved the game the way he did. Loved it too much, according to his mom. . . . Loved it more than anything or anybody.

(Porter; from *The Batboy* by Mike Lupica)

Novalee Nation, seventeen, seven months pregnant, thirty seven pounds overweight—and superstitious about sevens . . . By then Novalee knew there was something screwy about sevens, so she tried to stay clear of them. But sometimes, she thought, you just can't see it coming at you. And that's how she got stabbed.

(Payal; from *Where the Heart Is* by Billie Letts)

Leads

Memorable Wording

Like a skunk dog on the porch, whining to get in, and I'm afraid if I don't let it in, it will never go away.

(Madi; from *Learning to Swim* by Ann Turner)

The earth changed in the black sky. It caught fire. Part of it seemed to come apart in a million pieces, as if a giant jigsaw had exploded. It burned with an unholy dripping glare for a moment, three times its normal size, then dwindled to black.

(Kobi; from *Off Season* by Ray Bradbury)

I clung to the tree like it was a lifeboat from the Titanic.

(Alec; from *The Angel Experiment* by James Patterson)

Words have always swirled around me like snowflakes—each one delicate and different, each one melting untouched in my hands.

(Noah; from *Out of My Mind* by Sharon Draper)

She is blundering about like a daddy-long legs in a lamp light.

(Meaghan; from *Towards Zero* by Agatha Christie)

I can't walk. I can't talk. I can't feed myself or take myself to the bathroom. Big bummer. My arms and hands are pretty stiff, but I can mash the buttons on the TV remote and move the wheelchair with knobs that I can grab on wheels. I can't hold a spoon or a pencil without dropping it. And my balance is like zip—Humpty-Dumpty had more control than I do.

(Nina; from *Out of My Mind* by Sharon Draper)

Strongest Character Description

Mary was like an old photograph, faded, cracked, creased, all bent at the corners, those eyes are forever lost in shadows as they squint into the sun.

(Ryan; from *The Red Fox* by Anthony Hyde)

Rice paper thin/Model pretty and death camp thin/We are Scandinavian willows, with vanilla hair and glacier blue eyes and bone china skin.

(Arabella; from *Perfect* by Ellen Hopkins)

Sitting at Prim's knees, guarding her, is the world's ugliest cat. Mashed-in nose, half of one ear missing, eyes the color of rotting squash. Prim named him Buttercup, insisting that his muddy yellow coat matched the bright flower. He hates me. . . . Sometimes, when I clean a kill, I feed Buttercup the entrails. He has stopped hissing at me. . . . Entrails. No hissing. This is the closest we will ever come to love.

(Mrs. Rief; from *The Hunger Games* by Suzanne Collins)

Strongest Endings

Suddenly I realized the building was the one where grandma had been locked away. The old Central State Asylum. The figure was my mother. Sweeping the path, clearing the way for me to follow. I didn't.

(Ben; from *Stitches* by David Small)

In My Room I Read a Poem to Dad
If mom is a window, Dad is
a door, a sturdy screen
door that lets the breezes
in and keeps the bugs
out. The door is usually not
locked. When I read Dad my poem
'A Matter of Loyalty,' I see
that door start to swing out
toward me. When I get to the last
line, Dad throws the door open
and I step into the room
that his arms make. That's when
I see Mom, who's been listening
from the hallway. She comes in,
puts her arms around Dad and me,
and together we make a house.

(Arabella; from *The Secret of Me* by Meg Kearney)

He threw himself face downwards beside the corpse. The machine gun stopped. Then the sniper turned over the dead body, and looked into his brother's face.

(Raghav; from "The Sniper" by Liam O'Flaherty)

"They're not in District 12?" I repeat, as if saying it will somehow fend off the truth. "Katniss," Gale says softly. I recognize that voice. It's the same one he uses to approach wounded animals before he delivers the final blow. I instinctively raise my hand to block out his words but he catches it and holds on tightly. "Don't," I whisper. "Katniss, there is no District 12."

(Forrest; from *Catching Fire* by Suzanne Collins)

Then the green again; the deep green from the water coming up through the hole while we waited, waited for another fish, waited for deep winter, waited for the end of the white blanket that covered all things, waited for the end of cold, blue cold. Waited for summer and fishing to start again.

(Hunter; from "Fishhouse Dreams" by Gary Paulsen)

The general made one of his deepest bows. "I see," he said. "Splendid! One of us is to furnish a repast for the hounds. The other will sleep in this very excellent bed. On guard, Rainsford." . . . He had never slept in a better bed, Rainsford decided.

(Matt; from "The Most Dangerous Game" by Richard Connell)

Everybody said Dave Sanders lived for kids. Should've known he'd die for them too.

(Joey; from "The Big Hero of Littleton" by Rick Reilly)

Unique Style

You Remind Me of You by Eireann Corrigan is a memoir written in poetry form. Corrigan knew how to express her deep feelings, causing even me to shed a tear. I liked how every few pages she wrote a questionnaire and answered it. It helped me fill in all the questions I had.

(Megan)

Stieg Larsson writes in a way that I love in *The Girl Who Played with Fire*. He uses events that happen in the past to shape how the characters react to things in the future. He also crafts the story from multiple points of view, and has the different perspectives converge on one central point in the end.

(Peter)

Put a stack of index cards near the giant sticky notes so kids can jot down the leads, memorable wording, endings, character descriptions, or unique styles that they find in their reading. I ask the students to put their name in parentheses after the title and author of the writing. When we talk about these characteristics of fine writing, we can look at these examples to see what writers do when we are looking to revise our own writing.

We pay attention to these writers because we want to know how to emulate what good writers do in our own writing. But we can't emulate something if we don't notice it and pay attention to it. These are the examples we can use to actually see what Ralph Fletcher is talking about as he presents the specifics of what a writer needs.

Using Specific Revising Ideas

In addition to conferences, my own writing, and collecting the writing of professionals, I use the revision ideas of teachers and educators I admire to remind students about things they can do in their writing.

The most helpful resources I've found for helping students revise their writing are: Nancie Atwell's *Lessons That Change Writers*, Ralph Fletcher's *What a Writer Needs*, Georgia Heard's *The Revision Toolbox*, Barry Lane's *After the End*, Kate Messner's *Real Revision*, and William Zinsser's *On Writing Well*.

Once I know the students and know their needs, I turn to these resources for examples and lessons. Nancie's book is a comprehensive collection of writing minilessons that includes both revision and editing with examples from her students.

I love Ralph's book because he has such engaging stories that help students remember specifics of the craft of writing, while inspiring us to write. I can't bring Ralph Fletcher into my classroom every day, but I can bring in his stories. This is a book worth reading cover to cover. I am bringing in his "Latest Thoughts About Writing" at the end of his book to begin my year. His chapter topics include the art of specificity, creating a character, voice, beginnings, endings, tension, a sense of place, a playfulness with time, unforgettable language, writing nonfiction, and revision. I go back to this book and Nancie's for the specifics I notice my students need for whole-class lessons.

[handwritten margin note: Resources for helping students revise their writing ☆]

Kate's book weaves the revision strategies of many young adult authors throughout her book as she presents lessons for getting at the specifics of revision in accessible, classroom-specific ways.

I was at a table one day listening to a piece of writing from one student, and I noticed Sam hand his writing to Damian. It looked like a long piece, at least five pages, typed. Double-spaced, but still long. I watched as Damian read and flipped page after page. After about the fifth page I heard Damian ask Sam, "So what is this piece about?" Sam replied, "My trip to Florida." Damian turned the writing back to the first page, handed it to Sam and said, "Well, when you get there, let me know." (Ah, the directness of adolescents.)

Sam could use Ralph Fletcher's lessons on revision and where to start the writing. Fletcher says writing should always "begin at the roar of the waterfall, at the energy source, . . . the writer should cut the rest of the writing that meanders slowly toward the roar" (Heard 2002, 30–31). It's a metaphor and an image kids can remember. As a reader Damian was plodding through the river trying to get to the roar of the waterfall. He told Sam how to do it—albeit curtly but effectively. "When you get there, let me know."

I have stories of my own, like this one, to add to the stories I read and share from Ralph's book.

**Online
7.4**

Once students have written an abundance and begin to choose the pieces they like best to take to more extensive, finished pieces, we talk revision. My conferences are all about the content, helping the kids see their way to what they want to say and helping them find more powerful ways of saying it. The revision sheet that is on the website lists the things we talk about the most with respect to content: leads, titles, endings, specific wording, slowing the text to linger on the important scenes, or cutting the unnecessary, as in Sam's first five pages.

Ralph says the bottom line about revision: "When a teacher suggests a revision, the student should have the final say over whether or not to make the change in their writing. We open the door, the student decides whether or not to step through. However, if a writing teacher can create an atmosphere that values risk-taking, students are more likely to experiment with revision for their texts-in-progress" (2013, 170).

A note about editing: Once the student is satisfied with the content of the writing, we either have an editing conference where I go through the first page with the student, showing them the corrections and why, or I edit the first page and hand it back to the student. In both cases, they are responsible for editing the rest of the piece. In nearly all of their writing, they will make the same mistakes on the remainder of the writing as they do on the first page. It is their job to pay attention to the corrections and transfer them to all the subsequent pages. If they don't, their mechanics grade will reflect that.

The most common errors I am correcting and talking about as a whole class include the following: indenting and paragraphing, using quotation marks in dialogue, the use of a colon and semicolon, writing numbers, subject-verb agreement, apostrophes, capitalizing proper names and titles, pronouns in prepositional phrases, and pronouns as subjects of a sentence. These can be easily fixed. The content takes time, positive feedback, perseverance, and patience.

I do have to remember these are thirteen- and fourteen-year-olds. Too much feedback, again and again, can be too much. A student taught me that. On her third draft (I always seem to find something else after they have revised a draft) of a piece, she wrote in big, thick, red letters: THIS IS MY FINAL, FINAL, FINAL DRAFT.

What is the most important thing I've learned about revising and editing? Students revise and edit when they care about their writing, when it matters to them—therefore, they want to capture their thinking in the most compelling way and the most accessible way for readers. When the writing is for us, only as an assignment, there is little desire or effort to make it stronger. The urge to revise comes from having something to say. None of us revise things we don't care about.

Revision is about the content. Editing is about the mechanics, or conventions. There is no reason to edit a piece until the content is the way the writer wants it. I once heard Don Graves explain why editing should not come first. If you edit before the content is the way you want it, it's like dressing up the corpse. Sure, they have been dressed in a nice suit, makeup and hair are perfect, and the body looks great. But the bottom line is, the person is dead. Like that good-looking body, a piece of writing carefully edited before the content is even considered, is most likely dead. Make the content rich, compelling, and noteworthy, and then clean it up for a reader.

Assessment and Evaluation

> Many state writing assessments run the risk of undercutting good writing by scoring only for focus, organization, style, and mechanics without once asking judges to consider whether the writing is powerful, memorable, provocative, or moving (all impact-related criteria, and all at the heart of why people read what others write).
>
> (Grant Wiggins, in *Because Writing Matters*, by National Writing Project and Carl Nagin [2003, 67])

Assessment

Assessment focuses on the students' learning and my teaching. I constantly ask students what is working well for them as readers and writers in order to continue and build on those things that keep them moving forward, or let go of those things that don't help them. Many of them tell me they don't like having to maintain a WRN, but they realize how much it has helped them grow stronger as both a reader and a writer. They are astounded and proud of all they have read and all they have written by the end of the year. I will continue to use the WRN. But I will negotiate with kids as to how much writing and how much reading is too much.

We read several books together as a whole class. I watch, notice, and ask: Is this reading aloud in class taking too much time? Am I going too slow or too fast for the students? What are they taking from the reading and discussion that they didn't notice on their own? Am I killing the book and their enjoyment or understanding of it by asking them to notice/pay attention to the vocabulary, the author's craft, the big ideas in the writing? What could we do differently? What are the students taking from this reading together that they can't get on their own? Is it worth the time?

I carefully read through their WRNs every two weeks to see what they are understanding and learning as readers. How well can they communicate their thinking in writing? Are they noticing and picking up new words that they are beginning to own in their speaking and writing?

Students hand in all rough drafts with their writing. Have they truly relooked, rethought, revised their writing to make it stronger? What are they understanding about writing that makes it powerful, memorable, and provocative? How can I build on their strengths and help them work through their weaknesses?

All of these questions and the students' feedback help me monitor my teaching and their learning. It is continual assessment of all they do, and all I do as a result.

Evaluation

Evaluation lets the students know how well they are doing. They have to participate as writers and readers. I give a lot of consideration to their good faith participation in class (whether they come prepared with expected materials, actually write and read, give feedback to each other in conferences, contribute to class discussions, and respect each other as readers and writers). But I also grade their WRNs and their writing.

As mentioned in the chapter about WRNs, each time I read their WRNs I expect to find:

- a list of books they are reading (easy, just right, challenging)
- their thinking as readers, writers, and participants in the world
  - I am grading them on the quantity (thirty minutes of reading per night) and amount of writing (two to four pages per week).
  - I am grading them on the quality (my subjective opinion about the depth of their reading, writing, and thinking).
- vocabulary words they are noticing and writing down in context (two to four words per week from their reading)

No writing is graded until they have revised the content to the best of their ability (with feedback from peers and me) and edited the conventions of language to the best of their ability.

They hand in all rough drafts with their best draft on top and a process paper for at least half of the writing they do during the year.

On the process paper (included in the handouts on the website) students describe the process they went through to craft their writing, what helped them most, and how well they believe they did on the writing. They grade themselves on the process they went through, including considering feedback, questions, and suggestions in conferences on content and editing, the content (the product, the writing itself), and the conventions of language.

1. The process: By looking at the process paper and all the rough drafts that contributed to the final piece, I can see what the students did and how they did it. This does not mean I expect to see numerous drafts. The process paper explains what the student did, and much of it might have been in his head before he set his thinking to paper. Between the process paper and the rough drafts, I can see a relatively complete picture of everything that contributed to the work's growth.

2. The content: The content/product grade depends on the piece of writing—is it a book review, a personal narrative, a poem, an essay, an informational pamphlet, a cartoon, a letter to an editor?—and the different characteristics or elements that make that genre distinct. Throughout the year, we read many examples of various kinds of writing and describe the elements that make that genre distinct.

3. The conventions: The grade for conventions, or mechanics, is based on how well the students have edited the writing following our editing conference.

I average my grade on all three of these categories with the student's grade in each. Inevitably, my grade is usually higher than the student's grade. By grading in all three categories the students can better define their strengths, as well as their weaknesses. They might have worked very hard throughout the process, but the writing did not quite accomplish what it set out to do as an essay. The paper was well edited, with no mistakes. The grade on a piece like this might be: process = A, content = B, conventions = A. On another piece the grade might be A/A/C. The student worked hard, the writing is accomplished, but the conventions were not carefully edited.

I spend the most time giving students feedback on their writing as they are drafting. My teaching is concentrated on helping them move from that first to last draft; therefore, I don't feel compelled to write lengthy comments on the final draft. Grades should keep the writer writing and the reader reading. I wish I didn't have to give grades at all, but I do. I hope that what I do does keep them growing, but I have to pay attention to the result or reactions the students have to their grades.

[handwritten margin note: How do rubrics come into play?]

We are not the editors of a prestigious national magazine where we can cavalierly accept or reject a student's work. They depend on us to help them nurture their strengths and suggest ways of overcoming their weaknesses.

For my entire life, I either participated in sports (field hockey, basketball, and softball), watched hundreds of games (sons in T-ball through college soccer and hockey, grandsons and granddaughters in soccer, hockey, and lacrosse), or wrote articles as a sports correspondent for New Hampshire newspapers (high school soccer and hockey). I have seen many fine coaches and some not so fine. The two best coaches I ever watched were Paul Kerrigan and Tim Runk, coaching my grandson's soccer and basketball teams. I began to pay attention to how they talked to their players on the field and on the court.

They always played every child on the team. They liked having a range of kids with a variety of strengths. They trusted each one to do his best. They noted fine play. They applauded the players' efforts. No matter how many mistakes or how egregious the mistake the child made on the field or the court, they never mentioned it. They never yelled. Never. They found something first that the child did well. Then, and only then, did they give a suggestion for how the player might do something else in a certain situation and how he could do that. A strategy. And then the player went right back into the game.

A positive comment—a pat on the back. A suggestion—a way to overcome the weakness. The opportunity to try it again.

As teachers, we are always trying to nurture growth. We are coaches. I want to be the teacher and the coach, like Paul and Tim, and the conductor, like Benjamin Zander, who finds the positive, suggests alternatives and strategies, and gets out of the way to let the child play.

I may have to evaluate the writing, but I always try to think about that polished piece of writing in the way we always think of that particular performance, or that noteworthy sporting event: The first time I saw *Les Miserables* at the Kennedy Center in Washington, DC, and sobbed my way through "Empty Chairs at Empty Tables." That "Miracle on Ice" game when the United States hockey team, made up of amateur and collegiate players, defeated the Soviet team in the semifinals and then went on to beat Finland for the gold medal in the 1980 Olympics. That's how I want my students to write. Powerful. Memorable. Provocative. Moving. Human being to human being.

CHAPTER EIGHT

Whole Novels

For the Maxes in Our Classrooms

Max, an eighth grader who has already told me that his intent is to do nothing during the year because "it doesn't count 'til ya get to high school," is the first one to class every day. Every year I have several kids just like Max—it is just that their names change.

I am reading aloud *Holes* by Louis Sachar, a mystery that forces the reader to put together clues introduced in a variety of smaller stories that often don't seem connected but ultimately are tied together. It is the story of a boy unjustly accused of a "crime" and forced to endure inhumane treatment in a correctional institution at the hands of some mean-spirited adults. It's a puzzle that kids can connect to, especially adolescents who often feel that adults are not fair to them. With each chapter, more questions emerge and the reader wants the answers. It's a compelling story that forces even the most reticent reader to listen. Max is caught up in this story, in the voice reading to him, and in the thinking it forces him into.

Max enters the room each day with "I'm only here 'cause you're reading that book to us. You are reading that book today, aren't you?"

What can we learn from Max?

Max loves being read to. He enjoys hearing different voices, especially if he is only asked to follow along. He's not lazy. He just does not know how to read well, and he is not going to admit that. The first few times we read a book aloud as a class, he never volunteers for a part, no matter how small. When I force him to read aloud to me several weeks into the year (from a book of his choice, that he has been given time to practice reading), he reads in a halting staccato with a clear emphasis on decoding, not on meaning making. He "reads" thick novels but almost never writes a response or reaction to that reading. He tells me he reads fast, looking for the action of the story, and doesn't like to write what he thinks.

As a struggling reader who won't admit how little he understands, reading aloud helps Max hear and understand the pronunciation of single words, as well as whole sentences that lead to layers of meaning. Filling the classroom with thousands of books, having a day of silent reading for the entire period, and leaving Max to his own devices as a reader is not enough. Reading aloud is one way to help Max truly enter a book. When he finds the story compelling enough he tries to figure out what's going on; hearing it out loud helps him make hunches based on evidence in the story; it helps him relate to the characters, hating some, feeling compassion for others, in the instance of *Holes*.

Although Max seldom responds in writing to books read on his own, he asks substantive questions and offers pertinent information in class discussion when we read a text together. These oral responses tend to transfer into his writer's-reader's notebook (WRN) writing in response to each day's reading, when done in class and in response to these common readings.

One day Max rushed to class to tell me another student made his mother take him to the library to get the book *Holes* so he could read ahead. He wanted to know, "Whaddaya plan to do about that?" He didn't want the story to end any faster than I wanted *In the Fall* to end. And he didn't want the pleasure of daily listening and thinking out loud to end. He liked the predictability that our reading out loud each day for two weeks offered him.

It's because of the struggling readers, who don't really read on their own when given the choice, that I must find time to read the stories together aloud. I make sure all kids have the book in front of them, so they can follow along and see words as they hear words. When we read aloud books that the kids really enjoy, they look for more books by that author or similar story lines or genres on their own. They trust us with recommendations when we can say, "You really seemed to like *Holes*; I think you'd like this book, too." We can use their oral response to point out what thoughtful questions, what insightful comments, what great personal and worldly connections they made that they could also make in written responses to reading on their own.

For the sake of all of our students, I am suggesting we read at least two novels and/or a play a year as a whole class, so we can engage all of our kids in the process of real reading—thinking about the meaning of those words on the page, even as we are teaching some of them how to pronounce the words. In fifty minutes a day, it takes at least two weeks of reading to complete a short (around two hundred pages) novel. I suspend the writing, but continue to expect kids to write in their WRNs in response to the reading we are doing in class and the reading they are still doing on their own at night.

For the Fionas in Our Classrooms

I already mentioned I struggle with the idea of taking time to read whole novels. I know it is valuable to some kids, but not all kids. In the same way we notice the struggling students and try our best to engage them, we have to notice the exceptional students, like Fiona, and keep her engaged. She is reading *Jane Eyre* and *Sarah's Key*. She reads them deeply. She is a sophisticated reader who challenges herself to unravel her understandings of the most complicated human relationships, experiences, and situations and relishes literary conversations with several of her peers at every opportunity. Sitting through an all-class read-aloud is agony for her. Better to meet her needs by recommending much more challenging books, letting her go off to a quiet spot to read, and have written conversations with her in her WRN. Letting her do that says that you know her as a reader, and you trust her to challenge herself with her own choices. And she does.

If there are several kids like Fiona in the classroom, another alternative is to allow them to go off and read individually and to talk about or write about those books together, whether they are individual titles or the same book of their choice. All kids need choices. Certainly a main goal of mine is to keep kids reading and writing. So the question becomes, how do we make that appropriate for all kids? It takes knowing them, trusting them, and challenging them with alternatives.

Luckily for Fiona she is in a ninth-grade class this year with a teacher who understands and recognizes who she is as a reader. When Fiona told her she had read *Catcher in the Rye* numerous times, and talked it through again and again with family and friends, the teacher didn't hesitate to say, "What if we find another book for you; you might like *White Oleander*. Go read and we can talk later about your thinking." Kudos to that teacher! Fiona will continue to grow stronger as a reader because she is not being held back to satisfy a standardized curriculum mandated for all students.

[handwritten margin note:] How does this differentiated approach tend to play out?

Reading Aloud as Story Theatre

The most successful way I have found to read aloud is as reader's theatre, where I have labeled and highlighted the speaking parts of a particular character for one book. For instance, in *The Giver*, I have one book labeled "Jonas," where all his speaking parts are highlighted. Another labeled and highlighted for the Giver. Another for Fiona. Another mother. And so on.

Whatever book we are reading aloud, I have all the books prepared in this way. I list all the parts on the board and note whether each is a major, minor, or average amount of reading. Kids volunteer. We talk about listening to fluent readers and all we can learn from them. Each student gets the book highlighted with his part. All kids have a copy of the book. As the year goes on, more and more kids volunteer, including the struggling readers who dare to take a risk, who feel more confident in their reading abilities, and who like the idea of entering into a character through their interpretation of his or her voice.

I always read the narrator's part to keep the story moving. I put as much feeling into this part as I expect kids to put into their characters. In a class of good readers, I share the narrator's part, so more kids get a chance to read aloud.

This is not about testing kids to see how well they read aloud when it comes to their paragraph. It's about hearing voices of characters to understand the layers of a story. It's about helping all kids connect language and meaning by seeing and hearing it. By highlighting ahead, I am making a difficult task as easy as it can be so we can concentrate on the most important task—taking meaning to and from a text, as we are listening to a story.

Kids enjoy reading aloud this way. It is not a game. They don't have to look for parts, and they like listening to the voices of classmates as the characters. Following along while someone is reading aloud is also the best way I know to help kids connect sounds with symbols and to gain fluency in putting words together. Especially in adolescence, kids become defensive and say they hate reading before they will ever let us know they can't read. Giving kids watered down texts with simplistic language or didactic morals, or pulling them out for phonics instruction, are not the most helpful forms of instruction for struggling, adolescent readers.

In addition, by reading aloud in class, we can help kids take apart the layers of meaning through class discussion and questions that kids often miss when reading a book on their own.

We may have to abandon some of the major pieces of writing we hope to accomplish while reading whole novels together, but we can still do quickwrites in our WRNs as we read: questions, hunches, personal connections, reactions, responses to the characters, the plot, the implications, the craft of the writing. Even these quickwrites or illustrations (I often ask kids to draw out what they imagined in their heads after reading a particular chapter or section), whether to books the students are reading on their own or we are reading as a whole class, may be the seeds of ideas that lead to more thorough, polished pieces of writing or art once the reading is complete.

By listening to the sounds of words as we look at the words, and the intonations of the voices of those reading fluently, we are teaching reading and thinking to all of the students, but especially to the Maxes. It makes all of us more fluent readers. Beth, who I considered an exceptional student, a very thoughtful reader and writer, said in her evaluation at the end of the year:

> In the past year, I have definitely become a more fluent reader. Before I started eighth grade, I was terrified of reading out loud in class and couldn't read as fast as most of my peers. It really embarrassed me. But now, though it is still a little nerve-wracking, I can read in front of the class much better than before, and I don't stumble over words as often.
>
> What I wish I could say is that choosing our own books to read helped my reading the most. That didn't help my reading though, but it did help my

love of reading and my interest in books. What *helped* my reading was reading books out loud. I could practice following along and reading out loud at the same time, and it really helped me to become a better reader—and along the way, gave me great ideas for writing.

[handwritten margin note: Opening reading as ritual?]

Because I know how helpful it is to see and hear words in the context of a whole piece, I try to put anything I am reading aloud either on a screen for them to see or as copies in front of them. Poems. Short stories. Essays. Letters. Memoirs. Their own writing. My writing. They need to see and hear them all to develop their own reading voices.

We have eleven-, twelve-, and thirteen-year-olds in our classrooms who are still waiting for an introduction to the joy of reading. We may be the first adults in a child's life who offer her books. And connecting kids with books is hard work.

Years ago when a teacher poked his head into my classroom, stepped over kids sprawled on the floor—all reading—and sarcastically said to me, "Boy, you sure planned hard for this lesson!" I wanted to scream, "You bet I did!"

We have to know our kids as adolescents, we have to know the background of the community from which they come, and we have to know them as individuals to make good choices about the books on our shelves, the books we choose to recommend, and the books we choose to read aloud as a whole class. We have to know what interests the kids and what else might interest them. And we have to know books and how reading works.

We have to work hard at finding ways to surround kids with great reading—fiction, nonfiction, poetry; classic and contemporary literature; multicultural, male and female authors. Just knowing books is a daunting task. We have to build classroom libraries by belonging to professional organizations and subscribing to journals that keep us informed about the newest books. We often have to come up with innovative ways to purchase or obtain the books. We have to find the time to take kids to our school or community libraries if we don't have the resources in our own rooms.

We have to know books well enough ourselves to give book talks and author introductions or find trusted adults in the school and community who know books well. We have to learn to read aloud in practiced, theatrical voices that bring the books alive for our students. We have to find the time in our packed fifty-minute schedules for real reading—individually, in small groups, and as whole classes. We have to teach kids to find meaning in, and bring meaning to, all that they read through oral and written language. We have to take time to read ourselves.

Our students become readers when they are invited into books by adults and peers they admire and respect, who are passionate about reading and books themselves. They become passionate readers *and* writers when they are reading books that matter to them as human beings. I collect their thoughts about reading and share them with others. I post them around the room or put them on informational pamphlets I give to parents.

When I read a good book my brain does back flips. Suddenly there are possibilities to be explored—new ideas. Suddenly I have questions, thoughts.

Emma

I felt my soul tear and my eyes burn when I read *Night*. I felt the thunderous sound of fire drown out reality, and screams of their agony driven down my throat. I felt naked in the terror of what was, and what could be. As much as I understand Wiesel's terror, I knew I knew nothing. I think I hate this book. I find no joy in reading it. But I love this book for telling the truth.

Kaitlin

I am reading a mouthwatering book. . . . Just listen to this. A woman once asked John Viehman, "Why walk?" and he said, "Because the world looks different at two miles an hour? Because spring comes at you one flower at a time? Because a mountain only reveals itself to those who climb it? Because I like the drama of crags and gullies emerging from a curtain of mist?"

Seth

I think this is one of the most emotional books I've read. Every joy Torey and Sheila had was fragile, like a weak berry branch in a heavy storm. . . . I finished this book (*One Child* by Torey Hayden) standing in the bathroom and cried. My mom, who had been passing by, asked if I was okay and spoiled the moment.

Kaitlin

In Summary: Promoting Reading

In summary, what can we do as teachers to promote reading?

- Give students a balance of books that are easy to read, some that are just right, and others that are challenging. By reading books aloud to students, we can choose books that are more difficult and thought-provoking, because in the ensuing class discussions and written responses, we can help guide kids through layers of meaning, ideas, or innuendoes they may not pick up on their own.
- Keep a healthy mix of fiction, nonfiction, and poetry that is culturally rich and diverse.
- Provide varied genres of writing from women and men, dead and alive, classic and contemporary.

- Have a regular routine for reading. My standing assignment to the students is to read each night for a half hour and to read individually for thirty minutes every Friday. It is a schedule they love and look forward to.

- Allow lots of choice in what they read. Start right away to put lists up around the room of highly recommended books from each other, from the teacher, and from previous students. Pulling books off the shelves, giving book talks, and reading excerpts opens books to kids. When we trust our students to choose the reading that matters to them, they will trust our informed choices of books that might matter to them.

- Provide opportunities to hear reading we choose to read to them and with them. Kids love to be read to, and to read aloud themselves, if they are listening to fluent readers who easily take on the intonations and emotions of the characters they are reading.

- Give students books and the opportunity to read on their own, in small groups, and as a whole class.

- Introduce different authors, titles, and genres while at the same time encouraging favorite authors.

- Take time to write and time to talk about their thinking as readers.

- Expect both oral and written responses to their reading.

- Provide instruction in reading strategies and processes that allow them to experience close readings.

- Provide evidence of their teachers as readers.

Highly Recommended Books

These are the books that moved from hand to hand with, "You gotta read this!"

Sherman Alexie—*The Absolutely True Diary of a Part-Time Indian*

Julia Alvarez—*Before We Were Free*

Laurie Halse Anderson—*Speak, Wintergirls, Chains, Fever, Catalyst*

Jay Asher—*Thirteen Reasons Why*

Abigail Lynne Becker—*A Box of Rain*

Judy Blundell—*What I Saw and How I Lied*

Drew Brees—*Coming Back Stronger*

Dan Brown—*The DaVinci Code, Angels and Demons*

Orson Scott Card—Ender's series, *Xenocide*

Mary Higgins Clark—*Loves Music, Loves to Dance*

Suzanne Collins—*The Hunger Games*

Michael Crichton—*Timeline*

James Dashner—*The Maze Runner*

Nancy Farmer—*The House of the Scorpion*

Jonathan Foerr—*Extremely Loud and Incredibly Close*

Malcolm Gladwell—*Outliers*

William Goldman—*The Princess Bride*

John Green—*The Fault in Our Stars, Looking for Alaska, Paper Towns*

Lorie Ann Grover—*On Pointe*

Khaled Hosseini—*The Kite Runner*

Meg Kearney—*The Secret of Me*

Sue Monk Kidd—*The Secret Life of Bees*

Stephen King—*Pet Sematary*

Jon Krakauer—*Into the Wild*

Billie Letts—*Where the Heart Is*

John Marsden—*Tomorrow, When the War Began,* The Tomorrow series

Robert McCammon—*Boy's Life*

Patricia McCormick—*Sold*

Ben Mikaelsen—*Petey*

Michael Morpurgo—*War Horse*

Han Nolan—*Dancing on the Edge, Born Blue, If I Should Die Before I Wake*

Kenneth Oppel—*Skybreaker*

Christopher Paolini—*Eragon, Eldest, Brisingr*

James Patterson—Maximum Ride series

Gary Paulsen—*Harris and Me, How Angel Peterson Got His Name*

Jodi Picoult—*My Sister's Keeper*

Matthew Quick—*Silver Linings Playbook*

Rick Riordan—*The Lightning Thief, The Sea of Monsters, The Titan's Curse*

Tatiana de Rosnay—*Sarah's Key*

Veronia Roth—*Divergent*

Roland Smith—*Tentacles*

Nicholas Sparks—*Dear John*

Garth Stein—*The Art of Racing in the Rain*

Markus Zusak—*The Book Thief*

Suggested Books for Read-Aloud

(Several summaries are taken directly from the copyright page of each book.)

Anderson, Laurie Halse. 1999. *Speak*. New York: Farrar Straus Giroux.

A traumatic event near the end of the summer has a devastating effect on Melinda's freshman year in high school.

Curtis, Christopher Paul. 1995. *The Watsons Go to Birmingham—1963*. New York: Delacorte Press.

The ordinary interactions and everyday routines of the Watsons, an African American family living in Flint, Michigan, are drastically changed after they go to visit Grandma in Alabama in the summer of 1963.

Donnelly, Jennifer. 2003. *A Northern Light*. New York: Harcourt Books.

In 1906, sixteen-year-old Mattie, determined to attend college and be a writer against the wishes of her father and fiancé, takes a job at a summer inn in the Adirondacks, where she discovers the truth about the death of a guest. Based on the true story *An American Tragedy*, where Donnelly started asking "What if . . . ?"

Fleischman, Paul. 1999. *Mind's Eye*. New York: Henry Holt and Company.

A novel in play form in which sixteen-year-old Courtney, paralyzed in an accident, learns about the power of the mind from an elderly blind woman, who takes Courtney on an imaginary journey to Italy using a 1910 guidebook.

Fleischman, Paul. 1997. *Seedfolks*. New York: HarperCollins.

One by one, a number of people of varying ages and backgrounds transform a trash-filled inner-city lot into a productive and beautiful garden, and in doing so, the gardeners are themselves transformed.

Hinton, S. E. 1995. *The Outsiders*. New York: Puffin Books.

>Ponyboy is fourteen, tough, and confused, yet sensitive beneath his bold front. Since his parents' death, his loyalties have been to his brothers and his gang, the boys from the wrong side of the tracks. When his best friend kills a member of a rival gang, a nightmare of violence begins.

Lowry, Lois. 1993. *The Giver*. New York: Houghton Mifflin Company.

>Given his lifetime assignment at the Ceremony of Twelve, Jonas becomes the receiver of memories shared by only one other in his community and discovers the terrible truth about the society in which he lives.

Mack, Tracy. 2000. *Drawing Lessons*. New York: Scholastic.

>Like her father, Aurora is an artist. The great thing about art, Rory thinks, is you can bring back something you've lost and keep it forever. But when her father leaves the family, it's Rory who is lost.

MacLachlan, Patricia. 1991. *Journey*. New York: Delacorte Press.

>When their mother goes off, leaving her two children with their grandparents, they feel as if their past has been erased until Grandfather finds a way to restore it to them.

Paulsen, Gary. 1993. *Harris and Me*. New York: Harcourt Brace & Company.

>Sent to live with relatives on their farm because of his unhappy home life, an eleven-year-old city boy meets his distant cousin Harris and is given an introduction to a whole new world.

Philbrick, Rodman. 1993. *Freak the Mighty*. New York: Scholastic.

>Max thought he had never had a brain. All his life he'd been called stupid. Dumb. Slow. It didn't help that his body seemed to be growing faster than his mind. It didn't help that people were afraid of him. So Max learned how to be alone, until Freak came along. Freak had a little body and a really big brain. Together, Max and Freak were unstoppable.

Sachar, Louis. 1998. *Holes*. New York: Farrar Straus & Giroux.

>As further evidence of his family's bad fortune, which they attribute to a curse on a distant relative, Stanley Yelnats is sent to a hellish correctional camp in the Texas desert where he finds his first real friend, a treasure, and a new sense of himself.

Two books that sustain the attention of eighth graders are *The Outsiders* by S. E. Hinton and *The Giver* by Lois Lowry. All one has to do is look on the Internet for hundreds of ideas about teaching either of these books. What are some ways we have read these books and represented our understandings from them?

The Outsiders by S. E. Hinton

In a long-yellowed paper I've kept, labeled only "S. E. Hinton On Writing," Hinton says, "I always begin with character in mind and an ending I want to get to. I like my characters to grow, to show some change. So I know that in the middle of the book I'll have to figure out how to make the change happen. The middle is the hardest part for me."

In thirty years of teaching, I have worried that my students would outgrow this book. They have not. That the book would become old for them. It has not. They have as much enthusiasm for reading it this year as I've ever seen. For the characters. And I still love it. For the characters.

As I was standing in the hall monitoring the kids coming in from lunch and recess, Joey, a strapping, husky, well-liked, athletic, well-to-do, smart eighth grader, came up to me, breathless. "Tell me it isn't true. Someone from your last class said Johnny dies. Tell me it isn't true." Another eighth grader overheard him. "What?" she said. "What? Johnny died? Oh, no."

A few weeks ago five freshmen boys stopped in as they were headed to soccer practice on our field. As they left one of them said, "You know, I still have *The Outsiders* certificate from our tableaux on the wall in my bedroom. Are you reading that book again this year? You should, you know. I love that book." I assured him I would be reading that book again. All of them gave me a thumbs-up as they left.

It's about the characters. Hinton has given us characters with whom all of us can identify and with whom we can empathize: Johnny, Dally, Ponyboy, Darry, Sodapop. Like each of us, they all have their flaws, and perhaps that is why Hinton pulls us into their lives so fully and lets us live with them as they negotiate their world with all of their choices—the good and the bad choices. Even the few choices.

The handouts mentioned in the following pages can be found on the website.

■ We read *The Outsiders* as story theatre, aloud, in class.

Online
8.1–8.9

Each student reading a character's part has his or her own book with all the speaking parts highlighted. We talk about giving voice to the characters, once we figure out what they are like. I stole an idea from *'Tis* by Frank McCourt. When he wanted to teach his students how to read out loud with different voices and different emotions, he brought in several recipes and had them read the ingredients and directions in the way that the dish made them feel. I bring in a recipe for hot, hot chili, one for meatloaf, one for chocolate chip cookies, and one for tripe, sautéed gizzards, or tongue sandwiches. The kids read them with strong emotions. "Transfer *that* to your character," I tell them.

- Students keep a character storyboard. I give them a blank storyboard sheet and show them an example of what I mean from my storyboard.

Before we even read the first chapter, I give them a little bit of information about who the characters are and how they are related:

Darry, Sodapop, and Ponyboy; Johnny; Dally (Greasers)

Bob, Randy, Cherry (Socs)

I put the names of just the five Greasers in a basket (five times each as I have approximately twenty-five students per class), and students randomly choose the name of a character to follow. Ideally I would rather have students follow the character that intrigues them, but when I do that I have only two or three of the characters being followed. I want them to see that all of these characters are interesting in all the different ways Hinton has crafted them.

I show the kids a couple of frames from my storyboard—stick figures and key words of the first few things I find out about Johnny, supported with words from the text. (See Figure 8.1.)

First and foremost, I want students to enjoy this story. I want them to recognize how we treat each other as human beings, especially when we stereotype. I want them to enter into this story aesthetically. How does it make them think and feel, about themselves and about others in the world? How do they treat each other?

I also want them to notice what Hinton does as a writer to craft such strong feelings for her characters. What does she do to make us care so deeply? How does she do that? What we notice and talk about will carry us into our author-genre study.

In addition, I want to give kids a strategy for gathering information for themselves so that they can talk with authority—either in a discussion or in any kind of paper they might be asked to craft (analytical, imaginative, evaluative etc.)—about their understandings of any text.

- I instruct students to use a pencil to check information about their character in the margins as we read.

I tell kids that they can put a check or the first letter of the character they are following in the margin of the book as we read so they can easily get back to that information. They can't read, listen, and storyboard all at the same time. But they need a way to find that information again without having to reread the whole chapter.

Figure 8.1 *Johnny Cade Storyboard*

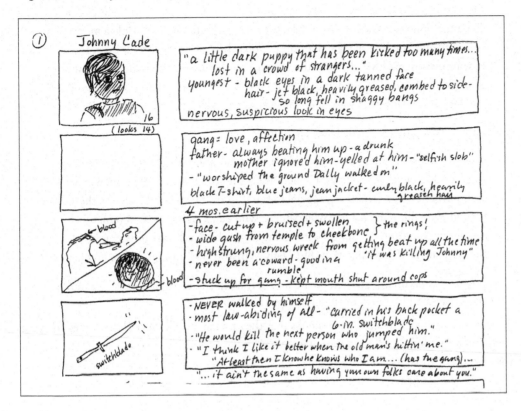

As we read I mention that if students are following Johnny, for instance, they might want to put a check next to that passage. At the end of each class, I give them five to ten minutes to storyboard what happened to or with their character and to collect the passages that support that.

■ I use passages from the story to stimulate the students' thinking.

I have typed out passages that I think will push students' thinking about these characters, their choices, and their emotional ties they will make to these characters and/or their situations. I use them as quickwrites. Or *slow-writes* as the kids tell me when we write for five, seven, ten minutes at a stretch. The writing is an entry into conversations we have as we read. I usually give them a passage to respond to after we have read the chapter in which it appears. I never use all of these passages—I vary them according to how our conversations are going as we talk about the book.

In her WRN, Anna wrote in response to what Johnny meant when he told Ponyboy to "stay gold."

Stay gold. Always keep your imagination. Press your face to the glass of the window and watch the first snowfall, amazed and silent. Gaze at stars and wonder about the universe. Make a wish. Make two wishes, both on 11:11. Ride a merry-go-round and laugh until your sides hurt. Don't think. Just close your eyes. Live in your own world. Never forget the happiness, thanks for the memories. Run through a field and feel the wind on your face. Swing on a swingset and pretend you are flying. Dance and wave your arms like you're walking on a tightrope. Smile!

In response to a passage about Dally she wrote:

I feel the most empathy for Dally. I don't want to sound like some typical teen girls, but I . . . like . . . badboys. I believe there's a little boy in Dally somewhere, and maybe it takes something special to see it in his eyes, but it's always there behind everything. He's a boy who can cry, who can laugh, who can remember a more simple time when he wasn't going through hell. Some girls can break through shells of boys like that, but Dally Winston was a tough kid to crack.

- Using their storyboard, students write an analysis in the form of an essay, a multigenre piece, or an art-biography of the character they followed.

Students write songs, poems, new scenes that they imagine took place, letters they imagine Sodapop wrote to Sandy, and more formal essays. They use the Character Analysis Guide I put together for them to show how the choices each character made affected that character and others and how the character changed throughout the book. Students had all the information they needed to craft their writing or art on the storyboard sheets.

- Students write a process paper that shows what they did and why.

**Online
8.8–8.9**

These process papers are often more interesting to me than the actual products the students create, because they show the thinking they went through to bring their ideas into a piece of writing or art. See Elizabeth's storyboard (on Johnny), art-biography, and process paper and Katya's art-biography and process paper (on Sodapop) on the website.

- In groups, formed based on the character students followed, the kids present their findings through a tableaux.

I show the students several sculptures—*The Pieta* by Michelangelo, Americans raising the flag over Iwo Jima, Thomas Franklin's photo of the three firemen raising the flag over Ground Zero on 9/11, and several sculptures from Duane Hanson, who has crafted realistic contemporary people in everyday scenes. We talk about a tableau being a freeze-frame that, in this case, will show us what they think are the most significant scenes portraying their character. They use the passages they have collected on their storyboard sheet to determine the most significant scenes.

We talk about choosing scenes that show what the character is like in the beginning, what affected change in them, and what they are like by the end. They need to get inside the head of their character. What are the feelings in each scene—fear, panic, anger, confidence, anxiety, sadness, disappointment, understanding—and how will their characters' gestures and facial expressions show that? What does *panic* look like? Each group of students has to type up the scenes they have decided to show, the passages they will use to narrate the scene, and why this scene is worth showing. (What does it show about the character?)

We practice, practice, practice—and present these scenes on Outsiders Day.

■ We have an Outsiders Day.

Students dress up as Socs or Greasers. We present all the tableaux scenes, present a number of art-biographies or pieces of writing, and watch the movie *The Outsiders*. Our entire team gives up other classes for the day so we can present and view everything together. At the end of the day, we give Stay Gold certificates for the strongest scenes in the tableaux presentations and the best outfits representing Greasers or Socs. More than half of the students receive these certificates. It is usually a great day—with 100% participation.

What do the students take from the reading, the writing, and the performing? I ask them several questions:

"What did you like most about the book *The Outsiders*?"

"What do you think Hinton is trying to get across in this book?"

"How do you 'stay gold'?"

All of the responses will keep me reading this book with students, but Hunter (see Figure 8.2) and Joey (see Figure 8.3) show us so poignantly that the real worth in what we as teachers choose to read is how deeply it affects our students.

Figure 8.2 *Hunter's Response to The Outsiders*

The Outsiders

I liked how the book relates to how kids label themselves in schools even today. It made it realistic. I also liked the characters—the way they interacted with each other and treated each other. Darry—I felt the most for him because he gave up so much to help Ponyboy. He gave up his college career, football, and working two jobs just to keep Ponyboy and Soda in the same house. I liked the way the Greasers treated each other. Even before the rumble they were humorous and laughing at each other. They got themselves pumped for it by joking around and having fun with each other.

I think Hinton was trying to show us how kids label other kids. She grew up in a school that labeled kids and she was frustrated with it. She was trying to show that both sides have their own problems. Reading the book out loud makes the characters sound more realistic. It makes it more active, instead of reading it by yourself. If you had a part you had to pay attention.

How do I "stay gold"? It's the moment of seeing the deer that you think you can get that only lasts for a short time. It's the look in Suzy's eyes

that says she wants to be with us again—asking why we had to put her behind the electric fence. It's recognizing the curiosity and intelligence that the buffalo seem to use to solve their own problems—sticking their heads through the corral gate to get to the salt lick. It's finding a buck's shed of antlers walking through the woods.

↑ *These are all wonderful "gold" moments!*

Response—70

Hunter

Figure 8.3 Joey's Response to The Outsiders

The Outsiders Feedback 1-30

Joey What I loved about this book is that it tells a story about something I never even knew of. It enlightens kids like me that life can be a whole lot worse than what we think is bad. I had no clue what a greaser or a soc was before I read this book. I had a little clue what a "hood" was, but nothing like the way Hinton puts them in the book. This was one of those books that I never wanted never to end. I was hooked by not only the plot of the book, but by the characters. I started to care for the characters and what happened to them. The story was filled with action from page one There was never a part in this book that I felt bored or satisfied, I always kept wanting to read on until the end, then I was wishing for a sequel.

Response–72

I think there are a lot of things Hinton was trying to show us in the book. The most obvious one is stereotyping. When I thought of "greasers" I thought more of a culture, or a religion. If you're catholic, you're catholic. You may never go to church, or never pray, but that doesn't mean you're no longer catholic. It's in your blood, you can't get rid of it you don't have a choice. For Ponyboy the question isn't, is he a greaser? But what kind of greaser? Their greasy hair symbolizes they're a greaser just like celebrating Christmas symbolizes you're catholic or christian. But "greaser" shouldn't be an adjective, it should just be a nown. Yes that's a book, but is it a good book, bad book, what kind of book? Yes that's a building, but what is it used for? Yes that's a door, but what's on the other side? That is a greaser, but what feelings does he have? Is he nice? Does he go to school? What kind of greaser?

Response–73

continues

Figure 8.3 continued

What I liked about reading The Outsiders out loud is, it was just more fun. I mean yes, we did screw up a lot but it was something different than what I was used to. It was also very useful to talk about the book after each chapter as well. You got to understand it more. This last year Oyster River didn't have a football team for 7th & 8th graders, so I had to play for another town. This was when I felt like an Outsider. I only had a few friends that came from Oyster River. We played with the Portsmouth team. I was difficult to fit in. The kids I was playing with had knew eachother for 5 years or more. They didn't want anything to change. The coaches yelled a lot, but

You have to imagine yourself inside the book, with the characters, feeling and seeing what they do as if you were really there. Not just reading words. Reading is painting a picture of what the author is trying to tell you.

—Shannon, eighth grader

Response–74

they were very welcoming. I found myself sticking with my Oyster River friends at the meetings. The year before, when I was on Oyster River, we lost every game we played so we didn't have a great reputation. Even though I was not originally on the team that didn't stop me from being me and do what I do best play football. I ended up starting on offense and defense, plus being on punt and punt return. The practice before our first game, my teammates, from Portsmouth voted me one of their captains. The kids are now one of my best friends. I might have came from a different team, but we were all their to do the same thing, play football. When Johnny told Ponyboy to "stay gold" I think what Johnny was trying to say was,

Response–75

Stay who you are. Don't try to change into someone you aren't, so you can impress people. Your true friends will like you for who you really are, and if they don't, then they are not your true friends. Johnny was telling Ponyboy to stay soft. Not to try to be hard like Dally or Darry. Be different, if different is who you are. You stay gold by once in a while you take a step back from life and ask yourself, "is this who I am?" The way you know who you really are is look back from when you were young. When you're young, you don't care what other people think, you just do what you do. Don't try to impress others, because you may satisfy them, but you're killing yourself. When I think of the first quote Ponyboy says, I think of time. Time is so valuable, but you have to make it count. No one gave me

Response—76

gave time to find out what Ponyboy was like. If they gave that time, they probably wouldn't mark him lousy. The second quote about the sunset really strikes me. But it makes sense. They may be from two different sides of town, but they all have the same purpose, and that's to live life to its fullest. They share way more things in common than they think they do, when they finally understand that, they will understand eachother. Hinton put life into the characters that I've never seen an author do before. I started to really have feelings and emotions I never thought before to a book. Hatred, sadness, wonder, impressed, etc. I never wanted to stop reading. I can't wait to read more of Hinton's books.

Response—77

The Giver by Lois Lowry

We usually read *The Giver* either right before or right after reading about social justice issues. What happens in a world when you have no choices in your lives. I give the students the following question: "If you were king of the world and could rid yourself or the world of any of the feelings or things that are disagreeable or destructive in any way, what would you abolish?" At tables they have eight minutes to come up with their list. I compile a comprehensive list from all of my classes.

The next day I give them the list and a sheet that asks them to categorize the list by placing each event or issue under one of two categories: Inconvenient and Disagreeable or Harmful and Destructive. Each table has one list to fill in. I suggest they add anything else that comes to mind and cross out those things they list so they don't repeat themselves. On a flip chart sheet, I gather their decisions in the two categories. The final list, after consensus, often looks like this:

Inconvenient/Disagreeable

Braces, body odor, bad breath, dandruff, hiccupping, colds, baldness, poison ivy, sunburn, frostbite, broken fingernails, glasses, zits, bad haircuts, homework, tests, taxes, chores (dishes, pets, laundry, babysitting, vacuuming, raking leaves, mowing lawn), mosquitoes, black flies, ticks, shedding animals, tooth decay, burping, farting, barfing, potholes, icy roads, rude manners, commercials, country music, taxes, expensive higher education, body image, high medical costs, censorship, politics, bad drivers, telemarketers, tailgaters, disgusting public bathrooms, bad singing, mad neighbors, birth pain.

Harmful/Destructive

War, terrorism, poverty, fatal diseases (AIDS, cancer), abuse (child, spouse, sexual), drug/alcohol, cigarette addiction, adultery, animal cruelty, crime, weapons (nuclear, biochemical, atomic), pollution, environmental damage (SUVs, unnecessary development), homelessness, hunger, poverty, crime (murder, rape), criminal use of guns, unemployment, birth defects, suicide, natural disasters (floods, hurricanes, tornadoes, forest fires, slavery, premature death, child laborers, torture of prisoners, obesity, anorexia, injuries (paralysis, burns, etc.), fanaticism, stereotyping, materialism, imperialism, communism, dictatorships, religious fanatics, discrimination, prejudice (racism, sexism, homophobia), the Ku Klux Klan, genocide, bullies, jealousy, envy, hatred, anger, rudeness, arrogance, paranoia, depression, sadness, road rage, gangs, embarrassment, boredom, laziness, greed, lying, fear, loneliness, inequality (class, gender, economic).

I then show them the book *The Giver*, with a bit of background about Lois Lowry and how this book came to be, using incidents from her Newbery Acceptance Speech from 1994. The book is an attempt to answer the question: What if we get rid of all of these inconvenient, destructive, and evil ways? What would society look like?

I don't tell students a lot more than this, as I want them to figure out what is going on in this book and what it means to a society, especially our society today and in the future.

Instead of making the students responsible for all of the vocabulary words, I divide the words among all the kids, giving each two or three. They must then put the word on a card in the sentence in which it was found (on the list I give them I tell them on which page they can find the word), with the definition based on the context of the sentence, and the etymology, or history of the word. They all do their words ahead of time so they are prepared. As we are about to read a chapter, those responsible for the words in that chapter tell us what the words mean and we put their cards on the wall. (The list of vocabulary from *The Giver* is on the website with other handouts, along with examples of vocabulary cards.)

**Online
8.10–8.14**

Several years ago I drew a storyboard (I have included that entire storyboard on the website after trying to have the students read and storyboard at the same time. Doing this for an entire novel is time-consuming and daunting. Now I use a large piece of poster board and insert my drawings that I have replicated on large index cards after we have read a chapter. The board is divided into four columns:

- what we learn from the chapter (especially about sameness)
- a space for my drawing of the happenings
- the advantages of the way this society is structured
- the disadvantages of the structure.

After we have read a chapter, I add the large index card of my drawing and we discuss what we noticed or found out and the advantages and the disadvantages of those things that are the same. In the meantime, I have given the students their own sheet that they have folded into four columns, headed by the passage: "The community was so meticulously ordered, the choices so carefully made" (48). "Like the matching of spouses and the naming and placement of new children, the assignments were scrupulously thought through by the Committee of Elders" (49). The columns are labeled:

SAMENESS   ADVANTAGES   DISADVANTAGES   LIKE TODAY

After each reading and discussion, they fill in their columns. I encourage them to talk this out so none of them miss anything.

As we read the novel, I frequently stop after a chapter and give the students a passage from the book, one that we have read and one that I know will stimulate their thinking and that may also lead to many different ways of drawing meaning from it. They glue this passage into their WRN and write a response or reaction to it. Sometimes I leave it at that—their response or reaction.

Following is my quickwrite in response to this passage about hair:

> Each child's hair was snipped neatly into its distinguishing cut; females lost their braids at Ten, and males, too, relinquished their long childish hair and took on the more manly short style which exposed their ears.
>
> Laborers moved quickly to the stage with brooms and swept away the mounds of discarded hair.
>
> (Lowry 1993, 46)

I think of my grandmother's hair—the white, tight curls that hugged her head after a perm. How soft it was to curl around my finger when I hung over her shoulder as she slept in a chair. I think of the long, black braid, coiled and stored in a tin box in her top bureau drawer.

And I think August—1944. While my grandmother was brushing and snipping, gathering and slipping those fine, blonde wisps of my hair from the linoleum floor into a tiny envelope, was some Nazi shaving the long, dark curls from Anne Frank's head at Bergen-Belsen? What did they do with the hair? ("Human hair will be processed into felt to be used in industry, and thread will be spun out of them . . . the cut-off women's hair will be used to make socks for submarine crews, and to make felt stockings for railroad workers . . . one kilo of hair was worth one-half Reichmarks." *The World Must Know*, p. 149.)

As the strands dropped to the dirt, what was Anne thinking? Could she find her curls swept into mounds? Did she reach down to save a strand, make a wish? Or was she too terrified, too embarrassed, too hungry to care? How much does a 14-year-old's head of hair weigh?

Other times I ask students to pass their notebooks around the table for response from their peers, a timed writing as the notebooks move from student to student. This is a written conversation of an issue. I am always in awe of the deep thinking from students who don't often speak aloud in class, but given the opportunity to voice their opinion in writing show sophistication and depth.

A write-around from one table of three students follows this passage about sameness and lack of color.

Passage from *The Giver* for Write-Around

"I'm right, then," The Giver said. "You're beginning to see the color red. . . . There was a time, actually . . . when flesh was many different colors. That was before we went to Sameness.

"We've never completely mastered Sameness. I suppose the genetic scientists are still hard at work trying to work the kinks out. Hair like Fiona's must drive them crazy.

"Why can't everyone see them? Why did colors disappear?"

"We relinquished color when we relinquished sunshine and did away with differences. . . . We gained control of many things. But we had to let go of others."

"We shouldn't have!" Jonas said fiercely.

(Lowry 1993, 94–95)

Write-Around Entry from Tom's Notebook

Tom: I don't really like the idea of sameness because I think people should be unique. Sameness is kind of like communism because they're trying to make everyone equal. I think that the decisions people make should decide the type of life they have. I think the government likes to take control of things in modern days.

William: I thought equality for everyone was good? But I guess that is what communism and this sameness started out as, but it never really worked. They sort of found out that everyone would never be equal. But they kept going and kept ignoring the fact that it wasn't really working. In most communist countries, everyone ends up poor except a few government officials.

Amy: I think that there is a difference between sameness and trying to make life more fair. For instance, when you cut a cake into an amount of slices so that everyone can have one, that is obviously a good thing. That is the same sort of concept as trying to meet everyone's needs. That's good. Trying to make people the same and take away differences, that's bad.

Tom: I guess communism and sameness are different but I don't really like either, especially sameness. I definitely wouldn't want everyone to be the same and without feelings. I think life would be boring and pointless without feelings. It would be like being a robot, you just do your job without feeling.

Write-Around Entry from William's Notebook

William: I guess the thought was that if there never was color, or sunshine, in a person's life, then they would never want any of those things. If you don't know of something it's very hard to miss it. But if you do, and you don't have it, then it is much more important. No one would even know that there could be colors the way it was set.

Amy: This is true. I wonder if people who are blind can understand the concept of color. They probably can't. And people who are deaf, that have never heard a sound, don't know what they're missing. But are they missing something? Or do they have a special gift that they wouldn't have without their disability? For example, would Steven Hawking still be such a phenomenal writer if he had no disabilities?

Tom: I don't think it really matters if there is because if you don't know about it you wouldn't miss it. It would be weird to find out that there's some weird thing out there that we can't see, like they couldn't see color. I wonder . . .

William: I guess sometimes I just sort of think about what could be better or more amazing than the world we have, and I couldn't think of anything. So maybe we are missing something but I sure don't notice if we are. And their lives were like that, they didn't know they were missing things. Maybe we are too. I don't know.

Write-Around Entry from Amy's Notebook

Amy: Genetic engineering. Those two words scare me. I picture a world full of people that have been designed, ordered, like you might order a hamburger at a restaurant. And I don't want that. I think it's sad that as a society we would choose to create our children to fit our likes. People are supposed to be born as individuals, individuals created from two people, not human beings whose genes have been altered. That's wrong, and the possibilities scare me.

Tom: I agree with you, I don't think people should be designed by other people. I think that they shouldn't mess with genes at all.

William: I don't think that we should tamper with genes either. But I think that for many people if they could choose exactly what their kids would be like they would do it. And now that they have figured out the genome code they will probably try changing genes, even though they say they are just using it for medicine. Maybe science is going too far.

Amy: I agree with what you said, Tom. And William, you bring up a good point about "maybe science is going too far." When you mentioned that parents will probably choose exactly what their kids will be like because of the info we have now, that's what scares me. Altering genes to create a "perfect society of people" is very similar to the premises of The Giver. But guess what, there is no such thing as a "perfect human being." Humans are full of imperfections and we should embrace those imperfections, instead of trying to do away with them.

Notice the variety and depth of the issues in which these three students engaged in this one write-around. These kinds of conversations work so well, especially when the piece of literature (a poem, or an op-ed piece, or an essay) is difficult to understand. The kids help each other deepen their thinking.

By looking back at the four-column chart the students kept as we read, we collect all the topics brought about in this novel:

euthanasia (mercy killing, care of the elderly, putting down animals, death penalty)

genetic engineering (genome code, test tube babies, birth defects and disabilities, surrogates, birth mothers and birth fathers, sperm and egg donors)

food (healthy eating, eating disorders)

drugs (use of, abuse of)

pollution

self-esteem

material possessions

crime

"Big Brother" control (news, video cameras, speakers, etc.)

sameness (no choices)

> no feelings

> no color

family (spouse/children, divorce, envy, child abuse)

volunteering

jobs

clothes

hair

culture

travel

one-generation memories

painful memories abolished (war, homelessness, hunger, poverty, envy, jealousy, fear, prejudice, homophobia, etc.).

By looking back at their charts, and at the class chart we keep with the storyboard, students have lots of notes from which to collect ideas for writing a personal or a more formal essay focused on one issue that fosters their curiosity. In their notes on these resources they have the issue, the advantages of doing what they do in this community, and the disadvantages. They can further extend their thinking by researching the ways we treat this issue in our society or in other societies today. The question often becomes, how close are we moving toward the society of *The Giver* with all the rules and abundance of choices, or lack thereof, in our lives?

These are developed as personal essays, often illustrated with a personal story. Alanna wrote a piece about a fallen tree deep in the woods that became her sanctuary, a place that never could have existed for her in *The Giver*. It begins:

> My family barely noticed when I disappeared for hours at a time. I went out to the tree to read, listen to music, write, and sometimes just lay over the water, self-absorbed or enjoying the sun. It's perfect. Secluded, private, and yet open and beautiful. Most days I lay out in the sun until it began to set, turning the opposite bank and the water golden and red.

**Online
8.15–8.18**

On the website you can read the full pieces of writing from Morgan, who I mentioned in the Introduction, writing about the beach, divorce and love. Isabelle tells us about the decision to put her dog Katie down, Yasmine, her first wake, and Jules, his uncle's connection to 9/11 on his way to his job near the World Trade Center. You can see the first to last draft of Jules' writing, where he began, and how this writing grew and changed. All connected to *The Giver* and the students' personal stories and beliefs drawn from all Lowry is saying about this dystopian community.

If I think we have spent an adequate amount of time reading, discussing, and writing about this book, I would rather leave the kids feeling good about the book instead of browbeating it to death and leaving them hating it. When the students tell me they understand the following big ideas (the points Lowry seemed to be making), I know they took more than I hoped for and they don't *need* to write an essay to test their knowledge.

However, if I want them to write an essay, these big ideas make the perfect "thesis statements" to begin the writing. They stem from the students. The students have a connection to these statements. They have the examples from the book that give them a context and support their thinking. They have stories of their own that personalize and extend all their thinking from the book.

When I ask, "What is this story about?" they say:

- Choices—we all want and need choices, even if we make some bad ones. Decision making helps us get better at what we do, even when we make mistakes. It is important to have options in life and not be forced to do and be things you don't like.

- Memories are important, both the good and the bad. They keep us happy remembering the good ones, and help us not to repeat the bad things.

- In an attempt to get rid of the bad, we often lose the good.

- There is no such thing as a perfect society.

- It is a bad thing when government gets too powerful. Individual peoples' lives become obsolete when that happens.

- Diversity makes the world interesting. It is not a good thing to isolate ourselves from others.

- If something is not the way it should be, try to change it and make things better.

It pleases me to see students build on some segment of this book when they choose topics of their own. I've shown them many times—in the quickwrites we do again and again—how writing from a short piece of writing or a quote often leads us into pieces we didn't expect to write.

We choose a book to read aloud with our students because we know it will make them think and feel something about themselves and make them pay more attention to the world. Just because there are twenty-five copies of a book in the storeroom does not mean that book is worth reading with kids.

CHAPTER NINE

Under the Influence of Writers: Author-Genre Studies

Goals for the Students

- Read and enjoy the works of a particular author or a variety of authors who write in the same genre.
- Notice and learn something about the craft of writing from these works (read deeply and intentionally).
- Try on some of the craft techniques of the authors in their own writing.
- Recognize and describe what a writer's technique does to affect the writing and the reader.
- Extend their understandings, their enjoyment, their range, and their success at reading and writing.
- Learn about the author's thoughts on reading and writing.

Throughout the year, I ask students to read like a writer; notice what writers do that make them sit up and say, "I wish I could write like that." It's why I ask them to find and collect leads, endings, unique phrasing, character or setting descriptions, unusual stylistic techniques that make them marvel at how writers engage us as readers. When we begin to read with an even deeper eye on authors as mentors, I ask them who their favorite athletes, coaches, musicians, or humanitarians are. What makes them a favorite? Why do they admire them?

Hannah says she admires Abby Ryne because "she really pushes herself and works really hard to make it to the U.S. team." Zack admires Chris Kyle "because he has helped the most people in military history. He has the most confirmed kills and is willing to give his life for his brothers." Abby, who loves to read, says, "Jane Austen really inspires me because in her books she is funny, intelligent, and a real feminist." Nate says he respects Rosa Parks for "her bravery, her toughness, and her pride." Katie, who wants to work in some area of astronomy or astrophysics, admires "Jerrie Cobb because she worked so hard to be able to get her dream to go into space. When she was told she couldn't, she didn't take it lying down."

As a teacher, I have mentor-teaching authors, who I greatly respect, admire, and want to emulate. I surround myself with their books and articles, devouring everything I can that they write. I travel hours to conferences to listen to these professionals speak. I look for their blogs on line. I love their writing for the stories they tell of their classrooms. I admire the rapport they develop with their students. I respect their honesty in admitting mistakes, constantly reflecting on their teaching and what they could do better to reach more kids.

Most of all, I am in awe of their ability to get their students to love reading and to produce such sophisticated, engaging pieces of writing. I respect the tenacity, patience, intelligence, passion, and heart they bring to their teaching. I notice and pay attention to what they do and how they do it. I want to bring the best of these teachers into my teaching, while still being myself. These are my mentors: Nancie Atwell, Penny Kittle, Tom Romano, Maureen Barbieri, Kate Messner, Tom Newkirk, Maja Wilson, Meredith Hall, Kelly Gallagher, and Jim Burke, just to name a few. I pay attention to what these educators do as teachers, whether in elementary, secondary, or college classrooms and how they think and write about their classrooms. They are my teaching, and my writing-about-teaching mentors.

The kids can always name the qualities of the people whom they admire (too often athletes and actors), and what it is they do that makes them so good. "So let's give the same attention to our reading," I say. "Who are the authors that you admire? What is it they do to keep you turning to their books or recommending them to other readers? What do they do as writers that you wish you could do, that you would like to try?" I want students to bring the best of the authors they read into their writing, while maintaining their own voices and styles.

Of course, they have been doing this in a more informal way for the entire year, as they read, collect passages and writing techniques they notice, and respond to that reading in their writer's-reader's notebooks (WRNs). Now we will go into more depth to notice, describe, and emulate what these authors do.

In her latest book, *Finding the Heart of Nonfiction*, Georgia Heard explains the origin of the word *mentor*.

> The word *mentor* comes from the ancient Greek poem *The Odyssey*, by Homer. Mentor was Odysseus' confidante, faithful friend, and reliable steward with whom he entrusted his home and family when he was away on his journeys . . .
> In a writing community, a mentor text is literature that is used by writers to study craft and genre, and to inspire writing as well as vision. (2013, 3)

What a wonderful story to share with kids—thinking of mentor writers as faithful friends and stewards from whom you are inspired and taught to develop your writing—in the same way you pay attention to and try some of the techniques learned from trusted athletes, artists, and musicians. (Actually, *I* find the faithful friends and stewards a wonderful metaphor. The kids yawn, shake their heads, and pretend they agree, asking each other what a "steward" is as they leave the classroom talking about their sports' heroes.)

They do understand *mentor*—someone you admire, who coaches you through something you want to do better. How to use the authors as mentors is where they need guidance. I help them pay attention to longer and more complicated writing by guiding them through shorter, simpler pieces that are more accessible. Why are they more accessible? Because the kids have already read some of these stories in a previous grade. ("Hey—we already read this," they say. "Why are we reading this again?")

This is intentional on my part. In their first reading in sixth or seventh grade, they were concentrating on the story. Now when we read them again, we are looking at the craft. What did this writer do and how did he or she do it? If rereading something is one of the best ways to comprehend it better, why aren't we reading more pieces of literature more than once?

I give the students the handout that describes an overview of our study with a list of recommended authors. We go through the requirements together, while I point out examples from previous years that I have posted of each kind of writing expected. I use several different samples from boys and girls, but I put up the strongest work. I set the standards high and I expect kids to give me their best effort. I will give them my best effort as I recommend authors to them, as I conference with them through their drafts of writing, and as we work together to take note of what writers do to craft memorable writing.

As we go through the recommended authors, I also hold up several books from each genre, with a quick book talk about some of these authors whom kids in the past have identified as some of their favorites. After going through these expectations, showing kids previous work and authors they might consider, I give them the interest sheet to gauge their thinking. They don't have to fill it in right away, but within a few days they should know what they want to read and with whom they will work. On the website, you will find all of the handouts I use for this entire study.

**Online
9.1–9.17**

Guiding the Students Through Models

I guide the students through a variety of models, before I turn them loose to gather all they find about craft from their own mentor authors. The first three stories on this list we read together and chart together, using the categories I want students to pay special attention to as they read on their own. I also want to give students a systematic way for gathering information from their reading. We read:

"All Summer in a Day" (science fiction) by Ray Bradbury

"Lamb to the Slaughter" (mystery) by Roald Dahl

"A Couple of Kooks" (realistic fiction) by Cynthia Rylant

It is only these first three stories that we chart together. Just to make sure they understand how to gather information on their own, I have them read either "Stray" by Cynthia Rylant (1985, 42–47) or "Going Steady" by Adam Bagdasarian (2002, 50–57), and have them chart their findings in partners—the partner with whom they will read for this author study. We go over their findings, along with my findings as I read and charted the story, so we can add to our findings.

Online
9.6

Let's take one of those stories, "Lamb to the Slaughter," to see how we talk about it, after we read it. We look at each of the categories, where we have collected Dahl's words and talk about what we notice.

Lead

How engaging is the lead? He describes the room and everything Mary Maloney is doing to get ready for her husband's return—she is calm, and methodical—caring—prepares everything for him—almost doting: drink ready, hangs up his coat, wants to get his slippers—the lead is almost boring, describing someone waiting for her husband to come home from work—maybe the lead is meant to make the reader think everything is normal, natural—and when she kills him we are in complete shock because it is so unexpected—maybe the author does that on purpose, to shock the reader as much as Patrick Maloney shocked his wife.

Characters

What do we know about the characters? Mary Maloney is six months pregnant, methodical, meticulous housekeeper, doting wife; Patrick Maloney is a policeman, never really says he wants a divorce but he insinuates he wants to leave without a fuss as it would be bad for his job—he is cold to want a divorce and to tell his wife this, especially since she is six months pregnant. We don't know much else about him. Why does the author tell us so many little details about all she does to straighten up the house and get things ready for her husband? Why don't we know more about him?

What hooks us now into the story? The questions: Why is her husband so silent, not talking to her? What does he want to tell her? What will she do now that she knows he wants to leave her? After she kills him with the frozen leg of lamb, will she get caught? So wanting to know the answers to questions that build seems to hook us into a story.

Memorable Wording

". . . watched him in dazed horror as he went further and further away from her with each word" (1995, 27). "All right, so I've killed him" (1995, 28). We wonder, is she in shock, or perhaps she is meticulous in all she does, certainly as she goes about coming up with an alibi, so quickly, so meticulously . . . she practices what she will say to the grocer, and then is so calm talking to him.

Ending

"Personally, I think it's right here on the premises . . . under our very noses . . ." (1995, 39). We talk about the irony of the ending, because the murder weapon is literally under their very noses as they are eating it. The evidence is figuratively under their noses also. This is an ambiguous ending because they might figure it out—but, what can they do, they ate the evidence. And they can't tell anyone even if they figure it out because it would certainly make them look stupid.

Unique about the Crafting

"And he told her . . ." (1995, 27). In four words we can imagine what he told her but we don't have to hear the way he did it—any other reasons, we ask?—maybe Mary Maloney is in such shock that she doesn't hear it either—only that he wants to leave her—other conversation with the detectives is not told in direct dialogue—as if Mary Maloney is hearing someone else talk to them—in shock still?—The irony of the ending, that the detectives ate the evidence.

Title

"Lamb to the Slaughter." Who is the lamb to the slaughter? What does that expression mean? Where did it come from? I tell them it originally came from the Bible, where the innocent lambs are brought to be killed, and now it means someone who is brought in to a situation not knowing it's going to be bad for them—again I ask, "Who is the lamb brought to the slaughter?" And these are all the different ideas the kids come up with:

- Mary Maloney, because she is so innocent and doesn't know her husband wants a divorce, but it could be
- Patrick Maloney, because he has no idea his wife will react the way she does, by slugging him with a frozen leg of lamb, but it could be

- The grocer, because she really fooled him into thinking she really was cooking a meal for her husband, but it could be

- The detectives, because even if they finally figure it out, they can't say anything because they ate the evidence, but it could be

- The unborn baby, if it's about someone innocent not suspecting something bad could happen to them—the baby's mother killed the father, and that could affect the baby someday—she'll have to tell it lies about its father for its whole life, it could be

- All of them—no one suspected what was going to happen—even us, the reader—maybe that's what makes a good story—we really didn't expect any of this. Do you think the author knew all this before he started writing the story? (Not my question—the students.)

In this author-genre study, I am trying to get kids to think about how authors craft a lead, create characters, use setting, choose unique wording and use dialogue, craft an ending, select a title. With each story read as a model, we talk about the way each of these elements is crafted and what it does to the writing. That's what I want kids to pay attention to—what does this do to the writing? How does what the author did in crafting the story make us think different things, draw different conclusions? Why does Ann Turner tell her story as poetry in *Learning to Swim*? Why is *Persepolis* told in pictures done with thick black lines? Why does Cynthia Rylant choose not to tell us the ending in *A Couple of Kooks*? What's the evidence in each of these stories that leads us to certain conclusions about what these craft techniques do to the story and the way if affects a reader?

These are big questions for kids as readers, but these are the questions that lead them to read deeply and critically. If we can teach kids to read with intent, it will help them write with intent.

In conjunction with reading and talking about many of the stories that follow, I give the kids a blank chart for their use as they read on their own. They do not have to use these charts. If it is more helpful to come up with their own way of gathering and organizing all they notice, they may do that. They have to show me what they will do, however. They have to have a plan, and they have to use it. Many of the students set up these charts on the computer and gather notes into a digital chart as they read. I want them to be able to compare findings from various books, which is why the chart works best—it is laid out in a visual format that helps kids see the comparisons and contrasts in their author's works.

Reading poetry, memoir, op-ed pieces, or graphic novels means the students have to tweak the categories (with my guidance) on the chart, although in most reading, they can make the categories work for any genre they choose to read.

We read these remaining pieces together, talk about them, and gather notes on a more open-ended chart—Summarizing Ideas for Writing (on the website). I include the first three stories

Online
9.6

and *The Outsiders* on this chart, because we have read them all and I want the students to think about how rich all of these pieces are with ideas for writing for them, as well as craft ideas.

Short Pieces that We Read Together

Excerpt (pp. 33–45) from *Boy*—"Mrs. Pratchett" (memoir) by Roald Dahl

"Fish Cheeks" (Holt 2008, 10–12) (personal essay) by Amy Tan

"It's All About the Lies" (op-ed essay) by Rick Reilly

"The Follower" (Scieszka 2005, 79–83) (personal narrative) by Jack Gantos

"Your Question for Author Here" (Scieszka 2010, 101–126) (realistic fiction) by Kate DiCamillo and Jon Scieszka

excerpt from *Persepolis* (memoir as graphic novel) by Marjane Satrapi

excerpt from *Stitches* (memoir as graphic novel) by David Small

excerpt from *Diary of a Wimpy Kid* (realistic fiction as comic) by Jeff Kinney

excerpt from *The Absolutely True Diary of a Part-Time Indian* (realistic fiction) by Sherman Alexie

excerpt (five poems) from *The Secret of Me* (creative memoir as poetry) by Meg Kearney

I use either Kinney's work or Alexie's work, as there isn't time to do both. Sometimes I don't make it through all of these because of time constraints. I want to give the students enough models that really excite them to read more on their own, but not so many that they are overwhelmed. By reading a variety of pieces such as these, I am trying to give kids examples of the kinds of writing they might want to try and, therefore, might want to read to gather even more ideas.

Planning and Timing of Author-Genre Study

What does each week look like during this author study, which takes a full quarter, a full eight weeks? For the first two weeks, I introduce the students to all we will do, showing them examples from previous years, reading the models, and charting our findings together. The routine for the next four weeks then becomes:

Monday Through Wednesday

- trying different kinds of writing through quickwrites and minilessons (fiction, memoir, poetry) and time for writing
- drafting writing
- homework: reading books and charting findings

Thursday Through Friday

- reading books in class, sharing and discussing findings with partners
- looking at book reviews, summarizing the genre, drafting reviews of recommended books
- homework: reading books and charting findings

If students choose to read novels, I expect them to read at least three. If they are reading short stories or op-ed pieces, I expect them to read at least seven to ten. While they are charting information about the craft of this writing, I am still expecting them to respond or react to the big ideas in these books and their connections to themselves or the world in their WRNs.

In the last two weeks of the study, we concentrate on developing their writing, completing process papers that describe the drafting of their writing and its connections to what they noticed from their mentor authors, and writing the book reviews or informational pamphlets to share their findings. (Some years I ask the students to do the book reviews; other years I ask them to do the pamphlets. I don't ask them to do both. Time becomes a factor, as well as what I realize the kids need to know and do better.)

During the entire study, I am constantly conferring with kids individually or in small groups and giving them time to write and to conference with each other.

We share their final pieces of writing in a reader's theatre format, meaning, if there is spoken dialogue in a piece, students gather peers to read those parts. We practice reading aloud with voice and feeling. Before they read their writing, students spend a few minutes telling the class what they learned from their author mentor and how they tried to incorporate those techniques into their own writing. This is a celebration of writing, honoring all they have done.

Minilessons During Study

I try to keep these to a minimum as I have set the study up so the students learn the most from their mentor authors, especially things we have not, and might not, touch on otherwise. That's the purpose of having mentor authors. But I do give them some guidance in these genres.

The professional books that are most helpful to me as I plan for lessons in various genres are Don Murray's *Crafting a Life in Essay, Story and Poem*, Georgia Heard's *Awakening the Heart* and *Finding the Heart of Nonfiction*, and Ralph Fletcher's *What a Writer Needs*. There are hundreds of others, and most of them line my bookshelves, each with tabs where I want to remember some splendid idea. But it is overwhelming to try to identify, let alone read, the thousands of books by good teachers and writers who have such great ideas. I use what I can get to. I am sure there is so much more I could be learning and doing.

Fiction: Short Stories

After reading several fictional stories together, specifically ones from the list earlier in this chapter, I ask the kids to list what they notice about these short stories. What are the characteristics inherent in this kind of writing that makes it different from poetry or essay or memoir? I gather their findings, which you will find on the website under Short Story Characteristics. After compiling this list from all classes, I give this to the kids, which they glue into the notes section of their WRNs and use when they are drafting this kind of writing. Nancie Atwell has a comprehensive description of helping kids develop fictional pieces, called "Some Elements of Fiction: A Writer's Decisions," in her book *In the Middle* (1998). I use Nancie's information based on the needs I see from the kids as they draft their writing.

Fiction: Let's Try Some

As the students are writing, I draw from the handout Fiction: Let's Try Some (on the website) at the beginning of several class periods—write about a flaw that has gotten you in trouble, describe yourself from the point of view of someone who dislikes you, and so on—during the week, intermingling the quick lessons with memoir, poetry, and writing with pictures. Although I plan on doing everything I've included here in this study, time often runs out. I base what I keep and what I let go of on all I see that the kids need in the time we have left. Sometimes we go over eight weeks. So be it. The kids are usually deeply engaged in reading and writing if that happens.

A very simple first step into developing a fictional piece is to take a piece of personal narrative and make up a name for the "I" character. It allows us to exaggerate, to lie, to build a character. When I first wrote "When I was 15 I believed . . ." (in *100 Quickwrites* [2003]) and changed the *I* to *she* ("When she was 15, she believed . . ."), I was amazed how easy it was to add things that were not true as I wrote about this "character" who was no longer me.

Using Pictures to Find Writing

Several weeks after school began this year, five of my former eighth graders, now freshmen, stopped in to visit. They asked how the book was coming (I've been working on this book for years and sharing parts each eighth-grade year). When I mentioned still having to write this chapter, Kobi immediately said, "I hope you told them about using pictures—those Harris Burdick pictures—I got my best piece of writing for the whole year from doing that."

The Mysteries of Harris Burdick by Chris Van Allsburg

This is a collection of black-and-white pictures, each accompanied by a title and caption that could be an introduction to the story. But the stories, if there were any, are missing in this original collection put together by Van Allsburg. I tell the kids the story behind these drawings.

Thirty years ago a man by the name of Harris Burdick brought his drawings to Peter Wenders, then a children's publisher, to see if he was interested in the work. Burdick left the fourteen drawings with Wenders, promising to return the next day with the stories that accompanied them. He never returned. Wenders spent many years trying to find this man with no luck. Van Allsburg first saw the drawings in Wenders' home many years later and reproduced them in a book in the hopes of inspiring children to write their own stories from them.

I took apart my copy of the book, carefully cutting the pages from the binding and gluing the title and phrase that accompanies each picture onto the back of the picture. I spread the pictures on the tables around my room, inviting the kids to wander from table to table looking at the pictures and the captions until something they see in one of the pictures inspires an idea for writing. I tell them, "Sit with the picture. Look at it carefully. Write what comes to mind in your WRN."

Fiona chose the picture titled "The Harp" and wrote:

> The misty sun filtered through the leaves, giving the thick, leafy woods a greenish-gold hue. The ground was damp, unable to dry itself through the layers of fallen leaves and marshy grass, the flowers choking on its forever moist, dark dirt. The boy knew there was no way for anyone to tell what secret horrors had happened here so long ago—the whole forest had an enchanted calm on it, as though the trees that had been bent out of shape all those years ago were healing themselves in the quiet. The boy loved the woods. Everywhere he looked he saw a story. Or, rather, he made a story for everywhere he looked. Usually he would bring a sailboat or toy soldiers on these secret excursions, flinging them into the river, marching them down rocks, burying them in soft riverbank sand. But today the boy had nothing with him but his dog—a companion to fight his new found feeling of eeriness when he stepped into the forest. Though he had been warned many times not to go to the brook in the heart of the woods, he had never had reason to fear it—until now.
>
> There he stood on the bank, walking stick shaking in his hand, his dog's ears pricked to the haunting music. Downstream was THE HARP.
>
> So it's true, he thought, it's really true. Down the babbling stream sat ripples, dark and alive. In front of them sat a harp, its strings plucking an invisible tune. Dropping his walking stick and covering his ears, he splashed

noisily through the shallow stream, jumping off the waterfall and stopping, dead still, next to the ripples. The delicate, golden strings of the harp continued to bounce over each other, their music a frightening sweetness.

He uncovered his ears.

Inspiration—a picture. Ten minutes of fast writing that she may or may not develop into a story. Tension. A boy. A dog. The frightening sweetness coming from the golden strings of a harp. Captured, in her WRN if she needs it. She decides.

Kobi used "Oscar and Alphonse," with the caption "She knew it was time to send them back. The caterpillars softly wiggled in her hand, spelling out 'goodbye.'"

In his process paper for the author study he wrote:

> The idea for the story came from a response I did to a picture by Harris Burdick. It was a picture of a girl, maybe 8 or 9 years old, standing at the edge of a forest, with sunlight and a breeze all around her. She held a caterpillar cupped in her hands, and she had a gentle smile on her face. This picture gave me the setting for my story.
>
> As I revised my writing, I used the information on my chart to make the next draft better. I read Ray Bradbury stories and noticed that in every single one of his stories there was something unexpected that you couldn't predict. I tried to put similar things in my story to make it more interesting. Also, Ray Bradbury added a lot of details, but often left the ends of his stories ambiguous, and left it up to the reader to connect the final dots of his plot. This is something that I realized was very difficult to do. I still tried, though, to add subtle clues and intriguing details to my story, without giving all of the answers at the end.

**Online
9.18**

His first-draft writing became his story for his author study, taking the idea from this picture and weaving in all he learned from reading Ray Bradbury. His writing "The Night Forest," along with his process paper explaining what he did, can be read in their entirety on the website.

There is another version of this book (*The Chronicles of Harris Burdick*) now out that includes stories by well-known authors, such as Jon Scieszka, Stephen King, Lois Lowry, Walter Dean Myers, and Kate DiCamillo, that were each written in response to one of the fourteen pictures. These could be read before or after showing the pictures to students to stimulate their ideas.

Another way to help students find writing, especially fictional ideas, is to have them start writing about a picture, write for three minutes, and pass the writing to the person on their right (if they are at tables of four and five). This is a write-around, a written conversation where kids are helping other kids extend their ideas. That person reads what the previous person wrote and continues the writing for three minutes. And so on all the way around the table. The original writer might be inspired to continue developing the piece, or any of the writers might find a phrase or paragraph that got them thinking about a piece of their own.

I have done this with the Harris Burdick pictures and with art postcards. With the post-cards, I ask kids to choose one from the hundreds I have collected and write a scene or create a character. Who is in this scene or could be in this scene? What is going on?

Or, they could write for three to five minutes, and pass their writing to the right, where the next person adds to the writing. Might be fiction. Might be real. It is just another way to help kids find and develop ideas. One method does not work for all kids, but many methods help most kids find ideas.

Or, they could recreate the postcard or a portion of it by drawing it. It is in the recreation of the card, the time it takes to draw it, that ideas often come to them. Once they draw it, I ask them to write from it. Step into the card, or your drawing. What is going on? Who is there? Not there? What is happening? Has happened?

No matter how and where they get their ideas, as they craft those ideas, we continually look back at what makes an effective fictional story—realistic fiction, science fiction, fantasy, mystery—and see if the writer is considering those elements as she drafts her writing. Of course, each genre has distinct elements that identify it as such: science fiction is set in the future, considering what we already know in science and technology and building on what seems plausible; fantasy is usually set in the past—but not always—building on elements of things that don't exist and most likely cannot (unicorns, wizards, magic, etc.). What I always want kids to keep in mind though, is not to let form dictate story. Let the story find its form as it develops.

Memoir

Students often ask me, "What's the difference between personal narrative and memoir?" I think personal narrative relates a story, just the happening, while memoir relates the story and includes a reflection on the meaning of the story. Why do we remember this? What did it mean to us? Why does this memory matter? What is the "So what?" of it?

Memoir is the uncovering of the significance or the truth of an experience. Which makes me ask, "What's the difference between memoir and personal essay?" If there are significant differences, I think they are too small to quibble over. (I am sure I will hear from a few people setting me straight on this.)

JoAnn Portalupi, in a workshop she did many years ago in my classroom, says memoir fuels all the writing we do. Living in New Hampshire most of my life, I know what she meant when she said, "Memory is like the rocks in New Hampshire, always rising to the surface. Memoir is picking up that rock, that memory, and turning it round and round, and asking, 'Why does this rock keep coming up?'"

"We write memoir," she said, "to have a better understanding of the experience and of ourselves."

Don Murray, in *Crafting a Life*, says,

> At first, most writers just write personal narratives—the fishing trip with father, the divorce, the death of a grandparent. These are not essays; they are simple chronological accounts . . . the writer needs to make the next step, turning this narrative into a personal essay. The essay looks at narrative experience critically—empathetically but evaluative—putting experience in a larger context, trying on the patterns of meaning hidden within the experience. This is critical thinking; the essay takes a broad experience and narrows it down so that it can be examined, or takes a narrow experience and discovers the broader issues that lie within it . . . it allows the writer to relive a personal experience of importance to the writer and discover a context and pattern of meaning that will make it significant to the reader. (1996, 57)

I need to know this so I can teach it to kids and answer their question as directly as possible: Memoir or personal essay is telling an experience while figuring out the reason or significance of remembering it.

We go back to several of the pieces we read together (earlier in this chapter) and talk about the significance of these memories. Why does Amy Tan remember this one meal so strongly? Why does this episode in *Boy* stay with Roald Dahl? In what way is he turning it over and over again in his memory looking at the meaning of this "rock"?

Several years ago in a graduate class I taught at the University of New Hampshire, Garret Hinebauch wrote "The Frogs of My Youth." Garret, now a teacher at the International School in Zurich, Switzerland, initially began this piece as a quickwrite in response to the poem "Bullfrogs" by David Allen Evans. He drafted the piece again and again—into a wonderful memoir, or personal essay, that I read with my students as a good example of how this kind of writing is crafted. (See Figure 9.1.)

Figure 9.1 *"The Frogs of My Youth" by Garrett Hinebauch*

The Frogs of My Youth

by Garret Hinebauch

I sold frogs for a living. Not ceramic ones painted with smiles and pastels, real ones looking up with forlorn eyes, trying to get away from my hand as I reached into the green wooden box to count out a dozen, hopping against the sides like muted popcorn.

I was ten and these frogs were sold for a $1.50 a dozen to be used for bait. My two cousins, my sister, and I would take to the paths of my grandparent's resort in Maine at dusk to search for the frogs needed to supply bait for the visiting bass fishermen. Frogs come out at dusk to eat the bugs that are active at night. They came out from their hiding places along the shore or amongst the low bushes and found their way to the footpath, an open space where they would wait for their dinner. In order to catch the frogs, we hunters would carry flashlights to locate and incapacitate our prey. Frogs, like a deer in the headlights, will freeze for several seconds when caught in a flashlight beam before hopping off. A good frog catcher can spot the frog, freeze it with his light, and scoop it up with his free hand in a matter of seconds. An accomplished frog catcher anticipates the frog's moves if the light doesn't do its job and becomes adept at grabbing at the spot where the frog is going. Sometimes even grabbing at a spot without actually seeing the frog, relying on the sense of hearing to locate and capture the little jumping creature. On most nights the four of us would catch between five and ten dozen frogs. Our all time high was fourteen dozen and seven, or one hundred and seventy five frogs, captured between 8:00 and 9:30 pm. Business deals took place after breakfast the following morning. Verbal contracts were made and deliveries to each cabin followed, transferring the frogs to a fisherman's own frog box.

Fishing with frogs entails hooking the frog through the mouth, bottom lip to top, with a gasp and a gurgle. It is then tossed overboard and pulled to the bottom with weights to be gummed and chewed by a passing bass. With any luck, the fish will feel comfortable enough with the frog to swallow it, hook and all. A well timed yank will set the hook and then the fight is on. However, sometimes the fish is missed and the frog is pulled right out of its mouth, reeled in with little skin left on its legs.

How could I have done this to the frogs of my youth? I struggle with the urge to tell my stories to Oliver as I show him the delicate features of a live frog for the first time, for these were the creatures that brought me together with my sister and cousins. Small webbed feet, almost

continues

It's helpful to give students a memoir like Garret's and ask them to point out the personal experience he is talking about and locate the place in the writing where he begins to shift his thinking to the significance of the experience. As a writer, how does he do that?

Lois Lowry's piece "1943" in her book *Looking Back* is a good memoir to look at also because of the simplicity of the piece but the clear reflection she is doing from which we can infer how she felt about the entire incident.

Figure 9.1 *continued*

fingers on the front. Creatures that helped create the memories and adventures of my youth. Strong powerful toes for jumping on the back. Who were a means to the money with which I funded the trips to the country store to buy candy cigarettes and bazooka bubble gum. Delicate ears are the circles to the rear of the eyes. Soft browns and muted greens of the skin help it blend in to its surroundings. Do I tell Oliver that I sacrificed these creatures for money and for sport? Do I tell Oliver the sordid history behind my interest in frogs?

I struggle with this same issue when we eat chicken or beef for dinner. What goes through Oliver's head when a chicken breast is put down in front of him while just moments before, we were reading his book about Henny and the Tomten. Just yesterday, he asked if the red thing hurt to eat. "What red thing?" I asked. "The red thing on the Daddy chickens," he replied, referring to the rooster's comb. What will I say when he asks where bacon comes from? Well, do you know the three little pigs or Toot and Puddle? He is starting to ask about death and killing. Does he make the connection between Buttercup in his book and the hamburger we eat for dinner? How do I explain to him where it came from?

Could I look a frog in the eye today and coldly hook it through its soft skin on the underside of its mouth, milky white like Elmer's glue, speckled with brown spots? Silencing him, sealing his lips together, and piercing his nose? I do not think so.

But have I really changed? Have I become more compassionate? or just more selective in how I choose to show my compassion? I still eat chicken and meat, but the killing is so far removed from my life. The killing process for these animals is humane, I hope, not a slow torture: reaching up with front legs, grabbing the hook with tiny webbed toes, trying to remove the object that is causing so much pain, being dragged to the bottom to await its death.

I still fish with Oliver, using worms or mussels, not frogs, for bait. There are no forlorn eyes to look up and to question why. With the worms, only an agonized wriggling at times. With the mussel, nothing. It just lies there as I crack open its shell and cut up its insides as bait. Have I changed? or have I transferred my cruelty to beings that elicit less guilt as I end their lives?

I used to sell frogs for a living. Now I kill creatures to provide entertainment for my son.

Poetry

I think the best way to teach poetry is to read it. Constantly. So many of the models I use for quickwrites all year are poems. The kids see how poems are shaped and hear how they sound as I read them aloud. They begin to shape their words into poetry. They internalize the patterns, the nuances, the shaping, and the line breaks before we even talk about it. I specifically read a collection of several poems from Meg Kearney's *The Secret of Me* because she has so much to teach kids about reading and writing poems in this one book. In the book's afterword, she talks about her own life as an adoptee. She also explains many of the forms and devices Lizzie (the fictional main character) uses to craft these poems and why she chose to write them this way. She includes a short "guide to poetics," which I use, with examples from her poems, to teach kids more specifically about poetry: end-stopped lines versus enjambed lines; free verse and list poems; rhyme, end rhyme, near rhyme, internal rhyme; alliteration, simile, and metaphor; repetition; and so on.

I show students several more poems that stand alone, usually from the poetry challenge we did at the beginning of the year or that students have written in the past. We talk about all we notice, why poets use line breaks and shapes, how they use or don't use punctuation, why they might have selected certain words, and what seems common to poems.

I want students to have some guidelines to hold onto as they write poems, but I don't want to limit their creative possibilities with too many restrictions. I share what I have learned from my students and from Meg Kearney, Georgia Heard, Ralph Fletcher, Naomi Shihab Nye, and Paul Janeczko, listed as Notes on Poetry Writing on the website. On the List of Recommended Authors for this study (also on the website), I note several authors who write novels as free verse poetry. By far, Meg Kearney's, Ann Turner's, Sharon Creech's, Patricia McCormick's, Sonya Sones', and Ellen Hopkins' books are the most compelling ones for my students as they study poetry as novel.

Additional resources available online

Online
9.3, 9.10

Using Pictures to Stimulate Poetry

In the same way that I use pictures to help kids find ideas for fictional writing, I use pictures and poems from *Something Permanent* (Walker and Rylant 1994), *Heart to Heart* (Greenberg 2001), *Songs of Myself* (Heard 2000), and *Clotheslines* (Tymorek 2001) to help kids find poetry. I choose a picture, show them the picture, and have them either write from the picture by stepping into it or by showing them the picture and reading them the poem that accompanies it and asking them to write from the poem (anything that comes to mind) or write from a line from the poem.

I return during the study to Meg Kearney's collection of poems to reinforce what we noticed in her poetry, coupling her story with several poems from McCormick's *Sold*, so kids can really see how the poems build the story. We also talk about why the author might have decided to tell this particular story as poetry. In what ways did the topic and the feeling lead to a format?

As with all the other genres, I expect the kids to learn the most from their mentor authors, which is why I give them so much time to read and write.

Graphic Writing (in Pictures)

As we look at the examples of graphic novels, we look at the lead picture, who the characters are, the hook that draws us in, something unique about the way the story is crafted, and the ending. But we also look at the differences in:

- style and design of the images
  - kinds of lines used: dark and heavy, or light
    - simple or complex
    - cartoonish or realistic
  - black and white or color
- layout and sequence of events
  - long shots or close-ups
  - full frames or open
  - depth of field: two-dimensional or three-dimensional
  - use of foreground and background
- use of text with the images
  - dialogue: in narration or word balloons

Mainly we are looking to see how the author tells the story and why he or she might have chosen this particular way. How does the design enhance the story?

I never thought I would like graphic novels because I enjoy the crafting of words so much. However, I began reading *Persepolis* and suddenly realized I was completely engaged in her story and wasn't even noticing the fact I was reading pictures or that it was any different from reading prose or poetry.

Recommended Graphic Novels

Timothy Decker: *For Liberty; Run Far, Run Fast*

Sid Jacobson and Ernie Colon: *The 9/11 Report*

Marjane Satrapi: *Persepolis I* and *II*

Brian Selznick: *The Invention of Hugo Cabret*

David Small: *Stitches*

Jeff Smith: Bone series

Art Spiegelman: *Maus I* and *II*

Stassen: *Deogratias: A Tale of Rwanda*

Marcia Williams: Chaucer's *Canterbury Tales; Greek Myths;* Shakespeare's plays

Gene Luen Yang: *American Born Chinese*

Recommended Resources About Graphic Novels

Will Eisner: *Graphic Storytelling and Visual Narrative*

Scott McCloud: *Understanding Comics*

On the website, I have added a page of notes I give the students, notes I gathered from Lincoln Peirce, the author of the Big Nate syndicated cartoon series, and notes I have gathered myself from reading about graphic novels. I draw simple illustrations to show kids that drawings to show emotions are best drawn as close-ups of characters' faces. Lincoln Peirce, who attended and graduated from the Oyster River School District, actually spent a day with us, showing kids drawing techniques and showing us that the Big Nate comic strip started when he was a student at our middle school. One Thanksgiving he found all his journals and notebooks at his parents' house and realized he had so many stories of school, adolescence, and teachers to tell through his cartoons. Big Nate was born—from his journal (his WRN) kept during middle school.

**Online
9.11**

Book Reviews
Short Recommendations

The short book recommendation is a lot easier for kids to read—and to write—if they really are looking for a book to read. I began doing these after realizing kids weren't reading the long reviews I had gathered and put in a three-ring binder near the bookshelves. They have enough information on them for someone to find the book and be convinced to try it: colored copy of book cover, title, author, genre, number of pages, short summary, excerpt to see the style of the writing, and why it is recommended.

I realized, watching kids milling around in the halls between classes and before and after lunch, that it might be a good idea to tape these reviews to kids' lockers. It works. I see kids reading the recommendations all the time. We also tape them to any blank walls near our classrooms. Laminating these first is helpful to keeping them intact.

Extended Reviews

As in all the other genres I have discussed previously, to understand what goes into a book review, which is a recommendation to read or not read a certain book, we read five to seven reviews from various resources—previous students, the *New York Times*, *Time for Kids*, *Time* magazine, local newspapers, *Teen Ink*, National Council of Teachers of English journals (*English Journal* or *Voices from the Middle*), and any other resource that publishes reviews. These reviews are more in-depth and require the kids to think more deeply about what the book has to offer a reader. In essence, a book review is an essay, an attempt to convince someone to read or not read a particular book.

After reading the reviews—I usually give the kids a packet of seven to ten and tell them to choose the five that really interest them to read—we list all the characteristics that a book review includes. I type up these lists into one sheet, Book Review Characteristics (on the website), that changes little through the years. Kids notice the same elements. I try to include their words in the descriptor each year so they know I paid attention to all they said. I add to the list anything they missed, and tell them what I added and why that's necessary to include. They glue this Book Review Characteristics sheet into their notes section of their WRN.

Book Trailers

Although we don't have the computer equipment for the kids to do book trailers, many of them do at home. Showing several examples of book trailers from the Internet and listing what they notice is most appealing and convincing helps them craft their own. They are short (one to three minutes), use music and lots of color to engage the ear and eye, feed short phrases or words in and out of the pictures, focus on compelling scenes, and show the book jacket several times through the trailer.

I can show them the book trailers; they have to show me how they crafted one.

Examples of Author-Genre Study Writing

On the website, you will find examples of the writing students did while studying a mentor author or genre. Feel free to read these to your students and use as examples of various kinds of writing, until you have collected similar work from your own students. You may not remember, as I mentioned it quite awhile back in this book, that Alden's piece about the NHL came from studying Rick Reilly as his mentor author. In addition, let's take a look at what several students said about studying Robert Jordan's writing.

Studying Robert Jordan

Rob, Jeremy, and Dave worked together to read and study Robert Jordan, author of The Wheel of Time series and other numerous novels. They each read at least one of his books of their choosing (all different titles), and all three of them read one book of the same title. (These are *long* books, anywhere from seven to eight hundred pages each.) In his WRN, during the study, Dave wrote in response to *The Lord of Chaos*:

> I have noticed that Robert Jordan is incredibly good at fight scenes in his writing. He's invented sword techniques, describing everything like he was a coach describing a student sparring. His writing seems to escalate when in a fight, and afterwards the writing seems to slump a little. I have been working on my fight scenes, because of the books he's written. I picked up that in no

major battle should the hero easily defeat the bad guy; they should be evenly matched or have the bad guy outclass the good guy. I now look for small tips (like these) when I read, and I use them in my writing.

I love this series! This book especially is great because the main character (Rand Al'Thor) finally starts doing stuff that if I were in his position, I would do, too. His character, as well as all the others, is growing and gaining new qualities; Rand now is stubborn and aloof, Mat is laid back and lucky, but he would go from jolly to murderous in a minute. Perrin is more remorseful, Egewene is more bossy, Elayne is nervous, confused, and sometimes even vulnerable (which is a total contradiction to the last book's portrayal of her).

Today I noticed that (although it is not very apparent straight off) Robert Jordan stereotypes a lot. In his books the men are all hand-to-hand combat masters, that hide their emotions; and all the women are bossy, stuck-up, power-abusing, lover-torn, sexist chameleons that are real jerks in one chapter and mushy, Bambi-eyed flirts in the next.

Each of the boys tried fantasy writing, based on what they learned from reading and discussing Jordan's work. One other technique that they noticed in his writing was that he often switches perspectives. Throughout his books, different characters appear and the story is told from their point of view. Until you figure this out, it is a bit confusing, they said. Jeremy tried switching perspectives through various characters—Radaiz, Sparrowhawk, Torledt—in his piece of writing titled "Hawk."

They were so fascinated with Jordan's books and how he wrote that they wrote him a letter, which unfortunately I do not have. But I do have a copy of his letter back to the three boys. This is an excerpt from that letter:

> The single most important bit of "technique" I use is to write what I like to read. (If you don't like to read it, you won't be able to write it well.)
>
> The second is to write what I want to write. No one can possibly catch the latest commercial or critical wave; the way the publishing of novels works, the wave you see today is actually already two years old.
>
> The third is to read everything I can get my hands on, non-fiction as well as fiction. We can learn from everything, whether it is "about" something (computers, religious festivals in ancient Greece, the way language changes, whatever; these things have a tendency to spark ideas simply because they make us think), or how a writer produced an emotion that especially caught me, or how he or she made me feel a certain way about a certain character, or how/why an author failed and so lost me at a particular point.

Fourth, remember that story always flows from character. Whatever the circumstances, people behave in the way that they do for a reason, and that reason always comes from, or is influenced by, the sort of person they are, by who they are, which in turn is always shaped to some degree by the life they have lived previously.

And finally, I write. No one can learn to write by thinking about it or talking about it or by listening to someone talk about it. The only real way to learn is to do it.

**Online
9.23**

Along with Jeremy's piece "Hawk," you will find Robert Jordan's letter to the boys and Jeremy's second letter back to Jordan on the website.

In his process paper about writing "Hawk," Jeremy said,

> This was one of the first pieces where I had a definite idea of the entire plotline. I knew how it would start, what would be in the middle, and how it would end. Because I had a plan, things worked very well for me. I think that, if I may say so myself, this piece was very well written. I used description in just the right amount, and subtly developed characters in the short amount of story that I had. I portrayed emotion and physical events with good style.
>
> I learned from Robert Jordan that it is an art to create a world of your own. The Wheel of Time series is a masterpiece that is in every way as intricate as our own world. I learned that to create a world like that, you have to love the world and live the world before you write about it. Jordan presents perspectives as if he really was inside each person's head, as if he really was there.

In his final evaluation for the year Jeremy said,

> I could write halfway decent stories when I set to work. But my stories were hollow. I could describe so well. I could be eloquent or I could be detailed. I could create such a mood with my words. I could not write plot or character, nor could I give my stories a point. . . . What finally brought me to the point where I could write character was Robert Jordan. He told me, "Remember that story always flows from character," in his letter to Rob, Dave, and me. I have, in the past year, read some 4800 pages of Robert Jordan and he is the master of character. I have learned so much about ways to make a plot real and continuous using what I think the characters would do. This is good for the plot and it develops the characters themselves.
>
> Of the three pieces in my portfolio that best represent me as a writer, the first one is "Hawk." This shows the side of me that is my imagination and emotion. In this piece I try to draw the reader through the pages into the

scattering perspectives that tangle into place as a story about hatred, pain, and revenge. "Hawk" also shows how I can learn from what I read. Perspective is a thing that I began to use because I liked how Robert Jordan used it. I tried to somewhat mimic his style. "Hawk" is different from my other pieces because of its intensity. No other piece that I have ever written has used emotion so much to enhance the piece. As I revised I made drastic changes in the whole story. There were problems with there being no build to a climax, but a steady high glow of intensity until the end, when everything crashes. I dispersed the flashbacks through the piece to make it more exciting, and rewrote some scenes and the entire ending to give the piece more direction.

My writing process has become much more refined. I have learned to revise as I write. When I write a phrase I run it through my head, sometimes I even say it to see if it goes down. I try to be as meticulous as I can in the beginning so I have to work less later. The first paragraph of "Hawk," for instance, has been barely changed at all. Before my first printed draft, I rolled around lots of phrases in my head and mouth.

My letter to Robert Jordan showed my analytical side and my imaginative side. It showed how I enjoy living in other worlds and questioning them.

I have grown the most as a writer in that the author study not only taught me to be analytical of other authors' writing, but of my own as well. I have a much sharper eye to cast at my essays and stories than I did at the beginning of the year.

I started approximately 40 books this year and I finished 30 of them. Best liked:

> The Wheel of Time (series) The creation of entire cultures, ideas, people, and worlds not like our own.

> *Boy's Life* (Robert McCammon) Hilarity and intense empathy. Believing the impossible.

> *Shadows of the Mind* (Roger Penrose) Exploring my own mind. Learning all about the workings of the universe.

> *Ender's Game* (O.S. Card) Scary, exciting, and intense view of a war-wracked future.

> *About Time* (Adam Frank) A masterpiece about the conclusions of the theories of space-time. Really a fun book!

Two things in my portfolio that show who I am as a reader are my letter to Robert Jordan and "Hawk." The letter shows who I am because it illustrates how I think when I read fantasy and what questions fantasy raises for me. "Hawk" shows who I am because it illustrates how I can incorporate styles

I have learned from my reading into my writing. The three most important things I am able to do as a reader are:

Analyze what I read: I ask questions all the time to myself. Sometimes I can answer them, other times I cannot.

Enter other worlds: When I read a fictional book I really like, I am traveling between the pages of the book. I can put my mind into the story.

Read something I almost completely don't understand, and still learn. When I read *A Brief History of Time* I was very confused. Nonetheless, I went away from it with more knowledge of cosmology and quantum physics.

My journal entries that I wrote during my author study changed how I think about writing fiction. It was through these journal entries that I subconsciously realized what Robert Jordan finally told me in his letter: story flows from character. This fact is evident in his writing, and responding to his writing helped me see that.

Learned from the Author-Genre Study

I learned how much everything an author writes is intentional. Every word is picked for a reason, every event contributes to the plot in some way. It made me look at my own writing and think about whether each word was really needed, if it really contributed to the overall feeling of the piece.

Molly, from Ann Brashares

I learned about changing point of view in a story. But I also learned about how to connect with a person by describing, the best you can, the emotions of the character until you can feel it yourself.

Kate, from Jodi Picoult

I learned to read the words in books more carefully.

Nicholas, from D. J. MacHale

I've begun to have more of a passion for reading. I appreciate writing, and I've gained a respect for authors and their words.

Evan, from Sharon Draper

I learned from Ralph Fletcher to "Do the writing only you can do." Don't be a writer that you are not. Write what is true to your heart.

Natalie, from Ralph Fletcher

I learned how to make fantasy believable by incorporating human emotions and writing about common events.

Emma, from J. K. Rowling, Stephanie Meyer, and Cornelia Funke

The most .valuable thing I learned from the author study was to make the reader feel for the character so that the whole story means a lot more. The best books make you cry, laugh, or think. The second best thing I learned was to describe deeply. It makes the reader feel like the reader is there.

Stefan, from D. J. MacHale

All fiction stories need to have something that makes them believable. Either the characters, plot, setting, or surroundings have to be semi-normal or the piece will just seem ridiculous. Fiction is not supposed to be completely true, but it can't be completely fake either.

Catherine, from science fiction

"Does George Orwell define us?" This question was posed by the *London Times*. The answer to this question, I have found, after reading *1984*, is yes. I found that Orwell's prediction for the world is very much like the world today. Like *1984* we are controlled by our government more and more. We also have become the very thing we were fighting against. That is to say that we are fighting a war against those who oppress but in the process oppress our own.

Dan, from George Orwell

Good mystery action books are like a movie playing in my head when I read them. I learned how to write a cliffhanger.

Sam, from Anthony Horowitz

Writing in any genre is not that easy. It may look easy, but getting an idea isn't easy. Developing it is even harder.

Joey, from Gary Paulsen

CHAPTER TEN

Exhibeo Humanitas *(Persuasive Writing)*

In real life, and in literature, what are the consequences of little to no choice in a person's life? What choices do these real people and these fictional characters make in response to their experiences?

Approximately ten years ago I met Miep Gies, the woman who took care of Anne Frank and her family while they were in hiding from the Nazis for nearly two years. She was speaking in Heidelberg, Germany, as part of a National Council of Teachers of English International Conference. She was a humble, soft-spoken woman, who said all of us would have done what she did because it was the right thing to do. I left that conference knowing that Miep was the hero for risking her life to protect and keep alive eight friends who had to go into hiding because they were Jewish. She did "nothing extraordinary," she insisted, instead, did what was "the right thing to do."

Just recently a story aired on the Sunday morning news program about a football team from Olivet Middle School in Olivet, Michigan. Unbeknownst to their coaches, parents, or the opposing team, the football players planned a play to help Keith, a member of the team who had never played, score a touchdown. Keith is small and profoundly learning disabled, but was still part of the team. To ensure Keith's touchdown, the players had to move the ball as close to the goal line as possible without scoring, even taking a dive if they had to. They took the ball to the one-yard line, and then surrounded Keith with a moving wave of players that helped him maneuver and carry the ball over the goal line. Keith had scored a touchdown. It was a life-changing moment for these boys, as much as it was for Keith, as the wide receiver explained in the story.

What seems extraordinary to me is that we find these stories extraordinary. Doing the right thing should not be unusual. It should be the norm.

In Latin, *exhibeo humanitas* means to show, to offer, to produce *kindness*. For many of us, trying to understand any of the atrocities that have happened throughout history is beyond our comprehension. Over the years, I have exposed my students to pictures and writing and "experiences" that I am ashamed to admit.

I have shown former students pictures from the Holocaust of some of the most appalling sights—including a pile of naked, emaciated bodies haphazardly layered like random piles of cordwood—thinking that would show them how horrific the Holocaust was. *An introduction to Anne Frank*, I thought. When one of my students bolted from the room, gulping for air, her stomach heaving when she realized this was a mountain of human beings, I stopped showing those pictures.

Another example: I had a copy of a book from a recommended Holocaust list on my shelf, until I read it. When I read the part about what was done to women by the enemy in the name of war, I heaved the book across the room, aghast at what one human being could inflict on another. I had nightmares for weeks. I removed the book from my classroom.

Instead, I am trying to turn our study to the kindnesses and courage people display in response to situations they can control or, too often, situations they cannot control. Those Olivet, Michigan eighth graders found a way to help a team member who might never play feel the thrill of scoring a touchdown. Helping Keith score left his teammates profoundly moved, realizing for the first time that all their lives had been focused on themselves, not others. A moment of kindness changed one little boy's life and yet positively affected the football players' lives, and probably many others after they realized what these kids had done. A simple act of kindness that may be remembered the rest of their lives and in situations in the future may impact others even more seriously.

I want my students to know they have choices in their lives, and those choices affect others as well as themselves. I want them to know that many of those choices are based on their personal beliefs and opinions that are grounded in their experiences. Their ability to share their beliefs and opinions can nudge the world a little.

We read portions of Anne Frank's diary, written while in hiding from the Nazis for two years. I show them a few scenes from the movie *Anne Frank—The Whole Story*. I stop the movie and have each of the girls in the classroom read a preselected passage that shows the intellectual astuteness, the personal issues, the frustrations, or the longing Anne lived and wrote about in her diary. Anne is extremely honest in this diary because she had no intention of ever letting anyone read it.

I want them to hear the voice of a fourteen-year-old who had no choice in her life, because someone didn't like her and chose to "exterminate" her. I cannot fathom that kind of thinking. Most of our kids cannot either. Thankfully.

I want my students to understand how Anne Frank's diary came to be, in the hope that events like that will never happen again, even though I know there are still many places in this world where genocide still occurs.

I tell them the story of Iqbal Masih, the Pakistani boy who was sold to rug makers at the age of four, for $12, and escaped the looms to protest child slavery. I tell them how this little boy risked his life to protest the enslavement of young children. How he came to America to receive a human rights award in 1994 from Reebok and subsequently spoke in Ron Adams' class in Quincy, Massachusetts, his legs not even touching the floor as he told Ron's seventh graders about his life chained to a loom and his eventual escape. I tell them about Iqbal's murder on his return to Pakistan and the response from Ron's students. How they have now built several schools in Iqbal's memory to honor this courageous little boy. Iqbal did what was right to do, and the students at Broad Meadows School did what was only right to honor him.

We read excerpts from *I Am Malala*, the fourteen-year-old young woman shot by the Taliban for speaking out for the right of girls to attend school. We listen to the haunting song, "Hana's Suitcase," written by eighth graders in Toronto after hearing the story of a Japanese teacher's two-year search for the little girl named Hana whose name appeared on a small brown suitcase, an artifact from the notorious death camp, Auschwitz. Karen Levine's book *Hana's Suitcase* tells the story.

In most cases, we cannot change events, but we can make a difference if we can just nudge someone else's thinking. We may never do things that change the world substantially, but learning these stories leads us into thinking about those things we do have opinions on and believe should, or could, change.

Vote with Your Feet: Getting Kids to Realize They Do Have Opinions

Despite the fact that most adolescents have strong opinions about many things, convincing them they have opinions worth writing about is another matter. Or it could be, "Good grief, don't anyone tell her you have an opinion or she'll make us write about it." Asked to simply list those topics that matter to them—personal or world issues—a lot of blank faces stare at me. I change my approach, and now start with a topic.

I toss out a topic and ask the kids to "vote with their feet," which in this case means if you agree, move to the left side of the room. If you disagree, move to the right. If you have no opinion, stand in the middle of the room. Topics I used this year were:

> The government should control and monitor the kinds and amounts of food sold in restaurants. (This came from the mayor of New York trying to control the supersize drinks sold in fast-food restaurants.)
>
> Athletes have a moral obligation to act responsibly because they are role models for kids.
>
> Parents should monitor the lyrics of all songs their teens listen to.

The U.S. government has the right to spy on any country, including its allies.

Football should be banned in all elementary, middle, and high schools because of the possibility of serious injury, especially concussions.

With each statement posed, the students move to one side of the room or the other, and then we talk. With each issue several students on each side offer their reasoning. I give them the chance to change sides if someone convinces them with their argument. The football question hits a nerve, because many of the students have begun playing for newly formed town teams in the hopes of becoming sanctioned by the school district as a varsity, not just a club, sport. There continue to be many opinions on both sides. Because the topic is close to home and personal for many of these kids, there are strong opinions.

Ahead of time, I put each of these topics as belief statements on large sheets of paper. As the kids give their reasons for support or nonsupport of the statement, I write down their reasons. After they go back to their seats, I spread these large sheets of paper on the wall and have student volunteers with two different-color markers indicate those reasons that support the statement in one color and those reasons that are evidence for nonsupport in another color.

I point out that this is the way we begin the process of identifying and gathering evidence for writing a persuasive piece that can lead to a solid argument in defense of our beliefs.

I ask the students to take out their writer's-reader's notebooks (WRNs) and jot down anything they feel strongly about—strong enough to defend their positions. They just need to be shown first that they do indeed have opinions. Here are just some of the latest belief statements the students wrote down after "voting with their feet" and searching their WRNs for ideas.

We as Americans need to eat healthier.

Abortion should be a parent's decision in the case of minors, not the governments.

Smoking is bad for you and should be completely banned.

No one should hunt or kill elephants for their ivory tusks.

Young horses, especially two-year-olds, should not be raced.

The NBA should not put ads on their athletes' jerseys.

The laws relating to the death penalty should be the same in every state.

PETA goes too far, to an extreme, in their protection of animals.

No animals should ever be used for human consumption.

If it is proven that an athlete does steroids/drugs, all their records and awards should be removed or taken away.

Public humiliation is not an effective form of disciplining from parents.

Chess should be included as an integral part of the core curriculum.

Parents should monitor what their kids do on Facebook.

Even if an athlete has three concussions in a sport, no one but the athlete has the right to remove that athlete from the sport.

Extinct animals should not be cloned, especially the woolly mammoth.

Texting while driving is dangerous and therefore should be illegal in every state.

Schools should start later to allow teenagers more sleep.

Guns are too accessible and therefore gun laws should be stronger.

The list goes on and on. Kids most definitely have strong opinions that can be developed well enough to nudge the world a little. These may not be the topics they eventually choose to write about, but it gives them something to hold on to and think about as we look at examples of this kind of writing.

What are the controversial issues or topics in which your students hold a vested interest? By giving students choice and models of this kind of writing, we give voice to those things they care deeply about.

Showing Students Examples of Opinion/Editorials

It is important to show students editorials, articles, op-ed pieces to which they can connect—something controversial or provocative for them, not just for us as adults. Although these are the articles I used this year, many others could be used. I use some of these pieces each year and add others, depending on what issues are current in the students' lives and in the media at large. We read:

Elizabeth White: "If Dress Code Doesn't Suit Teens, School District Will"
(The Associated Press 2008)

Rick Reilly: "Sis! Boom! Bah! Humbug!" (Caine 2008)

Leonard Pitts: "Our Destructive Love of Stuff" (2008)

As a reading strategy all year, we annotate various articles, poems, essays, or short stories so kids can see the value of looking at a piece of writing more closely with their comments, questions, connections that lead to fuller responses in their WRNs. I read aloud these first three articles while the kids follow along with a copy they can write on. They turn and talk with the person next to them, focusing on what they notice in the article. Then we talk as a class. See Figure 10.1 for an example of the annotations on one of the articles.

I choose one of the three to look at in even more depth based on how the students react to the piece. This year they were interested in the dress code article, so much so that they looked up the school on the Internet to see where in Texas it was and what the dress code actually said. We found pages and pages of rules on their school site. This led to a discussion about the

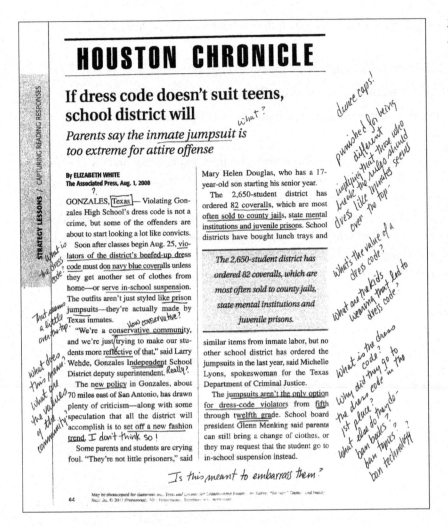

Figure 10.1 *Article Annotations*

differences they perceived in that school and our school. We also made a list of the reasons supporting a dress code in any school and the reasons for not supporting one. This listing can be done with any article, so that students can see the development of a persuasive piece.

Showing Kids How to Compare and Contrast Varying Viewpoints

This year we also read the following three articles, which I asked the kids to compare. I said, "Take a stand yourself about Lance Armstrong, based on what we've read and what you have already heard or read elsewhere. Then see what these three writers have to say. Would you stick with your belief about Armstrong or alter it based on the opinions and evidence in these articles?"

> Rick Reilly: "Armstrong Still Worth Honoring" (2012)
>
> Jim Vertuno: "Armstrong Says Last Few Weeks 'Difficult'" (2012)
>
> Marcus Hondra: "Lance Armstrong Could Not Put Up, Time Now for Him to Shut Up" (2012)

After showing the students how to differentiate the pros and cons by underlining them in different colors, I have them then list the comparisons side by side in their WRNs. Figure 10.2 shows one student's comparison based on his belief.

We discuss their findings from these three articles. "You know," one student concluded, "he did a lot of good, but the bottom line is, he built his entire career on a lie. He deserves having everything stripped from him." We then read Rick Reilly's "It's All About the Lies" and decided we, too, had had enough of Lance Armstrong.

Figure 10.2 *Comparison Based on Belief*

> I believe... that all the good Lance Armstrong has done does not outweigh the bad ∴ he deserves all the punishment he's gotten

In Support	Not in support
Reilly	
-gave up chance to prove innocence	-changed cancer from dread to hope
-companies have dropped endorsements	-14 of 17 TdF winners did performance enhancing drugs
	-"the man is a hope machine"
	-raised $475 million for cancer research
Hondro	
- Armstrong walked away so evidence would not be exposed	-set an example of courage by beating cancer
- USADA promised results of blood tests	-created successful research foundation (Livestrong)
-said "did not fail test" not "did not do drugs"	
Vertuno	
-international cycling union upheld charges	-mission bigger than Armstrong
	-"overcoming cancer is more important as a role model

Response—23

Using TED Talks to Enhance Students' Understanding of Persuasion

I want students to hear the persuasive power of the human voice, especially so well done in TED Talks. We watch Graham Hill explain his reasoning to his own question "Why am I not a vegetarian?" He grabs our interest immediately by putting himself in the same position many of us feel about eating meat: "My common sense and good intentions were in conflict with my taste buds." He presents the only solution most of us have faced also over eating meat—there seemed to be "only a binary solution: eat meat or eat only vegetables."

We watch the TED Talk twice—once to get the gist of what Hill has to say, the second time to take closer note of what he says and how he says it. On this second viewing, I ask kids to take notes on Hill's reasons for trying to stop eating meat. I have them write down his belief statement, and then several boxes in support, and several boxes that counter his argument. See Keerthi's page of notes in Figure 10.3.

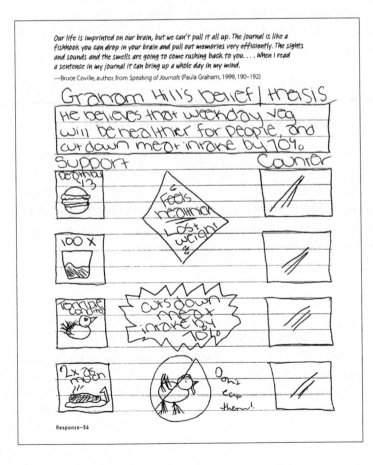

Figure 10.3 *Keerthi's Page of Notes*

We summarize his reasons for not eating meat:

- Increased risk of death is cut by one-third.
- Raising beef uses one hundred times more water than growing vegetables.
- Conditions under which most beef raised is horrific.
- We are now eating twice as much meat as we were in 1950s.
- Transportation for meat causes more emissions than all transportation combined. (Keerthi missed this last point, but many students heard it.)

Hill's solution to his dilemma: become a weekday vegetarian. Monday through Friday he eats nothing with a face. He has lost weight and feels healthier, it's better for the animals and the environment, and it is a structured, easy-to-remember solution.

What did the kids realize? That he had no counterarguments, but it didn't seem to matter because he had solid arguments for eating less meat and a reasonable solution that sounded appealing to those of us viewing his talk. Could this be another way of presenting an argument? We decided, yes. Presenting a solid argument through a personal story with a reasonable solution didn't seem to necessitate a counterargument. No one is hurt with the solution, and yet he produced a good solution for himself with an idea for others living with the same dilemma.

Using Previous Students' Writing as Examples

We read Sanam's essay defending her belief that the United States should not have compulsory voting (earlier in this book); Alden's essay (earlier in the book) in the more informal style of Rick Reilly; Peter's WRN entry thinking through his dilemma about cheering for Michael Vick as a sports hero, yet his belief that sports figures have a moral obligation to behave ethically and honestly; and Katya's piece objecting to racing two-year-old fillies, her process paper for the writing; and Jane's and Sophie's political cartoons in response to Katya's essay.

Sanam: A Formal Essay

I project Sanam's essay on a large screen so we can talk out what she did to craft this essay. Students note she began with two quotes by well-known individuals. She then stated her opinion, gave reasons for supporting it, and circled us back to the quotes in the end, as if taking the reader back to emphasize her points with the voices of these authorities to make the argument more convincing.

Alden: An Informal Essay

I project Alden's essay about the NHL cancellation for an entire year on the screen so we can see the differences in a more informal essay laced with the biting sarcasm he is emulating from studying Rick Reilly as a mentor author. His argument is still there, but in a very different structure from Sanam's. Is he convincing in his presentation? Absolutely. His belief that this was a selfish reason for cancelling the NHL for an entire year is based on the absurdity of how much money sports figures and owners make in the first place. Something all readers can relate to.

Peter: WRN Entry

I project Peter's WRN entry on the large screen with the direction to students to look for places where you have questions he might need to answer to develop this into a more extensive piece of writing that reaches some conclusions about his beliefs over this dilemma. (I want them to be able to do this when their peers share their drafts of writing with them, and they need to ask the questions that will help the writer more fully develop their beliefs more convincingly if they need to.) See Figure 10.4.

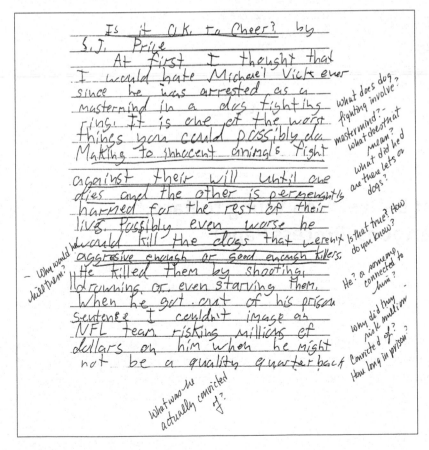

Figure 10.4 *Peter's WRN Entry*

continues

Figure 10.4 continued

> anymore. But the Eagles took
> that risk and it sure is
> paying off. After the trade
> Franchise quarterback Donovan
> McnNabb to the Redskins and
> week one starter Kevin Kobb
> went out with an ~~Knee~~
> ~~injury~~ Concussion Vick was
> in. He has been an electrifying *in what ways?*
> playmaker and by far gives *what is he good at?*
> the Eagles the best chance
> to win. It's really hard
> for me to cheer ~~on for~~ someone
> who has done ~~that~~ awful *What do you admire about him?*
> things. But as a sports
> fan he is a hero. His ability
> to scramble in the pocket
> and make plays running or passing
> is spectacular. It is a huge } *I wonder*
> morale delema for me to } *if this is*
> either love or hate him. There } *the thesis*
> is no inbetween with Michael } *statement*
> Vick. } *also*

Katya: Eight Belles, "Too Young to Race," Political Cartoons, Process Paper

I give students a copy of Katya's drawing of Eight Belles, the two-year-old filly who fell in the Kentucky Derby, her piece of writing "Too Young to Race," Jane's and Sophie's political cartoons in response to Katya's essay, and her process paper describing what she did to craft this writing. We read through her materials together, noting especially that her essay begins with a story, for the emotional impact it carries through her piece as she presents her argument against racing these young horses. I want students to have these models in front of them: Sanam's more formal argument, Alden's more informal, and Katya's piece that begins with a story. (See Figures 10.5 through 10.11.)

Before the students begin the serious work of writing their own persuasive pieces, I also show them Samrath's political cartoon about compulsory voting and Adelia's rant about all she believes about the sale of Girl Scout cookies. I want students to know they can draw an argument just as successfully as they can write one.

I also show them professional political cartoons and several ads from the J. Peterman catalog—the drawings and story that accompany each piece of clothing for sale. (This is the company that Elaine in the *Seinfeld* comedy worked for and yes, this is a real company.) I show them several pages from the catalog. We talk about the power of storytelling in advertising. Someday I might even be able to convince one of the many adolescents with whom I work, who have serious eating disorders, that a study of advertising and models used in teen magazines could force some changes.

Having an audience for their beliefs makes them work even harder on their writing. We will send these pieces to any writing contests that sponsor this kind of writing, including the Scholastic Art and Writing Awards, newspapers, and magazines. Their voices need to be heard beyond the classroom.

Figure 10.5 *Katya's Drawing of Eight Belles*

Figure 10.6 *"Too Young to Race"*
by Katya

Too Young To Race

I watched in horror as Eight Belles, a three-year-old filly racing in the Kentucky Derby, collapsed to the dirt track. Her fluid stride harshly ceased as her muscular chest, and then her smooth dark head, hit the ground. She had just galloped away, full of grace and athleticism, from finishing second in the three and one quarter mile horse race. My heart pounded as equine ambulances and nervous people surrounded the fallen horse, speaking brusquely into walkie-talkies and pacing back and forth. She had broken her two front ankles while running and could no longer support her own weight. The veterinarians made the decision- she had to be euthanized.

Eight Belles was not the only racetrack casualty that year. In 2008, 1,217 horses died at American racetracks. One reason for this considerably large number of deaths is that many of those horses were just too young to race.

Racehorses usually begin racing at the age of two. Their training may even begin as early as when the horse is one and one half years old, as opposed to regular riding horses, which start training around three or four years. At the age of two and even three, horses' bodies and minds are just not ready for the stress of racing. Their bodies, especially their legs, are not fully developed. The skeletal system and growth plates are not strong enough for the young horse to be ridden at a full gallop for a distance that can range to over three miles.

If a horse breaks its leg while racing, there is a great chance that they will be euthanized after the race because of the low chance of recovery from a severe leg injury. Many horses, with less serious injuries, are left permanently lame. Most of these horses can never race again and are often passed on at a cheap price to horse dealers and traders- over 5,000 horses yearly retire from racing in the U.S. They often end up neglected or abused, resulting in the large number of "off the track" thoroughbred horses at horse rescues around the U.S.

In addition to the physical strain of racing, the psychological strain leaves lasting negative effects on racehorses. Racing is not gentle. Not only are growing horses' bodies not fully developed, but their brains are still sensitive and maturing. They are forced to run as fast as they can, whipped into submission and speed, and surrounded by other terrified, galloping young horses. These experiences at such a young age leave many racehorses perpetually afraid, leading to health problems such as stomach ulcers. The time and money it takes to properly and carefully train and care for a horse is just too much for some owners and trainers. But the victory is what is thought to be important, even if the horse has to be sold or dies a few months later.

Strong supporters of racing argue that thoroughbred horses (the breed used for most racing) are "born and bred to race." If so, then why, according to the N.Y. Times, do an average of **24 horses die per week** at racetracks around the U.S.? Can we really make the excuse that they "were bred to do this" when so many are suffering and dying, as Eight Belles did before the eyes of millions that bright May afternoon? If we are going to have this sport of horse racing, we could at least try to make it safer by not racing horses before they are old enough to compete in the brutal way that they are now.

Resource:
Bogdanich, Walt. "Racing Economics Collide with Veterinarians' Oath." New York Times, Sept. 21, 2012.

Process Paper (Background History of the Writing) and Evaluation

Name __Katya__   Section __LA4__   Date __11/21__

Title or Topic: __Too Young to Race__

Tell me everything you can about **how this writing came to be**. You may write on the back of this sheet also.

How did you come up with the idea for the piece?

Jane Robinson and I were talking one day after the "agree-disagree" activity in class about topics we had strong opinions on. One was horse racing. I began to write my feelings and facts about horse racing. This eventually became my essay.

What parts of this writing are done especially well? (What qualities or characteristics make it an effective piece of writing?)

I think the personal, emotional part is really effective - my story in the beginning, about Eight Belles. That is the most important part of the essay, and I think the most effective because humans respond so much to emotion. I think I also did a good job tying fact and opinion together.

What did you do differently to revise this piece of writing-- the content-- as you went from each draft to the final draft? Name at least two suggestions you took and why you decided to try them?

1. I decided to include a personal story because I thought it would help the reader connect with the piece. It also helped me to believe in my piece more too.

2. I also included my source, for a fact which was more convincing to the reader because the source was the N.Y. Times. That helps the reader believe that the info is true

What kind of problems did you encounter and how did you solve them?

I didn't have too many big problems... I think the only notable one ~~was~~ was the need to include a personal story. To solve that, I shared the story of Eight Belles.

What helped you the most to make the piece as strong as it could be?

The story of Eight Belles. Also how strongly I believe in what I am saying. If you are trying to convince someone of something but do not have your whole heart behind the opinion and believe strongly in it, you will get nowhere. I believed in what I was writing.

Figure 10.7 *Process Paper*   *continues*

What do you want me to know about the writing of this that I might not know just from reading it?

I don't know what you don't know... I also don't know if there's anything to KNOW, really... Nothing important, I don't think. I don't think there's anything, actually. So no.

What have you learned to do as a writer that you learned from doing this piece?

I've learned that when you believe you do your best. When you believe what you're saying and willing to stand behind it 100%. That is the best writing. That is my best writing.

What did you learn/ notice/pay attention to with regard to editing comments given to you (or done on your own) about spelling, punctuation, paragraphing, and the construction of sentences in order to write this piece carefully?

I was reminded that numbers one through ten should be spelled out (seven not 7.). That's pretty much it except for 'just saying phrases differently which makes them more effective

Figure 10.7 *continued*

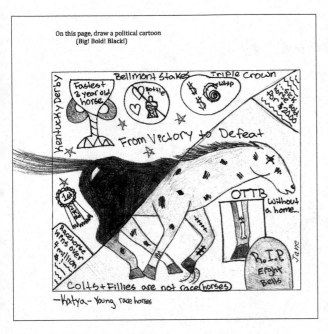

Figure 10.8 *Jane's Political Cartoon*

Figure 10.9 *Sophie's Political Cartoon*

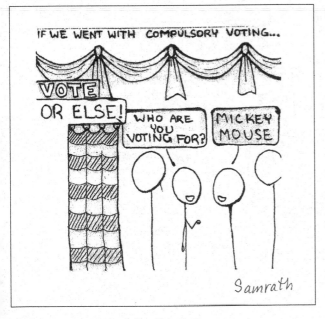

Figure 10.10 *Samrath's Political Cartoon*

Figure 10.11 *Adelia's Political Cartoon*

Beginning the Writing for Themselves

Malcolm Gladwell says, "Good writing does not succeed or fail on the strength of its ability to persuade. It succeeds or fails on the strength of its ability to engage you, to make you think, to give you a glimpse into someone's head."

I give the students a simple handout (on the website) summarizing a few of the things we have talked about. The expectation is that they will produce a persuasive piece of writing in response to a belief or opinion they hold, a political cartoon to accompany the writing, and a process paper describing all they did.

Online
10.1

Arthur: Chess Should Be Part of the K–12 Curriculum

Arthur's WRN was often filled with thinking about chess, what worked in a tournament or did not, how chess played into his thinking about life, and the following response to watching *Brooklyn Castle*. See Figure 10.12 for a look at the writing from his WRN.

---

chessboard can be en prise(free to capture) if one side is transfixed on one certain area on the board.

Response to the movie Brooklyn Castle
    After I watched a documentary movie, Brooklyn Castle, I was really inspired. The Intermediate 318 school in Brooklyn Chess had chess as an afterschool program. The school took kids to chess tournaments on Saturdays. Every minute and second the students have even when riding on a train, they play and study chess.
    The school issue in Brooklyn Castle was that many families were below the poverty line and the school was being attacked with budget cuts. The kids and the principal in school did not wait around for those budget cuts to affect them. They tried to solve the problem actively. One kid named Pobo was elected President of the Intermediate 318 school, and his primary and ambitious goal

was to raise one million dollars to compensate for the budget cuts. I admire Pobo's courage and thoughtfulness to help keep the education and chess program alive.
    One of the things that inspired me the most: Chess is so powerful it can help a ADHT kid to increase his attention span and win games in a chess tournament. There was a kid in the I.318 school named Patrick who had ADHT. The teacher in the school's chess program helped him with his opening and guided him to think about the consequences of each candidate move. Pobo also helped Patrick with his opening. Pobo showed him opening lines and went over games with him. After the guidance from both the teacher and Pobo, Patrick's rating went from the bottom to the top in the Under 1000 of his school.
    If chess didn't exist in the kids' life, those kids from disadvantaged families might be hanging out or fighting

Figure 10.12 *Arthur's WRN Entries*

continues

on the streets. This movie showed real examples of how chess turned outsiders into positive outliers. How does chess do this transformation? For me, chess also performed the magic of turning me from an outsider into an outlier. I didn't connect to most of my fellow students and teachers. The students talked about T.V. shows, video games, and I-pads, I-touches, etc... I am not interested in those. A few years ago. I had very little interest in school subjects and work, and my grades were below average. I lacked confidence about being myself. Chess gave me the focus. I built my confidence through chess. Now, math and language arts are both subjects I like. Science also became interesting to me. How could chess make me interested in school subjects and school work? Chess gave me a sense of purpose and helped me in my calculation, communication, and observation. Chess must have also gave those Brooklyn kids a sense of purpose so they could focus several hours everyday to study

~~was restore one-million dollars to compensate for the budget cuts.~~ chess and score national Junior High titles for their school. Through chess, these Brooklyn kids learn important lifeskills to succeed in life.

I recommend the whole ORMS school to watch the movie. I am going to donate ~~from~~ my chess tutoring earning to ~~buy~~ buy ~~this~~ this movie for ORMS. I hope everyone will learn from the movie not to give up in any poverty or disadvantage situations, but to work together to overcome difficulties.

~~Some~~ Rising to the top is like going up mount everest. Obstacles, dangers and risks are blocking your path. Overcoming them needs a true brave leader who is willing to take the risks, estimate the danger, and make the correct decision. If no one likes taking the risk they won't move on and will be stuck like they are stationary in midair. Boredom and fun may enter your

Figure 10.12 *continued*

It is no surprise that Arthur feels strongly about chess and that his persuasive essay takes that focus. His lead and the beginning to his essay, "Chess Should Be Part of the K–12 Curriculum in all Schools," starts with a story:

> It was November 24, 2012 at a chess tournament called Burlington Open. I had the Black pieces against the top seed. Our battle quickly developed. My opponent decided to go into an early endgame. He first offered an exchange of Queens, which I accepted, and immediately posted my Rook on an active square in his camp. He then led to trade off my pair of Rooks. I pictured the board to visualize the endgame. I had looked two moves ahead, three moves, four moves . . . Then I saw one move. The only one . . .
>
> * * * * * *
>
> Chess should be a subject in the K–12 education, just like math, language arts, social studies, science, world language, and gym. Why chess? Chess,

more than any other subject in school, equips you with important life skills, such as accurate decision-making, awareness, observation, calculation, imagination, and active attitudes and actions. When you learn chess, you practice all these life skills.

He goes on to argue each of these points, and concludes by circling us back to his story and the one move he sees. His story reinforces his argument by showing us how he uses those skills in each match.

Keerthi: Don't Talk to Strangers, Marry Them

Nearly all of the students' essays could be traced back to things that were important to them, mentioned in their WRNs. The website contains a series of writing examples from Keerthi that show how she returns to the subject of her cousin in India over a period of several months. Looking at all that is included, you can see the progression of the process that leads to her final piece, "Don't Talk to Strangers, Marry Them."

Online Student Resources

Online
10.2–10.7

- ten pages of WRN entries (This is where her thinking begins.)
- belief statement: write-around for questions (After deciding on her topic, with her belief statement, students do a write-around, jotting down questions they hope Keerthi considers answering as she develops the piece.)
- first draft—two pages (You can see my questions and comments in response to this first draft.)
- second draft—three pages (You can see that I have asked more questions, and added some editing corrections, because she is now close to the final draft.)
- final draft—three pages
- process paper—two pages (This explains her decision making that I might not know just by reading the paper itself. It also puts some of the responsibility for evaluating this writing herself for how well she believes she did.)

Political Cartoons

After the students are done with their persuasive essays and have read them aloud, we post them on the walls. I ask all the students to draw a political cartoon, either in support of their own essay or anyone else's. I show them several political cartoons, so we can figure out what the artist does with images and words to convey a point. Figures 10.13 through 10.15 show several of the cartoons they drew. These could also be done before they write their essays, as it is a good way to have students visualize what they believe, giving them a stronger entry into the writing.

Whatever it is that the kids believe, persuasive writing gives them a voice and lets others hear those voices. Devin researched the number of water bottles our schools were using and produced a video that showed the waste and the damage to the environment. He took his findings to the school board and the superintendent. All of the old water fountains have been replaced. We now have only water fountains in all four schools that allow kids to fill bottles and count the number of plastic bottles that have been saved. It is in the tens of thousands.

Devin's writing has nudged the world. He is taking ownership in the world and trying to convince others to care and act also.

Figure 10.13 *Isabelle's Belief that School Needs to Begin Later*

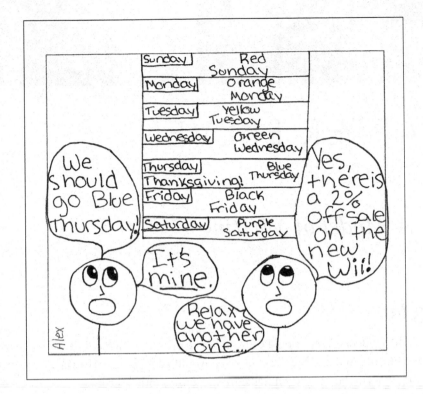

Figure 10.14 Alex's Belief that Shopping for Christmas Has Gotten Out of Hand

Figure 10.15 Daiyao's Belief that Humiliation Is Not an Effective Parenting Punishment for Bad Behavior

CHAPTER ELEVEN

A Model of Writing

Madi: Becoming Me

At the end of the year I ask the students: What would you still like to do as a reader and writer that you have not had the chance to do? What topic or issue would you like to investigate and present in a variety of ways? What choices do you make to nudge the world a little?

Although there are so many stories I can tell that encapsulate all that so many students decide to do at the end of the year, Madi's multigenre writing strikes me as the perfect ending to this book, mainly because her writing shows a new beginning for her.

Madi believes that telling her story of anorexia nervosa may help other young people with eating disorders. She continues to add to this piece with more writing and photographs. She plans to have this collection assembled in a small booklet that will be distributed to hospitals and schools in New England in the hopes that her story will help other young people overcome their eating disorders.

As a reader, she finished eighteen books during the year. She read *Twilight*, but called it "obnoxious." The best books she read: *The Help* ("fantastic"), *The Secret Life of Bees* ("unique"), *Sarah's Key* ("powerful"), *Fahrenheit 451* ("wonderful"), and *Learning to Swim* ("life-changing").

Like most of the writing for the students, it begins in her writer's-reader's notebook. Although she filled more than one hundred pages with quickwrites, responses to all she read on her own and pieces we read together, and her thinking about her life, I have included here only a few of the pages focused on her thinking connected to body image and her eventual time spent at an eating disorder center. Madi entrusted me with her words, and now she is entrusting you with them.

Each piece went through the process of receiving response from her peers and me. It took courage for Madi to read this writing aloud. But Madi lives, and writes, with honesty, integrity, and great respect for everyone around her. She knew this same respect would be reciprocated.

Figure 11.1 *Madi's WRN Entries*

"When I Was Young at the Ocean"   9-12

   Bryce, wide eyed and babbling, stares at me, smiling like some kind of happy, worriless child. Must be nice, to be carefree and happy, he's lucky. But he'll grow older, and there will come a time when that lovely smile will fade for long periods.
☆ He will learn the meaning of loss, regret, sadness. Now, the only reason he cries is when he's sick or falls *what has* down or misses mom, but someday, like the rest of us, *changed* that won't be the case. He'll think back to the time he *for you?* was young, just a baby

                                  What losses, regrets,
                                  sadness have been in your
                                  life? ☹

❋ Rambling Autobiography ❋
Born on November 17, on a gloomy, rainy day in 1997.
Fast forward: 11 months later and I'm fatherless, because he left us, no because he took his own life, which you can take however you wish. 12, almost 13 years later actually, and I'm
☆ still picking up the scattered pieces that are left, trying still
Tell to make sense of it. Does his depression, his illness, live on in
me me? Do I have similar problems, as I'm led to believe on occasion,
more! as he?   *My goodness - a lot of weight for a 13 yr. old*
       to bear. What makes you think you have
       similar problems? You know, this could be an
       article for a teen magazine!

                                            Response—3

Figure 11.2 Madi's WRN Entries

→ Of course, this is coming from someone (me!) who is

far too concerned with perfectionism

Perfection also. "let it go," I tell 1-24

myself. You are doing your best.

They say I'm too hard on myself. My mother says
that she's never had to put any kind of pressure on
me because I can do that all on my own. They say
I only expect the best from myself and that I don't
have to be perfect. Perfection. What a strange thing. certainly
not something that I am familiar with. She says it's
ok to be proud of myself or to take a break sometimes,
mom will say that I should not worry about dissapointing
everyone. She'll say its most important to just try hard
and accept what you get out of it. She thinks that
I'm too precise, ~~Raj~~ that I should lighten up on myself and not worry about always being the best.
~~She says that~~ As if I actually believe that she'll
love me less if I get a B, no I don't think that
if I let a goal in or don't win the race that my
family will be ashamed of me. And I don't really care
anyway. Then why? Why do I always push myself harder
and expect better? Maybe its because inside I know that
I can handle it or perhaps its because I think if I
just try hard enough or if I could be the best it would
make things better. Maybe if I could be the fastest or
the strongest or the smartest I wouldn't have to worry.
~~Not worrying Not worrying about~~ Maybe I could learn to love,
to love myself.

Response–63

Left margin (bottom to top): Ah "perfectionism" - we beat ourselves up for not being the BEST at everything - when we should realize it's about trying out best - giving something our all - sometimes it may be enough to try! That's all anyone can do!

Figure 11.3 *Madi's WRN Entries*

A-18

I don't know when I lost sight of myself. Maybe inbetween that awkward lines of ten-year-old chubbiness and pre-teen development Maybe it all started farther back than that, I can't tell exactly. Looking back now it all blurs the stages of my predicament. It started with eating healthier, excersing more, and trying to feel better. I had always been self consieus of my appearence. Body size and looks has never been an area of confidence for me It started innocently enough, loosing a little bit of baby fat and possibly feeling somewhat fit. But other than that, I can no longer recognize the difference. I do not know when the switch flipped from acceptable, to whatever this is. But suddenly things were different, foods like cake and goodies are off limits even though I often bake them for my family. Salad dressing is no longer used, condiments like ketchup and butter are not necessary. Water is the drink of choice and my answer to any offering of a treat became "no thanks, I'm not hungry." I no longer order what I'd like but consider which has fewer calories. The scale in my house was getting more use daily than in previous years it had seen in a week. If given the option I liked things plain, and suddenly calorie counting was a main hobby. I expected nothing but the best from myself, in school, in sports, in life. Exeersise was about pushing my self further than before and being

Response-69

continues

Figure 11.3 continued

Oh my goodness, Madi—
that is NOT you!

better all the time. I always consider myself lazy, non-athletic, and now-fatter than before. I did not even notice the impact this new way of thinking was having on my life, but less was always better. I do not understand how the things that happened to me did when I see how mild my case is compared to most girls with eating disorders. I certainly wasn't starving myself, I was just eating really healthy and restricting what I did eat. Part of the reason that I still did so much damage might be due to the fact that I should have been going through a major growth spurt during my period of restriction. While a lot of girls, even just the few cases at our school, starved themselves and lost lots of weight and hurt their bodies in very damaging ways, I got the same results (or similar) by not even having to try as hard. Maybe that's why both me and my mother didn't see it for so long, and why I still do not totally believe I have an eating disorder, because everyone could see that I was still consuming food. The biggest problem is probably that I chose the wrong time to restrict and therefore I lost over 7 pounds when I was supposed to be gaining weight and I've stunted my growth. I realize now that the reason I don't look like my friends, the reason that I don't have the shape of a young woman is because I messed with my

Response—70

Figure 11.3 *continued*

The two most useful things any writer can do is read widely and keep notebooks, writing on a regular basis. William Stafford, my favorite poet, believed that we must train ourselves to become more alert and attentive to all the messages, signs, and images around us, and that keeping an ongoing, regular notebook was one of the best exercises for maintaining alertness.

—Naomi Shihab Nye, author and poet, from *Speaking of Journals* (Paula Graham 1999, 206)

body. As a result I'm probably more body consiouse than I would've been and I feel gross most of the time now that I'm gaining weight. I try to avoid looking in mirrors and am dreading the day that I know is coming soon, the day clothes start feeling tight. Besides my appearence, my inner body was looking pretty sickly too according to the doctors. I was sent to the Boston Children's Hospital ER on Thursday January 24th and once there I was subjected to a lot of tests and finally went to sleep in a hospital bed. They hooked me up to a heart monitor and had to come check up on me because it went off a few times during the night alerting them that my heart rate had dropped dangerously low. The scariest part I think was knowing that I had never even felt like there was anything wrong with my heart, and if I hadn't gone to see my pediatrician earlier that week to get some blood taken and tests done I might not have ever realized that my heart was slowly shutting down. In fact, until Thursday afternoon when my mom pulled me out of school after 1C, I had not even been aware that any of this was going on. I knew that my mom was insisting that I go to a place in

Response—71

continues

Figure 11.3 continued

Bedford, NH that helped people with eating disorders through an outpatient program. This had been her idea and she had brought it to my doctor's attention when we went in that Tuesday and saw that what my mom had been suspecting was true, I'd lost more weight. My doctor agreed then that something more needed to be done. When I was pulled out of school Thursday it was because my mom had just been contacted by my doctor. The tests that the doctor had run had come back looking not-so-good. When my doctor called the Eating Disorder Center in Bedford and spoke with the doctor there, the eating disorder specialist told her that the test results looked really bad and that there was no way Bedford could accept me at the state I was in. I needed professional medical care, apparently soon. Then my doctor called my mom and sent us to Children's. I stayed there for a week, attached to a heart monitor every night, restricted to bed rest most of the day, and allowed to leave my room only for small periods of time via wheelchair. I'm still not really grasping how all of this happened when I felt just fine leading up to all this. Ironic how resistant the body is. Anyway, after a week of re-feeding, counselling, doctors visiting me, nutritionists, long discussions with many people, and spending a LOT of time with my amazing mother, I was sent to CEDC (Cambridge Eating Disorder Center). Now I've been here for about

Response—72

Figure 11.3 *continued*

two and a half weeks, continuing to be re-fed, participating in many helpful groups, talking, journaling, and dealing with my feelings, visiting with family, making new friends, and reading. It's a very nice facility all things considered, although I do not appreciate having to ask every time I want to use one of my Q-tips (some of the rules here are a little extreme). I have become more aware of my emotions and am now trying to work on improving how I think of myself (not always easy like you would think). I've met so many beautiful, wonderful, intelligent girls since being here; none of which deserve the position their in. I will soon be moving down to the partial program here which means I'll only be at the center for six hours instead of 24/7. But including travel time I'll still pretty much live here except on the weekends. The reason I'm moving down is kind of because it's not taking me as long as some to recover but more so because my *Oh, no!* insurance hates me and doesn't want to have to pay for my treatment. Well, that is the basics of what's been going on in my life, sorry

Basically, quite a bit, dear Madi!   Response—73

continues

Figure 11.3 continued

to throw this all at you, I guess I just
needed to see it all out there in ink. The
most important thing I've learned from this
whole experience is how wonderful and caring people
I have in my life, and I am grateful for
every one of them. Top on my list is certainly
my mother who has done everything and then
some for me. I love her more than anything else
and I ~~couldn't~~ couldn't survive without her.
Signing off for now, Madi

Where The Heart Is
2/15 -2/19
4 hours (8x ½ hours)

Where The Heart IS
2/20/
2 hours (4x 30 mins)

Where The Heart Is
2/21/
2 hours (4x 30 mins)

"Go confidently in the direction
of your dreams. Live the life
you've only imagined."

→ Madi, I appreciate knowing all you've told me.
I am *so* grateful that your pediatrician did those blood
tests and knew what to do— getting you to Children's.
You know, Madi, I cannot imagine all the trauma you
have been
through—
physically and emotionally.
I do know that you are an intelligent,
spirited, energetic, kind and thoughtful young
woman who is loved by so many people, especially your
mom! You are loved for who *you are*. You give of yourself →

You have to imagine yourself inside the book, with the characters, feeling and
seeing what they do as if you were really there. Not just reading words. Reading
is painting a picture of what the author is trying to tell you.
—Shannon, eighth grader

Response—74

Figure 11.3 continued

<u>Where The Heart Is</u>   2-21

   I finished <u>Where The Heart Is</u> today. I really enjoyed this book, it's funny because I'd never heard of this book before or the author-Billie Letts-but it seems like every person I've met and talked to about it recognizes the title. I have heard so many people say "Oh! That's the movie with the teenage girl who gets dumped at Walmart and has her baby there." I was not even aware that there was a movie out about this book but apparently there is, and apparently, it's very good. So my plan now is to see that and <u>Sarah's Key</u>. I loved the characters in this novel, each one was so unique, and so quirky! I admire the amount of detail and thought the author put into each one, from the blue tint of Sister Husband's hair to the sliver of a scar on Novalee's bottom lip. I feel like I know what these characters look like, how the feel, and who they are. I was scared when Americus was kidnapped and horrified when Lexi and her children were abused by Roger. I almost cried when Sister Husband died and laughed when Novalee finally realized she loved Forney. I really felt connected and present in this book and admire all the traits and details Billie Letts captured. I'm really glad you recommended this book to me Mrs. Rief and I will definitely remember it for a long time.

with your <u>entire heart in all you do</u>. And that is what matters. Look at that book title — where the Heart Is- and that's you - you give 100% of all you do because that is where your heart is. (I'm just so happy it is healthy again- Response-75

or getting healthier!

Figure 11.4 *Final Draft of Madi's Multigenre Piece*

Becoming Me.

Can she pull through? Will the fear be gone?
Or will the girl disappear, and the shell live on?

What is Beauty?

Beauty is not being so thin that people can see your spine. Beauty does not come from not eating. Calorie counting, the inability to be present with your family, and loneliness are not beautiful things. Constantly weighing yourself on the bathroom scale and doing workouts in your room do not give you a glow. There is no award for losing yourself. Empty smiles, being short-tempered and anxious, these things do not grant superiority.

And were you hoping for confidence? Did you expect a sense of pride and accomplishment from your struggles? Did you believe that control would come out of this? No, there is nothing involving happiness or greatness when the topic is eating disorders. Binging and purging, restricting, over-exercising, they do nothing to fill the hole. The temporary feeling of control is just that, just temporary.

But there is a way, there must be a way to be real again. And it is not by continuing the cycle and further increasing the harm you inflict on yourself and others. Relief only comes when you finally say *enough*, when you learn the true meaning of beauty.

Residential

Sometimes I lay in bed at night, staring at the ceiling, trying to figure out how it all came down to this. They tell me I am strong, my mom says that she believes in me. I don't feel strong though, strong would be at home not here. Strong would be deciding for myself what to eat, how much of it, and when. Not being told because I'm deemed "incapable". No, I am not strong for being in treatment, I am weak. I am weak because I can't be in school like normal kids, can't be in sports or activities right now. I feel weak because I can't tell when my body is in a danger zone. And I feel weaker still because even when I am informed by doctors that I'm malnourished and that my heart has slowed, I still don't believe that I have a problem.

I often feel like I don't deserve the life I've got. My wonderful, caring family, my friends, the opportunities I have. I don't feel like I deserve praise for accomplishments. Sometimes I don't feel like I deserve to eat. Eating to me seems like weakness, and I am so weak already. But I guess that's why they say I have a problem. I feel like a monster, getting attention for a problem that doesn't even seem like a problem compared to what these other girls have gone through. Attention from my mom, my family, everyone. I just want to go unnoticed, then I can hurt myself without affecting others. Sometimes I think I would do anything if only to not burden anyone else. I look in the mirror and can quickly pick out lots of things that I dislike about my self.

I've never starved myself, never gone a day without eating, and yet I'm labeled anorexic? How can that be true when I see girls here who would clearly

Figure 11.4 *continued*

not eat anything if they were allowed. I look around and see very, very thin girls. Girls who go days without eating, girls who have had eating disorders for most of their life. I just feel fat and piggish most of the time.

Why was it so hard for me to just do what the pediatrician said? Why didn't I just gain weight? I know why. Because every time I stepped on the scale and it showed that I had gained weight, I didn't think of that weight as muscle and curves. No, I thought of that weight as fat that I couldn't afford to have. And every time the scale read lower, every time I had lost more weight I felt like I had won.

But it was never enough, when the scale said 84 pounds, I knew I could go lower. Then came 80 pounds, then 78. And still it wasn't good enough. I always needed to lose more. The mirror always showed that I was still too big. My mind had rewired itself. Now less was always more. Less weight, less food. And as a result less energy, less ambition, less me.

But everything is getting better, much better. I'm starting to understand my real goals, and not the ones that my eating disorder set for me. I remember now how much I care about the world, and the people and creatures around me. My desire to change the world is no longer dimmed by the obsessive haze I was in before. Maybe someday I'll even like what I see in the mirror and I will judge myself as I judge others, not by unhealthy standards. Maybe I'll learn to love myself as much as I love everyone around me. Maybe someday I'll be who I want to be, and then I can stop pretending.

Enough.

Fat, gross, worthless, pig. These words hurl themselves around in my mind, torturing me with their harsh intentions. I cry, silently now, hoping not to disturb the fragile wall of isolation I've built around myself. My eyes stare blankly but inside I'm in turmoil. One part of me begs to forgive, wanting only to move on and discover my purpose. This part wishes to be set free from the prison I've created within myself. It whimpers, wanting to return to the place I was before, to the happiness I once had. The other half sneers, there is no going back. I can never be that way again. I was not happy before, only a pathetic, chubby girl who was unable to accomplish anything. The only way to be good, the only way to succeed, is to be thin. I must eat less, I must do more. No exceptions, no breaks.

I observe this internal rage with a type of removed wonder. And I cringe at what I have become. Emotions I did not know I possessed reveal themselves, thoughts I would never have believed were my own are suddenly present. Looking in the mirror is too painful, talking about my fears too great a risk. And the greatest fear, the one that is always there. Even when I recover, how will I stop this from happening again? Or, how will I prevent my problems from coming out in other areas of my life?

What would they think if they knew? My family, my friends? They would not believe it was me. Curling up in a ball and wishing I could disappear is not uncommon, and I've realized that caring for myself is not nearly as simple as taking care of others. Still the concern is, will I be enough? I know the answer

continues

Figure 11.4 *continued*

to that is no. I will never be enough. When I am done with this, when I look back on what I've done and what I do, I will never be able to say I AM ENOUGH.

Empty

A shell remains of what was before,
of what was there exists no more.

The eyes are dull, no light shine through,
her laughs are numbered, her smiles few.

The girl no longer cries because,
she can't recall just who she was.

Unable now to get things right,
she lies awake in bed at night.

Trying again to find her way,
keeping emotions once more at bay.

She reaches out and calls for aid,
as the girl she was appears to fade.

Can they help her, will they know the cure?
Can they stop her bleeding, her internal war?

With love and hope they try their best,
there is only one thing now, the final test.

Can she pull through? Will the fear be gone?
Or will the girl disappear, and the shell live on?

Taking Action

There is a sense of change blown in with the warm Spring breeze. My ways are to be altered, my health and happiness restored. I am uncovering the true reasons for this problem and taking steps to change behaviors.

I choose to be true to myself and those around me, and to not limit myself with trivial complications. I choose to be part of this world, to hold nothing back and to go forth with purpose and determination.

I will not sit back and allow myself to be created into an unhappy creature. I vow to be my best. I want to give and enjoy. I wish not to harm or to be harmed but to love and receive it. I promise not to give up, I promise to persevere and pull through. I will live.

Happiness

I feel...happy. It's a strange feeling and one that has been to some extent absent from my life for some time. True happiness that is. I am excited

Figure 11.4 *continued*

to go to school again, excited to see friends. I don't feel quite so alone, and certainly not as down all the time.

It's so strange to think that just a few weeks ago I was watching as doctors hooked me up to a heart monitor. I remember the first night that I was in the ER, I could not sleep for a while and even when I did fall asleep, the alarm on the monitor kept going off as my heart rate dipped into a danger zone. Now I'm able to look in the mirror and not have to turn away because it brings on tears. Not that I love the way I look, but I am starting to appreciate all the things my body does for me. I feel stronger, not as likely to blow away in the wind. And the warmth, it is so nice to not be shivering and freezing all the time anymore. I am grateful for how my body has bounced back and is operating in ways I could not have imagined, it appears that even when I did not believe in myself my body did and was waiting for me to catch up.

And still stranger is the absence of the feeling of guilt. I do not hate every mistake I've made/make, and I have even been gentle with myself lately.

As I approach my ideal body weight, my brain has started to operate properly, or at least that is the explanation according to my doctors. My psychiatrist is also thrilled to hear about the change in thinking and self-judgement.

It was very difficult for me to agree that I would start taking the medication, and harder still for me to allow myself to tell others about it. As of now I have not informed many people that I am on antidepressants, but I might tell some of my friends once I work up the courage. The first step was admitting it to my grandmother, and now to you Mrs. Rief. I struggle with the idea that people will think of me differently, since I myself think of my change in attitude as somewhat artificial. But the drug has provided me with a new sense of self, and other things for which I am grateful. My mood continues to improve as the medication fixes the unbalanced chemicals in my brain.

Something I wasn't even aware of, not only is depression hereditary (and it runs on both sides of my family), but children with parents who have emotional problems/ imbalances are much more likely to have eating disorders. And, as I have recently discovered, since the antidepressant has kicked in, it is much easier to accept my weight gain. This, as my therapist has explained, is because I really don't have an eating disorder (or not a very serious one) but rather mild depression.

It's interesting to me that I denied this for so long. The reason being that when I thought of depression, an image of someone who is constantly sad and has trouble getting out of bed popped into my mind. When in fact, there is a wide range of things that may classify a person as depressed, and I have experienced a few of them for a long time, much longer than the span of my eating disorder.

I was often very emotional, and felt overwhelmingly guilty or unworthy at times. More than anything though, my depression is present in my sense of accomplishment, and the feeling that nothing will ever be good enough. But the medication is helping with this as well, and like I said before I have even been gentle with myself lately. I'm relearning to listen to my body, synchronizing myself again. And I honestly have NEVER felt happier.

Online
11.1–11.3

When students write about those things that matter most to them, the writing (and their lives) matters to others. In addition to her writer's-reader's notebook writing, on the website you will find her rough drafts of writing with my response and questions, her final drafts, process paper, and her end-of-the-year self-evaluation.

Through her writing Madi not only has found her voice, but also has found herself. In the process, she is giving so many other kids voice when they see themselves in her words. It is a gift she gives courageously.

AFTERWORD

In her poem "The Teachers," May Sarton says:

> History happens in small rooms. And people grow
> In your large hands like states patiently won
> From wilderness. But the work is slow.
> You do not see the end and it is never done . . .

For my entire professional life I have been incredibly fortunate to have been able to live and teach in a school system (Oyster River schools) and at a university (University of New Hampshire) with colleagues who believe and practice teaching with their heads and their hearts. Teachers who knew, and continue to know, that the students in their classrooms are their best teachers, and listen patiently, plan intelligently, and teach intentionally. Yet, as teachers, we seldom see the result of our work.

> . . . This is your mystery.
> You plant knowing that you will never bear
> The harvest in your hands. You have no history.
> You lose what you have won and do not care.

As teachers, we know the work is slow and we never see the end. But it's the lives of the students—those who are with us in the moment of teaching and those who have moved on—that keep us going back into our classrooms year after year: the note from Duncan working with special needs adults in Ireland, Nahanni on a fellowship in Israel filming and writing for Seeds of Peace, Jim with his own computer business, Jennifer, a principal, Sarah bookbinding, Tricia teaching English to second language adults, Rob on stage in New York, Erica at McGill—the ones we occasionally hear from, but the hundreds whom we still think about and hope are successful, having found what makes them happy.

What begins with a celebration for writing her full name "in cursive" in first grade becomes a triumph at explaining her fifth-grade invention to a group of adults at the invention convention, continues with her own surprise at reading a three hundred-page book in a week in eighth grade ("Mrs. Rief, that book you gave me, I couldn't put it down last night. Have you got any others by that author?"), and blossoms into her valedictorian speech at high school graduation, or simply becomes the pride and satisfaction that she made it through to graduation. We know, but we seldom see it.

I ran into Patrick who was back for a high school reunion. I wondered if he remembers the time in seventh grade when he approached me, brows furrowed, genuine concern in his words. "Mrs. Rief, in this freewrite we're doing you said, 'Just write fast, don't take your pen from the paper.' Well, I'm having a terrible time crossing my *t*'s and dotting my *i*'s since I can't take my pen from the paper. How can you do that?" I smile over the incident. In his chosen profession, orthopedic surgeon, his patients want a perfectionist, a doctor who is concerned about the smallest detail. As his teacher for just a split second in his education, I have "lost what I have won" but it does not matter.

The students we have had, have now, and will have in the future have touched our lives, with the choices and challenges they face in the lives they live. They are what keep us teaching through the choices and challenges we face.

> For this largesse, this gift, words are too narrow.
> They are not needed: the praise is afterwards.
> For you who are the future, wearing love at marrow,
> The praise is later and found in lives, not words.

REFERENCES

Adams, Douglas. 1980. *The Hitchhiker's Guide to the Galaxy*. New York: Harmony Books.

Alexie, Sherman. 2007. *The Absolutely True Diary of a Part-Time Indian*. New York: Little, Brown and Company.

Alvarez, Julia. 2004. *Before We Were Free*. New York: Laurel Leaf.

Anderson, Laura Halse. 2009. *Wintergirls*. New York: Viking.

———. 2008. *Chains*. New York: Simon and Schuster.

———. 2003. *Catalyst*. New York: Speak.

———. 2000. *Fever 1793*. New York: Simon and Schuster.

———. 1999. *Speak*. New York: Farrar Straus Giroux.

Anderson, Richard C., et al. 1985. *Becoming a Nation of Readers*. Champaign, IL: NIE.

Anne Frank—The Whole Story (DVD). 2001. Walt Disney.

Asher, Jay. 2007. *Thirteen Reasons Why*. New York: Penguin Books.

Atwell, Nancie. 2007. *The Reading Zone*. New York: Scholastic.

———. 2002. *Lessons That Change Writers*. Portsmouth, NH: Heinemann.

———. 1987. *In the Middle*. Portsmouth, NH: Boynton-Cook.

Austen, Jane. 1979. *Pride and Prejudice*. New York: Modern Library.

Bagdasarian, Adam. 2002. *First French Kiss*. New York: Farrar Straus Giroux.

Becker, Abigail Lynne. 1995. *A Box of Rain*. Self-Published.

Berenbaum, Michael. 1993. *The World Must Know*. Boston, MA: Little, Brown and Company.

Blundell, Judy. 2010. *What I Saw and How I Lied*. New York: Scholastic.

Bolin, Frances Schoonmaker, Ed. 1994. *Poetry for Young People: Emily Dickinson*. New York: Sterling Publishing.

Boyne, John. 2007. *The Boy in the Striped Pajamas*. New York: David Fidding Books.

Bradbury, Ray. 1993. *The Trilogy of Terror Series* ("Off Season" Vol. 7). New York: Nantier, Beall, Minoustchine Publishers.

———. 1986. *Fahrenheit 451*. New York: Ballantine Books.

———. 1954. "All Summer in a Day." *The Magazine of Fantasy and Science Fiction*. March 1954.

Brees, Drew. 2011. *Coming Back Stronger*. New York: Tyndale House Publishers.

Bronte, Charlotte. 1897. *Jane Eyre*. London: Service and Paton.

Brooklyn Castle (DVD). 2013. Millenium Studio.

Brown, Dan. 2009. *The DaVinci Code*. New York: Anchor.

———. 2003. *Angels and Demons*. New York: Atria.

Bryson, Bill. 1999. *I'm a Stranger Here Myself*. New York: Broadway Books.

Cabot, Meg. 2008. *The Princess Diaries*. New York: Harper Teen.

Caine, Karen. 2008. *Writing to Persuade*. Portsmouth, NH: Heinemann.

Card, Orson Scott. 2008. *The Ender* series: New York: Tor Science Fiction.

Christie, Agatha. 2011. *Towards Zero*. New York: William Morrow Paperbacks.

Cisneros, Sandra. 1991. *Woman Hollering Creek*. New York: Vintage Books.

———. 1989. *The House on Mango Street*. New York: Vintage Books.

Clark, Mary Higgins. 1992. *Loves Music, Loves to Dance*. New York: Pocket Books.

Codell, Esme Raji. 1999. *Educating Esme: Diary of a Teacher's First Year*. Chapel Hill, NC: Algonquin Books.

Collins, Billy. 2001. *Sailing Around the World*. New York: Random House.

Collins, Suzanne. 2009. *Catching Fire*. New York: Scholastic.

———. 2008. *The Hunger Games*. New York: Scholastic.

Connell, Richard. 1924. "The Most Dangerous Game." Available online at www.classicshorts.com/stories/danger.html.

Corrigan, Eireann. 2002. *You Remind Me of You*. New York: Push.

Couch, Dick and George Galdorisi. 2012. *Tom Clancy Presents: Act of Valor*. New York: Berkley.

Creech, Sharon. 2001. *Love That Dog*. New York: HarperCollins.

Crichton, Michael. 2003. *Timeline*. New York: Ballantine Books.

Crutcher, Chris. 1987. *The Crazy Horse Electric Game*. New York: Greenwillow Books.

Curtis, Christopher Paul. 1995. *The Watsons Go to Birmingham—1963*. New York: Delacorte Press.

Dahl, Roald. 1995. *Lamb to the Slaughter and Other Stories*. New York: Penguin.

———. 1984. *Boy*. London: Penguin Books.

Daniels, Harvey, and Nancy Steineke. 2011. *Texts and Lessons for Content-Area Reading*. Portsmouth, NH: Heinemann.

Dashner, James. 2010. *The Maze Runner*. New York: Delacorte Press.

Decker, Timothy. 2007. *Run Far, Run Fast*. Honesdale, PA: Front Street Boyds Mills Press.

———. 2009. *For Liberty: The Story of the Boston Massacre*. Honesdale, PA: Calkins Creek.

Donelson, Kenneth L., and Alleen Pace Nilsen. 1989. *Literature for Today's Young Adults*, 3d ed. New York: Scott Foresman.

Donnelly, Jennifer. 2003. *A Northern Light*. New York: Harcourt Books.

Downham, Jenny. 2009. *Before I Die*. New York: Ember.

Draper, Sharon. 2012. *Out of My Mind*. New York: Atheneum Books.

Durrell, Ann and Marilyn Sachs, Eds. 1990. *The Big Book for Peace*. New York: Dutton Children's Books.

eGFI. 2011. "Marshmallow Design Challenge." Available online at http://teachers.egfi-k12.org/marshmallow-design-challenge/.

Eisner, Will. 2008. *Graphic Storytelling and Visual Narrative*. New York: W. W. Norton & Company.

Elbow, Peter. 1973. *Writing without Teachers*. New York: Oxford University Press.

Essley, Roger. 2008. *Visual Tools for Differentiating Reading and Writing Instruction*. New York: Scholastic.

Estes, Eleanor. 1972. *The Hundred Dresses*. Orlando, FL: Harcourt Brace and Company.

Evans, Walker, and Cynthia Rylant. 1994. *Something Permanent*. New York: Harcourt Brace and Co.

Farmer, Nancy. 2004. *The House of the Scorpion*. New York: Atheneum.

Feelings, Tom. 1993. *Soul Looks Back in Wonder*. New York: Dial Books.

Fitch, Janet. 1999. *White Oleander*. Boston, MA: Little, Brown and Company.

Fleischman, Paul. 1999. *Mind's Eye*. New York: Henry Holt and Company.

———. 1997. *Seedfolks*. New York: HarperCollins.

Fletcher, Ralph. 2013. *What a Writer Needs,* 2nd ed. Portsmouth, NH: Heinemann.

———. 2005. *Marshfield Dreams.* New York: Henry Holt and Co.

———. 1996. *Breathing In, Breathing Out: Keeping a Writer's Notebook.* Portsmouth, NH: Heinemann.

———. 1994. *I Am Wings.* New York: Atheneum.

Foer, Jonathan. 2005. *Extremely Loud and Incredibly Close.* New York: Houghton Mifflin Company.

Fox, Mem. 1984. *Wilfred Gordon McDonald Partridge.* New York: Viking Penguin.

Franco, Betsy, Ed. 2000. *You Hear Me?* Cambridge MA: Candlewick Press.

Frank, Adam. 2011. *About Time.* New York: Free Press.

Frank, Anne. 1952. *The Diary of a Young Girl.* New York: Random House.

Frost, Robert. 1969. *The Poetry of Robert Frost.* New York: Holt, Rinehart and Winston.

Gallagher, Kelly. 2009. *Readicide.* Portland, ME: Stenhouse.

Gendler, Ruth. 1988. *The Book of Qualities.* New York: Harper and Row.

Gladwell, Malcolm. 2008. *The Outliers.* New York: Little, Brown and Company.

Glenn, Mel. 1982. *Class Dismissed!* New York: Houghton Mifflin.

Goldman, William. 1973. *The Princess Bride.* New York: Ballantine Books.

Graves, Donald. 1983. *Writing: Teachers and Children at Work.* Exeter, NH: Heinemann Educational Books.

Green, John. 2012. *The Fault in Our Stars.* New York: Dutton Group.

———. 2006. *Looking for Alaska.* New York: Speak.

———. 2009. *Paper Towns.* New York: Speak.

Greenberg, Jan, Ed. 2001. *Heart to Heart.* New York: Harry N. Abrams.

Greenfield, Eloise. 1978. *Honey, I Love.* New York: Harper and Row.

Grover, Lorie Ann. 2008. *On Pointe.* New York: Margaret K. McElderry Books.

Gutkind, Lee, Ed. 2008. *Keep It Real.* New York: W. W. Norton & Co.

Hall, Meredith. 2007. *Without a Map.* Boston, MA: Beacon Press.

Hawking, Stephen. 1998. *A Brief History of Time.* New York: Bantam Books.

Hayden, Torey. 1980. *One Child.* New York: Avon Books.

Heard, Georgia. 2013. *Finding the Heart of Nonfiction.* Portsmouth, NH: Heinemann.

———. 2002. *The Revision Toolbox.* Portsmouth, NH: Heinemann.

———. 2000. *Songs of Myself.* New York: Mondo.

———. 1999. *Awakening the Heart*. Portsmouth, NH: Heinemann.

———. 1995. *Writing Toward Home*. Portsmouth, NH: Heinemann.

Hill, Graham. 2010. "Why I'm a Weekday Vegetarian." TED Talk video. Available online at www.ted.com/talks/graham_hill_weekday_vegetarian.html.

Hinton, S. E. 1967. *The Outsiders*. New York: Puffin Books.

Hondra, Marcus. 2012. "Lance Armstrong Could Not Put Up, Time Now for Him to Shut Up." *Digital Journal: A Global Digital Media Network*. Available at http://digitaljournal.com/article/331443. August 24.

Hopkins, Ellen. 2013. *Perfect*. New York: Margaret K. McElderry Books.

———. 2012. The Crank Series (1–6). New York: Simon Pulse.

Hosseini, Khaled. 2003. *The Kite Runner*. New York: Riverhead.

Hyde, Anthony. 1985. *The Red Fox*. New York: Knopf.

Jacobson, Sid, and Ernie Colon. 2006. *The 9/11 Report*. New York: Hill and Wang.

Janeczko, Paul. 1990. *The Place My Words Are Looking For*. New York: Bradbury Press.

———. 1991. *Preposterous*. New York: Orchard Books.

———. 1982. *Poetspeak*. New York: Bradbury Press.

Jordan, Robert. 1994. *Lord of Chaos*. Wheel of Time Book 6. New York: A Tor Book.

Kaufman, Doug. 2000. *Conferences and Conversations: Listening to the Literate Classroom*. Portsmouth, NH: Heinemann.

Kearney, Meg. 2005. *The Secret of Me*. New York: Persea Books.

Kent, Richard. 2012. *Writing on the Bus: Using Athletic Team Notebooks and Journals to Advance Learning and Performance in Sports*. New York: Peter Lang Publishing.

Kidd, Sue Monk. 2002. *The Secret Life of Bees*. New York: Penguin Books.

Kindig, Joan Schroeder. 2012. *Choosing to Read*. Portsmouth, NH: Heinemann.

King, Stephen. 2001. *Pet Sematary*. New York: Pocket Books.

Kinney, Jeff. 2009. *Dog Days*. Diary of a Wimpy Kid series. New York: Amulet Books.

Kittle, Penny. 2013. *Book Love*. Portsmouth, NH: Heinemann.

Knudson, R. R., and May Swenson, Eds. 1988. *American Sports Poems*. New York: Orchard Books.

Koch, Kenneth, and Kate Farrell, Eds. 1985. *Talking to the Sun*. New York: Henry Holt and Company.

Kooser, Ted. 1985. *Flying at Night*. Pittsburgh, PA: University of Pittsburgh Press.

Krakauer, Jon. 1997. *Into the Wild*. New York: Anchor.

Kunhardt, Dorothy. 2001. *Pat the Bunny*. New York: Golden Books.

Lane, Barry. 1993. *After the End*. Portsmouth, NH: Heinemann.

Larsson, Stieg. 2011. *The Girl Who Played with Fire*. New York: Vintage.

Lent, Jeffrey. 2000. *In the Fall*. New York: Atlantic Monthly Press.

Levine, Karen. 2003. *Hana's Suitcase*. Park Ridge, IL: Albert Whitman and Co.

Letts, Billie. 1995. *Where the Heart Is*. New York: Time-Warner.

Lewis, Michael. 2007. *The Blind Side*. New York: W.W. Norton and Company.

Lowry, Lois. 1998. *Looking Back*. New York: Houghton-Mifflin.

———. 1994. *The Giver*. Boston, MA: Houghton Mifflin Co.

Lupica, Mike. 2011. *The Batboy*. New York: Puffin.

Maberry, Jonathan. 2012. *Dust and Decay*. New York: Simon and Schuster Books.

MacGowan, Christopher, Ed. 2004. *William Carlos Williams: Poetry for Young People*. New York: Sterling Publishing Co.

Mack, Tracy. 2000. *Drawing Lessons*. New York: Scholastic.

MacLachlan, Patricia. 1991. *Journey*. New York: Delacorte Press.

Marsden, John. 2006. *Tomorrow, When the War Began* series. New York: Scholastic.

McCammon, Robert. 1992. *Boy's Life*. New York: Pocket Books.

McCarthy, Cormac. 2007. *The Road*. New York: Vintage Books.

McCloud, Scott. 1993. *Understanding Comics: The Invisible Art*. New York: HarperCollins Publishers.

McCormick, Patricia. 2006. *Sold*. New York: Hyperion.

McCourt, Frank. 1999. *'Tis*. New York: Scribner.

Messner, Kate. 2011. *Real Revision*. Portland, ME: Stenhouse.

Meyer, Stephanie. 2008. *Twilight*. New York: Little, Brown Books for Young Readers.

Mikaelsen, Ben. 1998. *Petey*. New York: Hyperion Books.

Miller, Arthur. 2008. *The Crucible*. Logan, IA: Perfection Learning.

Miller, Donalyn. 2009. *The Book Whisperer*. San Francisco, CA: Jossey-Bass.

Morpurgo, Michael. 1982. *War Horse*. New York: Scholastic.

Murray, Donald M. 1996. *Crafting a Life in Essay, Story, Poem*. Portsmouth, NH: Boynton-Cook.

———. 1990. *Write to Learn*. Fort Worth, TX: Holt, Rinehart and Winston.

National Writing Project and Carl Nagin. 2003. *Because Writing Matters: Improving Student Writing in Our Schools*. San Francisco, CA: Jossey-Bass.

Newkirk, Tom. 2012. *The Art of Slow Reading*. Portsmouth, NH: Heinemann.

Nolan, Han. 2003. *If I Should Die Before I Wake*. New York: HMH.

———. 2003. *Born Blue*. New York: HMH.

———. 1997. *Dancing on the Edge*. New York: Harcourt Brace and Co.

Nye, Naomi Shihab. 1998. *Fuel*. New York: BOA Editions.

———. 1994. *Sitti's Secrets*. New York: Simon and Schuster.

O'Flaherty, Liam. 1923. "The Sniper." Available online at www.classicshorts.com/stories/sniper.html.

Oliver, Mary. 1992. *New and Selected Poems*. Boston, MA: Beacon Press.

Opdyke, Irene Gut. 1999. *In My Hands*. New York: Alfred A. Knopf.

Oppel, Kenneth. 2007. *Skybreaker*. New York: EOS.

Paolini, Christopher. 2012. *Eragon* series. New York: Knopf Books.

Patterson, James. 2010. Maximum Ride series. New York: Little, Brown and Company.

Paulsen, Gary. 1999. *Hatchet*. New York: Aladdin Paperbacks.

———. 1994. *Father Water, Mother Woods*. New York: Delacorte Press.

———. 1993. *Harris and Me*. San Diego: Harcourt Brace and Co.

———. 1991. *The River*. New York: Delacorte Press.

———. 1989. *The Winter Room*. New York: Orchard Books.

Penrose, Roger. 1996. *Shadows of the Mind*. London: Oxford University Press.

Pickering, James H. 1978. *Fiction 100: An Anthology of Short Stories*. New York: MacMillan Publishing Co.

Picoult, Jodi. 2006. *The Tenth Circle*. New York: Washington Square Press.

———. 2005. *My Sister's Keeper*. New York: Washington Square Press.

———. 1995. *Harvesting the Heart*. New York: Penguin.

Pink, Daniel H. 2006. *A Whole New Mind*. New York: Penguin Group.

Pitts, Leonard. 2008. "Our Destructive Love of Stuff." *The Miami Herald*. December 3.

Philbrick, Rodman. 1993. *Freak the Mighty*. New York: Scholastic.

Quick, Matthew. 2012. *The Silver Linings Playbook*. New York: Sarah Crichton Books.

Quindlen, Anna. 1998. *How Reading Changed My Life*. New York: The Ballantine Publishing Group.

Reilly, Rick. 2013. "It's All About the Lies." ESPN.com. Available online at http://espn.go.com/espn/story/_/id/8852974/lance-armstrong-history-lying. January 17.

———. 2012. "Armstrong Still Worth Honoring." ESPN.com. Available online at http://espn.go.com/espn/story/_/id/8310275/armstrong-worth-honoring. September 4.

———. 2003. *The Life of Reilly—The Best of Sports Illustrated's Rick Reilly.* New York: Time, Inc.

———. 1998. "Next Time Stop the Freaking Race." Originally published August 17, 1998. Available online at http://www.si.com/vault/article/magazine/MAG1013694/index.htm.

Reynolds, Vicki S. 1999. "When 'Harry' Met My Nephew." *Lincoln Star Journal*, Sunday October 24.

Rief, Linda. 2007a. *Inside the Writer's-Reader's Notebook.* Portsmouth, NH: Heinemann.

———. 2007b. Writer's-Reader's Notebook. Portsmouth, NH: Heinemann.

———. 2003. *100 Quickwrites.* New York: Scholastic.

———. 1992. *Seeking Diversity: Language Arts with Adolescents.* Portsmouth, NH: Heinemann.

Riordan, Rick. 2006. *The Lightning Thief* (Percy Jackson and the Olympians series). New York: Disney-Hyperion.

Roessel, David, and Arnold Rampersad, Eds. 2006. *Poetry for Young People: Langston Hughes.* New York: Sterling.

Romano, Tom. 2004. *Crafting Authentic Voice.* Portsmouth, NH: Heinemann.

———. 1987. *Clearing the Way.* Portsmouth, NH: Heinemann.

Rosen, Michael J. Ed. 1993. *Speak! Children's Book Illustrators Brag About Their Dogs.* New York: Harcourt Brace and Co.

Rosenthal, Amy Krouse. 2005. *Encyclopedia of an Ordinary Life.* New York: Three Rivers Press.

de Rosnay, Tatiana. 2007. *Sarah's Key.* New York: St. Martin's Press.

Roth, Veronica. 2013. Divergent Trilogy. New York: Katherine Tegen Books.

Ryan, Pam Munoz. 2010. *The Dreamer.* New York: Scholastic. Sidman, Joyce. 2003. *The World According to Dog.* Boston: Houghton Mifflin.

Rylant, Cynthia. 1994. *Something Permanent.* Orlando, FL: Harcourt Brace and Co.

———. 1990. *A Couple of Kooks.* New York: Orchard Books.

———. 1989. *But I'll Be Back Again.* New York: Orchard Books.

———. 1985. *Every Living Thing.* New York: Aladdin Books.

Sachar, Louis. 1998. *Holes.* New York: Farrar Straus & Giroux.

Salinger, J.D. 1945. *The Catcher in the Rye.* Boston: Little, Brown and Company.

Sarton, May. 1945. "The Teachers." *Queen's Quarterly, A Canadian Review* 52, no. 3.

Satrapi, Marjane. 2003. *Persepolis*. New York: Pantheon Books.

Schaefer, Jenni. 2003. *Life Without Ed*. New York: McGraw-Hill.

Schoonover, Ruth C. 1937. "The Negaunee Reading Experiment." *English Journal* 26.7 (September).

Scieszka, Jon. 2012. *Guys Read: The Sports Pages*. New York: Walden Pond Press.

————. 2010. *Guys Read: Funny Business*. New York: Walden Pond Press.

————. 2008. *Knucklehead*. New York: Penguin Group.

————. 2008. *Guys Write for Guys Read*. New York: Penguin Group.

Selznick, Brian. 2007. *The Invention of Hugo Cabret*. New York: Scholastic.

Seuss, Dr. 1960. *Green Eggs and Ham*. New York: Random House Beginner Books.

Shan, Darren. 2010. *The Cirque du Freak* series. New York: BMI Publishing.

————. 2007. Demonata series. Boston: Little, Brown and Company.

Silverstein, Shel. 1974. *Where the Sidewalk Ends*. New York: HarperCollins.

Small, David. 2009. *Stitches*. New York: W.W. Norton and Company.

Smith, Jeff. 2005. *Bone: Out from Boneville*. New York: Scholastic.

Smith, Roland. 2009. *Tentacles*. New York: Scholastic.

Sparks, Nicholas. 2007. *Dear John*. New York: Grand Central Publishing.

Spiegelman, Art. 1973. *Maus I: A Survivor's Tale*. New York: Pantheon Books.

Stafford, William. 1998. *The Way It Is*. Saint Paul, MN: Graywolf Press.

Stassen, J. P. 2000. *Deogratias: A Tale of Rwanda*. New York: First Second.

Stein, Garth. 2008. *The Art of Racing in the Rain*. New York: Harper.

Stockett, Katheryn. 2009. *The Help*. New York: Amy Einhorn Books/Putnam.

Tan, Amy. 2008. "Fish Cheeks." *Elements of Literature: First Course*. Orlando, FL: Holt, Rinehart and Winston.

Tolkien, J.R.R. 1967. *The Lord of the Rings*. Boston, MA: Houghton Mifflin.

Trueman, Terry. 2000. *Stuck in Neutral*. New York: Scholastic.

Turner, Ann. 2000. *Learning to Swim*. New York: Scholastic.

Tymorek, Stan, Ed. 2001. *Clotheslines*. New York: Harry N. Abrams.

Ulin, David L. 2010. *The Lost Art of Reading*. Seattle, WA: Sasquatch Books.

Van Allsburg, Chris. 2011. *The Chronicles of Harris Burdick*. New York: Houghton Mifflin.

————. 1984. *The Mysteries of Harris Burdick*. New York: HMH Books for Young Readers.

Vertuno, Jim. 2012. "Armstrong Says Last Two Weeks 'Difficult.'" *Foster's Daily Democrat,* October 21.

Wallace, David. 2006. *Infinite Jest.* Boston, MA: Back Bay Books.

———. 2004. *The Broom of the System.* New York: Penguin.

Wiesel, Elie. 1986. *Night.* New York: Farrar, Straus and Giroux.

Wilbur, Richard. 1988. *New and Collected Poems.* Orlando, FL: Harcourt Brace Jovanovich.

Williams, Marcia. 1998. *Tales from Shakespeare.* Cambridge, MA: Candlewick Press.

Wolf, Dennie Palmer. 1988. *Reading Reconsidered.* New York: College Entrance Examination Board.

Wujec, Tom. 2010. "Build a Tower, Build a Team." TED Talk video. Available online at marshmallowchallenge.com/TED_Talk.html.

Yang, Gene Luen. 2006. *American Born Chinese.* New York: First Second.

Yousafzai, Malala, and Christina Lamb. 2013. *I Am Malala.* New York: Little, Brown, and Company.

Zander, Benjamin. 2008. "The Transformative Power of Classical Music." TED Talk video. Available online at http://www.ted.com/talks/benjamin_zander_on_music_and_passion.html.

Zinsser, William. 1980. *On Writing Well.* New York: Harper and Row.

Zusak, Markus. 2006. *The Book Thief.* New York: Alfred A. Knopf.

Praise for *Read Write Teach*

Linda Rief is my teaching hero. For thirty years she has brought her formidable intelligence to the challenges of middle school—meeting young adolescents where they are, immersing them in compelling versions of literacy, inviting them to make choices as writers and readers, and teaching them how to make good ones. *Read Write Teach* is nothing less than a manifesto, Linda's passionate yet practical account of the transformative goals she sets for her students and the powerful methods she creates to nurture them as "world-ready" writers and readers. Her curriculum goes beyond state and national standards. It inspires students to think, attend, engage, produce, and excel as readers and writers.

—Nancie Atwell

In the long-awaited book, we can see what it truly means to have high standards—not ones simply imposed from above, but ones that come from true engagement. Linda Rief shows us how to tap the passions, angst, and interests of adolescents, and how this driving force can lead students to do amazing work in a variety of genres, guided by the best mentor texts. She offers her students the best gift of all: to be taken seriously.

—Tom Newkirk

Reading Linda Rief's *Read Write Teach* has energized and challenged me. Linda hopes that students will write with the power to nudge the world and, as she says, for the world to nudge them a little as they read deeply and then respond with their ideas, values, and experiences. The student work she shares in this book must awaken us all to the potential of our students. Linda shows us how to achieve clear, effective writing through time, choice, response, and modeling as daily practices in workshop teaching. Meaningful choice can only operate with a system of structures, models, standards, norms, and a culture and values that students actively engage in. Linda exposes all of this scaffolding for readers, allowing us to imitate her practice to deeply engage students. It is my hope that *Read Write Teach* will nudge us all.

—Penny Kittle

In 1992, Linda Rief's *Seeking Diversity* was a blockbuster for those driven to teach adolescents to read and write. Now this master teacher, perceptive reader, and compelling writer has written *Read Write Teach* (no periods, no commas, no hyphens. Just one integrated act). The book is filled with a lifetime of Linda's immersion in reading, writing, and teaching. In these pages, you'll experience a philosophy of literacy instruction that deepens and widens your own. You'll find handouts and prompts, strategies and activities that Linda has created to engage students in continuous literacy growth. You'll follow her logic and her heart as she explains how she evaluates students' writing—from expressive thinking in their reader's-writer's notebooks to sophisticated persuasive essays. You'll gain a companion to accompany you on that long, rewarding road of teaching students to be the strongest readers and writers they can. With *Read Write Teach*, Linda Rief has once again busted the block.

—Tom Romano